RUSSIA'S WORLD TRAVELER POET

The poetry of Nikolay Gumilev (1886–1921) is part of the life of every educated Russian. Children read him in school for his appealing adventure tales—notably "The Discovery of America," where he shows Columbus guided by the same spirit that gave life to the Russian poet's own lifetime work—the "Muse of Distant Travel." To young Russians Gumilev plays a role like that of Antoine de Saint-Exupéry for the youth of France. Yet, characteristically, the "Discovery" is filled with meaning for every mental traveler. One of the central poets of the 20th century, a celebrator of love and risk, heroism and passion, a psychological explorer of deep acuity and a wanderer whose work could nearly serve as a poetic world atlas, Gumilev was an officer in the White army and co-founded the influential poetic movement of Acmeism. Contemporary with Joseph Conrad, he devoted a book to his pioneering journeys in Africa—where he mapped uncharted terrain. There is nothing like this African panorama in modern Western verse. Gumilev needs to be better known in America for his lyrical work—mellifluent, vigorous, and riveting.

The eight unabridged Gumilev collections offered here in form-true renderings will at last allow speakers of English a chance to acquire a thorough acquaintance with one of the finest and—to native speakers—best-known poets of the Russian canon. *Romantic Flowers* (1908) offers a kaleidoscope of the poet's early interests, mainly in the Symbolist tradition. *Pearl* (1910) adds a more detailed realism and offers outstanding narrative poems on Odysseus and Adam. The five-part *Alien Sky* (1912) combines the vivid concrete imagery of Acmeism with passionate lyrics often conveying a religious dimension, as in "The Prodigal Son" and the Islamic poem "Pilgrim," and ending with a hilarious one-act comedy in verse, "Don Juan in Egypt." *Quiver* (1916) is filled with European travel postcards and character sketches. In *Pyre* (1918) many lyrics are tenderly personal. In the brief *Porcelain Pavilion* (1918) we find vignettes of domestic life in China and Indochina, while *Tent* (1918) is an epic-scale travelogue of Africa, blending realism and boys' adventure fantasy. *Fire Column* (1921) achieves a culminating religious and philosophic depth.

RUSSIA'S WORLD TRAVELER POET

EIGHT COLLECTIONS BY NIKOLAY GUMILEV

Romantic Flowers, Pearls,
Alien Sky, Quiver,
Pyre, Porcelain Pavilion,
Tent, Fire Column

Translated with Foreword by Martin Bidney

Introduction and Illustrations by Marina Zalesski

Dialogic
Poetry
Press

VOLUME VII IN THE SERIES:
EAST–WEST BRIDGE BUILDERS

Copyright © 2016 by Martin Bidney
Dialogic Poetry Press
Vestal, New York

All Rights Reserved

ISBN 13: 978-1537320137
ISBN 10: 1537320130

Printed in the United States of America

Available from Amazon at
http://www.amazon.com/dp/1537320130

With esteem and affection
we gratefully dedicate this work
to our dear friend and colleague

Katharina Mommsen

on the occasion of her
ninety-first birthday:

Zum Geburtstag viel Glück!

Contents

Translator's Foreword	xv
Introduction	xxiii
ROMANTIC FLOWERS	1
1. Sonnet	2
2. Ballad	2
3. Ossian	3
4. Rat	4
5. Dawn	5
6. Death	6
7. In the Heavens	7
8. Thoughts	8
9. Cross	9
10. Masquerade	10
11. After Victory	11
12. Choice	12
13. Sly Devil	13
14. Refusal	13
15. Memory	14
16. Dreams	15
17. Glove	16
18. I Dreamed	16
19. Sada-yakko	17
20. Suicide	18
21. Princess	19
22. Cave of Sleep	20

23.	In Love with the Devil	21
24.	Lovers	22
25.	Spell	23
26.	Hyena	24
27.	Ship	25
28.	Jaguar	26
29.	Horror	28
30.	Beyond the Grave	29
31.	Lion's Bride	29
32.	Soul Gardens	30
33.	Contagion	31
34.	Sindbad's Eagle	33
35.	Giraffe	34
36.	Rhinoceros	35
37.	Lake Chad	36
38.	Pompey and the Pirates	38
39.	Founders	38
40.	Manlius	39
41.	Games	40
42.	To the Emperor	41
43.	Caracalla	42
44.	Mariner Pausanias …	44
45.	Neoromantic Tale	45

PEARLS 49

46.	Magic Violin	50
47.	Descendants of Cain	51
48.	Rock	52
49.	Possessed	54
50.	Duel	55
51.	Portrait of a Man	57

Contents

52.	Forest Fire	58
53.	Queen	59
54.	Comrade	61
55.	In the Library	62
56.	On the Way	64
57.	Semiramis	65
58.	Old Conquistador	66
59.	Barbarians	67
60.	Soldier of Agamemnon	69
61.	Androgyne	70
62.	Eagle	71
63.	Submission	72
64.	Knight with Chain	73
65.	Christ	74
66.	Marquis de Carabas	75
67.	Trip to China	77
68.	Testament	79
69.	Lakes	80
70.	Rendezvous	81
71.	Remember the palace ...	82
72.	Antiquity	83
73.	He had sworn ...	84
74.	Gates of Paradise	85
75.	Backwaters	86
76.	Kangaroo	87
77.	Maestro	88
78.	Don Juan	89
79.	Parrot	89
80.	Book Reader	90
81.	I can never ...	90

82.	It Wasn't the First Time	91
83.	Prayer	92
84.	Groves of palm ...	92
85.	Evening	93
86–89.	Beatrice	93
90-92.	Return of Odysseus	96
93–96.	Captains	102
97.	Adam's Dream	107

ALIEN SKY 113

I

98.	Guardian Angel	114
99.	Two Roses	115
100.	To a Girl	115
101.	At Sea	116
102.	Doubt	117
103.	Dream	117
104.	Fragment	118
105.	That Other One	119
106.	Eternal Things	120
107.	Constantinople	121
108.	Contemporaries	122
109.	Sonnet	122
110.	One Evening	123
111.	She	124
112.	Life	125
113.	From a Snakehole	125

II
DEDICATED TO ANNA AKHMATOVA

114.	I Thought, I Believed ...	126
115.	Dazzling Dreams	128

116.	Rhodes	129
117.	Pilgrim	131
118.	To the Cruel One	133
119.	Love	134
120.	Ballade	135
121.	Animal Tamer	137
122.	Poisoned	138
123.	By the Hearth	139
124.	Margaret	140
125.	The Ragged One	141
126.	Generals of Turkestan	142
127–130.	Abyssinian Songs	144

III
BY THÉOPHILE GAUTIER

131.	On the Seashore	147
132.	Art	148
133.	Anacreontic Ditty	150
134.	Rondeau	151
135.	Hippopotamus	153

IV
NARRATIVE POEMS

136.	Prodigal Son	154
137.	The Discovery of America	158

V

138.	Don Juan in Egypt	168

QUIVER — 185

139.	In Memory of Annensky	186
140.	War	187
141.	Venice	188
142.	Old Country Estates	189

143.	Fra Beato Angelico	191
144.	Conversation	193
145.	Rome	195
146.	Iambic Pentameters	196
147.	Pisa	200
148.	Judith	201
149.	Stanzas	202
150.	Return	203
151.	Leonardo	204
152.	Bird	205
153–154.	Canzonas	206
155.	Perseus	208
156.	Spirit Sun	209
157.	Middle Ages	210
158.	Cathedral of Padua	211
159.	To One Departing	212
160.	Again the Sea	213
161.	African Night	214
162.	On the Offensive	215
163.	Death	216
164.	Vision	217
165.	Courteous ...	218
166.	What a peculiar ...	219
167.	I've not so much ...	220
168.	Happiness	221
169.	Eight-Liner	223
170.	Rain	223
171.	Evening	224
172.	Genoa	225

173.	Chinese Maiden	226
174.	Paradise	227
175.	Islam	228
176.	Bologna	229
177.	Tale	230
178.	Naples	232
179.	Spinster	233
180.	Postal Clerk	235
181.	The Sick Woman	236
182.	Ode to D'Annunzio	237

PYRE   239

183.	Trees	240
184.	Andrei Rublyov	241
185.	Autumn	242
186.	Childhood	242
187.	Small Town	243
188.	Ice Drift	245
189.	Nature	246
190.	You and Me	246
191.	Dragon	247
192.	Peasant	249
193.	Worker	251
194.	Sweden	252
195.	Norwegian Mountains	253
196.	On the North Sea	254
197.	Stockholm	255
198.	Creativity	256
199.	Solace	257
200.	Prememory	258

201. First Canzona	258
202. Second Canzona	259
203. Third Canzona	260
204. Victory of Samothrace	261
205. Rose	261
206. Telephone	262
207. South	262
208. Star Scatterer	263
209. About You	264
210. Dream	265
211. Ezbekeeyeh	266

PORCELAIN PAVILION — 269

CHINA — 270
- 212. Porcelain Pavilion — 270
- 213. Moon on the Sea — 270
- 214. Heart so joyful ... — 271
- 215. Nature — 271
- 216. Road — 272
- 217. The Mandarin's Three Wives — 273
- 218. Happiness — 274
- 219. Unifying — 274
- 220. Stranger — 275
- 221. The Poet — 276
- 222. Home — 276

INDOCHINA — 277
- 223. Annám — 277
- 224. Girls — 278
- 225. Song of a Child — 278
- 226. Laos — 279
- 227. Kkha — 280

TENT — 281

228.	Introduction	282
229.	Red Sea	283
230.	Egypt	285
231.	Sahara	290
232.	Suez Canal	294
233.	Sudan	296
234.	Abyssinia	300
235.	Galla	304
236.	Somalian Peninsula	306
237.	Madagascar	308
238.	Zambezi	310
239.	Damara	312
240.	Equatorial Forest	314
241.	Dahomey	318
242.	Niger	319

FIRE COLUMN — 323

For Anna Nikolayevna Gumileva

243.	Memory	324
244.	Woods	326
245.	Word	328
246–248.	Soul and Body	329
249.	First Canzona	331
250.	Second Canzona	332
251.	Imitation of the Persian	333
252.	Persian Miniature	334
253.	Sixth Sense	336
254.	Young Elephant	337
255.	Strayed Streetcar	338
256.	Olga	340

257.	With the Gypsies	341
258.	Drunken Dervish	343
259.	Leopard	345
260.	Prayer of the Masters	347
261.	Ring	348
262.	Bird-Maiden	349
263.	My Readers	352
264.	Starry Horror	354

Translator's Foreword

Nikolay Gumilev (1886–1921) is Russia's best-known travel poet. His work—always meant to be acted aloud—is part of the life of every educated Russian. Children read him in school for his engrossing adventure narratives such as "The Discovery of America," where he shows Christopher Columbus guided by the same spirit impelling the Russian poet's own lifetime work—the "Muse of Distant Travel." To young Russians Gumilev plays a role like that of Antoine de Saint-Exupéry for the youth of France. Yet characteristically the "Discovery" is filled with meaning for every mental traveler, young or old. One of the central poets of the 20th century, a celebrator of love and risk, heroism and passion, Gumilev was a psychological explorer of deep acuity, an adventurer and military officer (in the White army during the time of troubles) whose work could nearly serve as a poetic world atlas. Contemporary with the Africa-traveling novelist Joseph Conrad, Gumilev devoted a book to his own exploratory trips to that continent—where he mapped uncharted terrain and did valuable ethnographic research. There is nothing like this Russian poet's African panorama in modern Western verse. He needs to become better known in America for his lyrical work—mellifluent, vigorous, and riveting.

The eight unabridged Gumilev collections offered here in form-true renderings will at last allow speakers of English a chance to acquire a thorough acquaintance with one of the finest poets of the Russian canon. Though Gumilev (pronounced Gumilyóv) may be less known in the anglophone world than Anna Akhmatova, to whom he was married from 1910 to 1918, his works are as colorful and lively as the life that nourished them was dramatic and perilous. Nurtured in the dreamy Symbolism of the late 19th century, with Osip Mandelstam and others he co-founded in 1911–12 the Acmeist movement, aiming for a terse and vivid concreteness. Between 1907 and 1913 he took four trips to Africa (Egypt, Sudan, Abyssinia, Somaliland)—and the literary results were astonishing. It's odd that his epic-scale vision in *Tent*, a book entirely composed of 16 vividly detailed (realistic *and* phantasmal) lyrical presentations of Africa, is rarely mentioned even by readers who are minutely familiar with Conrad's "Heart of Darkness" (1899). Marina Zalesski's biocritical introduction will survey the panorama of the explorer-poet's life and works, and her evocative illustrations, each a frontispiece for one of the eight collections, will set the mood for what's to come.

If you read the book straight through, you will be swept along by an animating verve, coupled with a variety of genre and experience, all rarely equaled in Russian lyric writing. But it's also enjoyable to browse, in relaxed fashion, as you may prefer. What I'll do in these few pages is simply give an indication of what distinctive pleasures each volume will provide, while noting some of the most remarkable poems they respectively offer—the highlights of the book as I've lived it.

Romantic Flowers (1908) couples an idealizing fantasy (1. Sonnet) with sinister motifs left over from the "decadent" movement (2. Ballad). The dramatic tension produced can be delightful (9. Cross, 10. Masquerade). Moods range from morbid humor (13. Sly Devil) to troubled pathos (15. Memory), or an enjoyable neo-Gothic horror (16.Dreams). Sometimes the experimental rhythms are dazzling (23. In Love with the Devil, 33. Contagion, 37. Lake Chad). Travels range from the Middle East and Africa (poems 33–37) to ancient Rome (poems 38–44).

Pearls (1910) moves fantasy a bit nearer to the daylight

world we think we know. The initial poem (46. Magic Violin) makes the transition, or achieves the blending, with winsome whimsy. Sinister intimations continue to haunt us (poems 48–51) but move from imagined scenarios to a more realistic film-like jungle scene (52. Forest Fire). Horror and adventure variously combine (poems 53–55), to be summed up in the vigorous and stoical 56. On the Way. Rhythmic virtuosity resurges in the galloping beat of 59. Barbarians. The psychological study of domination (62. Eagle) alternates with that of being humbled or subjected (60. Soldier of Agamemnon, 63. Submission), or the two opposing conditions contrasted in one man's life (64. Knight with Chain). Then suddenly comes a vision exhilaratingly or soberly sublime (65. Christ, 74. Gates of Paradise), or one endearingly amusing (66. Marquis de Carabas, 67. A Trip to China).

I love to recite 75. Backwaters for the charmingly unpredictable ending. Still more important, and on a far larger scale, are Gumilev's brilliant, deeply personal rewritings of a classical scenario (90.–92. Return of Odysseus) and a biblical one (97. Adam's Dream). These two poems are treasures of world literature, but there is a sadness at the heart of each one's triumph. A preoccupation throughout this volume of Gumilev is solitary heroism and its hazards. In general, romantic love is not a happy topic in his work. Love (though not passion) is increasingly distrusted.

In *Alien Sky* (1912) Gumilev has become explicitly an Acmeist, and the focuses are more on reality than fantasy. In Part I, whatever the realm of being, passion prevails: it animates the skeptical parable 99. Two Roses and the polite yet telling rebuke in 100. To a Girl. The superb little debate in 104. Fragment defends the poet's passion against that of the preacher. But something like the expectation of a religious thinker or would-be quester animates 105. That Other One and 106. Eternal Things. Daylight and mythnight are effectively contrasted in 108. Contemporaries. In

Part II my favorite work is 117. Pilgrim, one of the most moving Islamic poems I have ever had the privilege to read. There's a strange power of a different kind in 127-130. Abyssinian Songs. Part III of *Alien Sky*, poems 131-135, contains translations from Théophile Gautier. Because the Russian versions are, like the French originals, perfectly made and entirely successful, I render Gumilev's lyrics directly from his Russian.

Part IV is the finest part of *Alien Sky*: poems 136. The Prodigal Son and 137. The Discovery of America are among the most effective lyrical narratives to be found anywhere. The first is the biblical squanderer's dramatic monologue, the second an account of Europeans' encounter with the New World from Columbus' point of view in three richly descriptive cantos—here not only is the psychology fascinating, but the employment of the intricate stanza pattern shows the highest melodic mastery. The fifth and final section of *Alien Skies* contains a one-act comedy in verse, *Don Juan in Egypt*. How I'd love to see this clever sketch performed! Nothing in Gumilev's earlier, more serious writing prepared us for the sparkling, hilarious wit.

In *Quiver* (1916)—with groups of poems about Italy, the war, religion, and Russia—one may see a greater depth to Gumilev's personality in lyrical monologues. Having visited St. Mark's Plaza myself, I responded with pleasure to 141. Venice. Both poems 143. Fra Beato Angelico and 151. Leonardo are powerful in their loving simplicity—while in 157. Cathedral of Padua the ironic distance lends force, and in 176. Bologna and 178. Naples the gentle humor is touching. Pictures of Old Russia surviving today are offered with complexity and without sentimentality (142. Old Country Estates, 180. Postal Clerk). It is fittingly invigorating that Gumilev suddenly introduces a reaffirmation of his favorite theme of solitary heroism (160. Again the Sea). His war songs are stirring for this reason (163. Death). In the

Translator's Foreword

varied ironies of the sketches constituting 168. Happiness we appreciate the paradoxes in every human fate. As for religion, 174. Paradise recalls to me the bemused fantasies on the afterlife in Goethe's *West-East Divan*.

Pyre (1918) is a short book, yet hard to summarize, containing many short masterworks on varied themes. Thus in 183. Trees we find an idyllic vision of Mary in the palms and Moses in the oaks, in 184. Andrei Rublyov a tender tribute of a modern thinker to the medieval prince of Russian icon-painters, and in 185. Autumn the poet's walk with his dog, a moving epiphany presented in what might be called free verse, though it is still intensely musical, like the semi-metrical free verses of Goethe (e.g. "Prometheus," "Ganymede"). The overall level of writing in this collection is so high in the first half that I'm tempted to mention nearly every poem in that section for some specially attractive feature. I will single out the candid parable 186. Childhood, the delightful trio of poems 187–189 which are at once consoling and energizing, the passionately liberated parable 190. You and Me, and finally the historically foreboding 192. Peasant and 193. Worker. The second half of the book contains a collection of love poems that I don't rate among the poet's best work. But the final monologue, 211. Ezbekeeyeh, is a gripping inner drama with the last word suspensefully unwritten—though maybe guessable. I recited this poem to a friend who had been to Ezbekeeyeh, and I still picture the suddenly changing expressions on his face while he listened.

The brief collection *Porcelain Pavilion* (1918) contains adaptations of Chinese poems in Part I and of Indochinese ones in Part II. Some of the Chinese poems remind me of those used by Gustav Mahler in his *Song of the Earth* (*Das Lied von der Erde*). They are most delicately made, and they paint varying moods. The poet's liking for unusual rhythm appears in 214. Heart so joyful ... Poem 214. Road is grimly realistic, poem 217. The Mandarin's Three Wives startlingly funny, and poem 220. Stranger is transfixingly beautiful, showing, as do so many songs in our book, mastery of melodic unrhymed verse. The final three lyrics, 225–227, are superbly actable Laotian monologues.

Tent (1918) is an unprecedented achievement in Russian poetry—an entire book about Africa. Like the work of Joseph Conrad cited earlier, it combines observation and fantasizing, imaginative vigor and colonial bias. Earl D. Sampson, in *Nikolay Gumilev* (New York: G. K. Hall, Twayne series, 1979), rightly notes that the first half of the book is chiefly place description, the second half adventure, so that the second half is more obviously fictional or fantastical than the first (think of boys' adventure tales, the cowboy-and-Indian plottings of Mayne Reid). But observation and imaginative urgings—ideological, literary, or personal—are blended throughout (Sampson 108–111). *Tent* is a literary work of its era, complex and ambivalent, highly energetic and wide-ranging. Everyone will likely have mixed feelings about it, but no student of early twentieth-century literary and cultural history should ignore it.

What I called "mixed feelings" will be immediately aroused. In the opening poem of *Tent,* 228. Introduction, we are told (1) that Africa's historical woes are related to its having been guided by an inexperienced apprentice angel (no reference here to colonial exploitation), and (2) that the poet would love to die in Africa, near the sycamore tree where Jesus and Mary had rested. (I'm glad to be reminded in this touching way that most biblical stories take place on the African continent.) Poem 229. Red Sea is filled with wonders and troubles, 230. Egypt with awe and tenderness, and we are charmed by the latter poem's benignly humorous conclusion. My favorite piece in the group—and one which I've recited in public with great pleasure—is the thrillingly symphonic 231. Sahara, where both the beauty and the disturbing drama of the sublimely forbidding landscape

Translator's Foreword

appear continually to increase until our wonder is climaxed in entertaining if sobering fashion by a sci-fi ending that is not only clever but perhaps ecologically prescient. The ingeniously constructed poetic forms in this volume vary as does the changing topography—poem 232. Suez Canal in short quick lines, 233. Sudan in long unrhymed stanzas of melodious motion, and 234. Abyssinia where galloping rhythms add vigor and speed. The adventurous action lyrics offer the solitary heroism of 236. Somalian Peninsula, the boatride dream of 237. Madagascar, and then the melodramatic adventure fantasies of 238. Zambezi and 240. Equatorial Forest. Poem 239. Damara (Hottentot Cosmogony) condescendingly posits a too-simple myth of white peacemakers. But 242. Niger, the farewell tribute, bespeaks an earnest ardor—a deep and passionate attachment.

Lastly, *Fire Column* (1921) strikes most people as the culmination of Gumilev's achievement, largely on account of its religio-philosophic depth. In poem 243. Memory the speaker tells of the souls he had been in former lives. Poem 245. Word gives an ontological dimension to living speech; in 246–248. Soul and Body, the unnamed third entity—Imagination, I'd call it—reveals a transcending of the other two. Poems 249–252 lend new psychological insight to the presentation of Gumilev's recurrent disabusals by love. Poems 253. Sixth Sense and 255. Strayed Streetcar are considered among the poet's finest. The latter features a surreality emergent from deep dream-layers and repays repeated readings. Poem 257. With the Gypsies takes dream-logic into the half-dreamt tavern world.

The most purely entertaining, jaunty, and melodious poem in *Fire Column* is 258. Drunken Dervish—definitely my favorite to read aloud. Yet it's equally true that 260. Prayer of the Masters gives me courage and determination every time I think of it: this, too, could be read every day with deep satisfaction. Poems 244. Woods, 261. Ring, and

262. Bird-Maiden are, like Ludwig Tieck's "Blond Eckbert," oneiric fairy tales for adults, but with an Acmeist concision replacing earlier languid Symbolist reverie.

I have been shaping my translations of the engrossing lyrics of Nikolay Gumilev for over a decade. One reason I undertook the project was to acquire practice—and, I hoped, mastery—in the writing of poems both visually powerful and melodically appealing. Gumilev could equally sustain my prolonged interest by the abundance of contradiction and conflict in his personality. His love poems are so often blended with doubt, irony, and dislike (of himself or the loved one or both) that I think he may have ventured on his risky African trips partly, or largely, out of love-frustration. A jocoserious line from William Blake's *Jerusalem* keeps coming back to mind: "I must rush again to war, for the virgin has frowned and refused" (*J* 68:63). In Gumilev we have a man who wrote his life into his poetry with a shocking directness. An explorer of the inner as of the outer world, Gumilev is a composer, a painter, a dramatist—and one of the best lyric poets who ever wrote Russian.

Introduction

NIKOLAY GUMILEV, POET-ADVENTURER: A BIO-CRITICAL OVERVIEW
by Marina Zalesski

... now catch sight of her
Swifter gaze than blazing meteor

With predictable inconstancy,
Muse of Distant Travel—patron, she.

Let's begin with an evocation of the poet by his devoted friend:

> There was something about him reminiscent of a wild and proud migratory bird, topped with a small, rounded head perched loftily atop his neck. His face was dominated by a large straight nose standing beneath a pair of round, bulbous eyes, which threw alert sidelong glances with inquisitive, unhurried movements.
> Just like a bird, he loved space and freedom, his affection manifested not in any metaphorical or theoretical sense, but with a love whose origins lay in the spirit. His joys were to be found in long journeys. ... He traveled to Africa, where from the Negus of Abyssinia he received generous (though unneeded) permission to hunt elephants and dig for gold in Abyssinian lands. He had been in the

far north, to the island of Vaygatch and the archipelago of Novaya Zemlya, in the enchanted lands of silence, the six-month darkness, and the majestic Northern Lights. In the winter of 1919 I sometimes met him on the streets of Petersburg, draped in a long Lapland coat made from the skins of caribou calves, with glass-bead embroidered trim. Tall, with a serious face, walking in a dawdling and condescending manner, his countenance would have been more appropriate on one of the slender, stern high priests of an exotic land.

His life was always one of solitude, and like a large, freedom-loving bird, rather than acknowledging the rules of the flock, he opted instead to build his nest in the places least accessible to others. Few knew him personally, and (consequently) few spoke of him. One would be hard-pressed, for example, to find someone aware that he had served throughout the Great War [WWI] in the Sumsky Cavalry Regiment, an experience that he mentioned briefly but about which (despite an astonishing display of valor that earned him two St. George crosses) ... he never shared a single significant detail. ... I have no doubt that this bravery was reserved, cold and silent.

As if it were not enough to enter willingly a modern (and increasingly deadly) conflict, his greatest merit was that he and he alone was able to realize its poetic potential.

He was, admittedly, no stranger to the antiquated notions of the previous era, such as love for one's motherland, an awareness of owing a living duty to her, and a sense of personal honor. Yet most old-fashioned of all was his readiness, without a

Introduction

moment's hesitation, to pay for all three with his life.[1]

This passionate description of the poet Nikolay Gumilev, composed by A. Kuprin in his essay "Winged Soul" shortly after the poet's death, was, along with the majority of Gumilev's poems, banned by the Soviet authorities for nearly seventy years. Any one of several factors—his birth into the aristocracy, service in the White Army, open upholding of royalist views, and composition of poetry solely for the sake of art—could have led to an individual's execution in the wake of the blood-soaked 1920s. He died as another of the countless victims of the Red Terror whose stories became the mute stones making up the walls of Soviet prisons. An ordinary manila folder, kept in the archives and scrawled with a terrifyingly long number above the simple inscription *"Delo N. S. Gumileva"* ("The Gumilev File"), remains the only detailed account of his final silent sufferings.

Nikolay was born in the town of Kronstadt on April 3 (15 by the Gregorian calendar), 1886 to aristocratic middle-class parents, Stepan Yakovlevich Gumilev (1836–1920) and Anna Ivanovna L'vova (1854–1942). His childhood years were spent in St. Petersburg (his father's place of work) and Tsarskoye Selo, and he stayed in Tiflis (during the 3-year treatment period of his tuberculosis-afflicted brother) or at his family's summer residences in Slepnevo (in Tver Region), Popovka (near Moscow), and Berezki (in the Ryazan region).

A fragile and sickly child, Nikolay crafted for himself an imaginary world inspired by the tales of his uncle (an

---

1. Luknitskaya, V. *Nikolay Gumilev: Zhizn' poeta po materialam domashnego archiva sem'i Luknitskikh* (Leningrad: Lenizdat, 1990), 298.

admiral) and father (a naval physician), as well as adventures drawn from the works of James Fenimore Cooper, Thomas Mayne Reid, and Jules Verne. Nikolay began composing fables before learning to write, and made his debut in the "Tiflis Pamphlet" with the poem, "I Ran from Cities into the Woods" (1902). An ancient city surrounded by biblical mountains, Tiflis (today's Tbilisi) captured the young Nikolay's imagination, arousing it with ruins of Georgian palaces, legends of ancient invaders, sounds of Asian music, and the noise of colorful markets, which formed currents of poetic imagery in Nikolay's as yet unskilled but passionate verses. His love of geography and zoology, combined with a passion for drawing, once led him to transform his room into an exotic underwater garden, covering the walls with murals populated by sea monsters and mermaids, even constructing a functioning shell-covered fountain at the room's center. His mother considered the nurturing of kindness and the development of good taste to be the most vital aspects of parenting. Little concerned about her son's poor school grades, she cared primarily about his spiritual growth, encouraging him to read copiously and unhurriedly, and urged him toward thoughtful conversation. It may be owing to her that Gumilev developed an "ability to see in any object its heavenly beauty; to see how every object is an eye through which one can look and get a glimpse of perpetuity."[2]

Gumilev's time in Tsarskoye Selo and the village Popovka was particularly influential in the early development of his poetic talent. Tsarskoye Selo, the verdant poetic paradise "where so many lyres are hanging on branches,"[3] was closely tied to the great Russian poet Alexander Pushkin. There Nikolay attended high school under the

---

2. Luknitskaya 19.
3. A. Akhmatova, "Verses of Tsarskoye Selo," 1921.

INTRODUCTION

direction of Innokenty Annensky, an influential Symbolist poet whom Gumilev would later lovingly refer to as "the final swan of Tsarskoe Selo" ("In Memory of Annensky," 1912). Annensky's encouragement, direction, and leniency toward Gumilev's lack of academic enthusiasm helped the budding poet to concentrate on his early experiments with verse, a labor whose fruits became apparent in 1905 when he presented his teacher with his first book, *The Way of the Conquistadors*. (Poem 1. Sonnet [see below] refers to this theme.) Popovka, by contrast, was a small summer residence purchased by the Gumilevs in 1890, and it became the cradle for Nikolay's aspirations to become a brave explorer. Not one to be bound by mundane reality, in Popovka Gumilev discovered his first "new lands." Through his eyes, a pond, a patch of birch trees, and a creek were transmuted into mysterious seas, virgin lands, and nameless rivers unsailed by living soul.

Painfully conscious of physical weakness, Nikolay continually tested his endurance and will power. Even as a child he became an able horseman and an impressive marksman, despite the double affliction of lameness and strabismus. While explaining his often reckless stunts, Gumilev quipped that "Bravery substituted for [his] nonexistent strength and agility."[4]

Self-discipline and the ability to triumph over weaknesses of body and spirit were qualities that Gumilev never ceased perfecting. As a young man, however, he paid equal heed to refined appearance and to the daily exercise of exquisite manners. Idealistic, sensitive, and withdrawn, young Nikolay was nonetheless acutely aware of what he deemed his own unattractiveness, and he carefully compensated for it with an air of eccentricity, enigma, wit, and gallantry. But these social tactics proved useless when

---

4. Luknitskaya 21.

in 1903 he was introduced to the sister of one of his friends, 14-year-old Anna Gorenko, who would grow up to become the great poet Anna Andreyevna Akhmatova. For the next six years Gumilev would persistently ask for her hand in marriage, and her repeated rejections would push him to several suicide attempts. As they both had strong, independent, freedom-loving natures, they would feel the visceral connection between their two poetic souls, yet would always yearn for the open air of a bohemian existence characterized by autonomy of choice, nonconformity in relationships, and the absence of worldly attachments. Despite involvement in other romances and, later, marriages, their feeling of true love and deep caring for one another would pervade the works of both poets until the end.

Though Anna eventually surrendered to Gumilev's proposals and subsequently gave birth to a son, Lev, the boy's tragic fate served for her as a living and tormenting reminder of her first marriage.[5] Lev was raised by his erudite grandmother, who, as did his father, educated him in the old-fashioned aristocratic atmosphere of long evenings spent in reading and study, allowing an ample amount of freedom and time in which to daydream and play. At age 16 Lev became a hostage of the regime and ultimately spent nearly 25 years of his life in prison for the "transgressions" of his "bourgeois" and politically nonconforming parents. Lev's captivity, as well as that of Akhmatova's second husband (literary critic N. Punin, who died behind the walls of a state

---

5. Nikolay Gumilev had two more children: a son, Orest Nikolaevich Vysotsky (1913–1992), with actress Olga Vysotskaya, whom Gumilev met at the artistic café "Stray Dog" during the jubilee of the Russian poet K. Balmont, and a daughter, Elena (1919–1942), with his second wife, Anna Engelgardt (the daughter of historian and noted literary critic A.N. Engelgardt), whom he had met at one of V. Bryusov's poetic evenings in 1919. Tragically, Anna, her parents, and Elena died during the Leningrad blockade in 1942.

Introduction

prison), became the inspiration for Akhmatova's famed "Requiem" (1935–1940), an elegy dedicated to the mothers and wives who suffered, along with their innocent loved ones, from the Stalinist oppressions. Lev eventually became a historian-ethnographer known for his works on ancient ethnic groups and for his controversial theories of ethnogenesis and "passionality."

The majority of the poems in Gumilev's *Way of the Conquistadors* are dedicated to Anna. In this youthful, romantic work, thoroughly imbued with themes drawn from Gumilev's favorite poets and writers (Balmont, Annensky, Nietzsche), Gumilev's most significant fascination is with the beautiful armor worn by the Spanish conquerors whom the title exalts. The costume of the conquistador, which projected an air of fearlessness, determination, and invincibility, had protected Gumilev's vulnerable poetic personality during its temperamental development. The sheltering armor let him explore the spaces of imagery that intrigued him: historic legends, knightly adventures, and explorations of lands afar. His poetic debut was noticed by the coryphaeus of poetry, Valery Bryusov, who, despite his stern review, found some encouraging words for the aspiring poet, noting prophetically that that all the young "conquistador's victories and conquests lay ahead."[6] An artist distinguished by exceptional literary discipline, Bryusov may have sensed the degree of diligence and will power in the young poet that he felt in himself. Always open to criticism, Gumilev was grateful for the honesty of the review. Bryusov's poetry, as well as his views on art, resonated with Nikolay's still intuitive ideas, prompting him to initiate a correspondence of more than eight years that had a crucial influence on his poetic growth. In each piece of advice from Bryusov, Nikolay could vastly amplify the

---

6. Valery Bryusov, "Put' Konkvistadorov," *Vesy* 11 (1905): 165.

constructive meaning, while at the same time nurturing his own theory about the "making of a poet." His conclusion was that the inborn gift for poetry must be nourished and cultivated, and he began the meticulous endeavor not only to improve the poetic form but also to cultivate the "poetic soul."

After completing his education at the high school in Tsarskoye Selo in 1906, Gumilev traveled to Paris, where he spent his days meeting Russian and French poets and artists, as well as attending exhibitions, concerts, and literary evenings. At the Sorbonne he studied poetic theory, read noteworthy French poetry, and zealously worked on his own lyrical technique, aiming at a complete knowledge of the "anatomy of a poem."[7] In Paris he also tried his hand at publishing his own literary journal, *Sirius*, in which he implemented his idea about the symbiosis of painting and poetry by publishing works by artists M. Farmakovsky, S. Danishevsky, and others, and even sent his articles to a popular literary magazine, *Scales* (*Весы*), in St. Petersburg. One such article described an art exhibition in France featuring paintings by Russian philosopher-artist Nicholas Roerich, in whose sweeping murals Gumilev recognized his own poetic landscapes, comparing them to recently viewed works of Paul Gauguin. "They both," Gumilev wrote, "fell in love with the world of primal people, with its basic yet potent chromatic scheme, and with the line-work which surprises by its almost crude simplicity; with its stories both wild and sublime. Just as Paul Gauguin opened the tropics, Roerich opened for us the true North, so beloved and so daunting."[8] During this trip Nikolay spent considerable time visiting the Jardin des Plantes and Jardin d'Acclimations, where he

---

7. Title of N. Gumilev's article, published in the literary magazine *Dragon* in 1919.
8. Nikolay Gumilev, "Dva salona," *Vesy* 5 (1908): 103.

often came during the night to observe the plentiful fauna, both woodland and avian. His childhood dream of reaching distant and unexplored lands was fueled by his Parisian surroundings highlighting both masterpieces of western civilization and historic layers of human creativity. He felt that what people had dreamed of throughout the ages was within his grasp, that he had the capacity to become another Columbus or a Russian Théophile Gautier. Critic A. Pavlovsky wrote that one of the most definitive traits of Gumilev's personality was his ability to turn dream into reality, to "actualize what appeared to be nonexistent, unreachable, or was not given by nature or destiny,"[9] and to do this by sheer force of will.

While in Paris, Nikolay published his second book of poetry, *Romantic Flowers* (1908), which he dedicated to Anna Gorenko. The theme of exotic lands, which would to some extent become Gumilev's poetic signature, first appears in this collection, as well as qualities of what Gumilev would later develop into a new poetic movement called "Acmeism." Despite the sentimental titles and themes of some of the poems, in this volume Gumilev moves away from the romantic musicality so widely applied in *Conquistadors*, trying instead to depict life in an almost prosaic, detailed, and "earthy" way. All this he achieved while simultaneously (and with some mastery) exchanging his Spanish armor for a jaguar pelt (*«И к людскому я крался жилищу / По пустому сумрачному полю»*) ("Jaguar," 1907), a captain's uniform (*"Нас было пять ... мы были капитаны"*) ("Captains," 1907), or the precious jewels of a sacrificial maiden ("Lion's Bride," 1907). Some of the poems boast a decidedly epic tone (as heard in "Giraffe," 1907), revealing what would also distinguish Gumilev's particular style: his

---

9. A. I. Pavlovsky, "Nikolay Gumilev," *Stikhotvoreniya i poemy* (Leningrad: Sovetskiy pisatel', 1988), 16.

gift for "painting" (*живописать*) a story or staging it in a poetical form, a trait which would eventually lead him to playwriting. Though *Romantic Flowers* received an enthusiastic welcome from Bryusov, Gumilev was not satisfied. His own standards had exceeded the requirements of his teacher, and his self-criticism became harsher than that of his critics. In every letter to Bryusov he requested advice and immediately provided it himself.

"The silence and emptiness"[10] that saturated Gumilev's soul after the publication of *Romantic Flowers*, as well as another marriage proposal declined by Anna upon his return from Europe in April of 1908, crystallized Gumilev's already growing design to depart. Africa, which had lived and breathed in his heart and poetry since he was a small boy, now called him with the irresistible enticement of a siren. By a short, almost touristic journey that lasted roughly six weeks, Africa captivated Nikolay, and for the remainder of his life his soul would unfailingly reverberate with that enthralling call of the Muse of Travel. She would become his unquenchable thirst, his inextinguishable love.

Upon his return to St. Petersburg Gumilev settled down in Tsarskoye Selo with the rest of his family. A meeting with writer Sergey Auslender led him to the home of prominent Symbolist poet and philosopher Vyacheslav Ivanov, in whose turreted house the artistic elite met regularly for evenings of discussion and poetry reading. During the early years of the 20th century, Russian literature and arts bore a mark of decadence that found its reflection not only in Symbolist poetry but also in the intelligentsia's perception of the world—its philosophic thought. Rapid sociopolitical changes brought into the artistic consciousness feelings of the ephemerality and futility of life. These emotions were augmented by the rejection of historically established morals

---

10. Luknitskaya 66.

and values, an undermining of ideals in a vein akin to the so-called "nihilist movement" during the reign of Alexander II. Writers and artists further isolated themselves into an exalted space of "pure art," searching for new themes, forms of expression, and their niche within a world in flux. The feeling of stagnation in literature and art generated frustration, which gradually led to the birth of a cluster of new literary movements and the inception of new experimental forms. The new period, marked by the rise of exceptional creativity, would later acquire the label of a "Silver Age," on par with the "Golden Age" of a century earlier. Aspiring young writers, musicians, and artists joined creative workgroups, attending lectures, concerts, exhibitions, and performances of experimental theatre. Social life burst with novel forms of entertainment as a politically interested middle class began hosting intellectual parties where state policy was discussed with the same enthusiasm as the latest performances of Isadora Duncan. Such gatherings would readily be followed by occult sessions, poetry readings at small basement clubs, dinners at restaurants, or all-night walks along the embankment of the Neva. Young intellectuals eagerly awaited the printing of new magazines, and even while making prodigious use of their capacity for traveling abroad, were frequently drawn back by the richness of cultural life in their native land, the eruption of an amazing array of new artistic opportunities which made Europe, as Gumilev put it, "seem provincial compared to St. Petersburg."[11]

Gumilev found himself in the heart of the city's artistic life, an environment animated by its frenetic excitement. In August 1908 he commenced his studies at Petersburg University, initially at the law school, then relocated to the historical linguistics department and the department of

---

11. Luknitskaya 73.

Romance and Germanic studies, where he organized his first interest group. With the help of the writer A. Tolstoy and the poet P. Potemkin, Gumilev coordinated and published a literary journal, *The Island*, which, regrettably, saw only one issue in print. With untiring enthusiasm, Gumilev turned his energy towards a new magazine, *Apollo*, under the editorship of poet and literary critic S. Makovsky. This literary almanac would reflect the idealistic views of the artistic elite, prophesying the missionary role of art and its spiritual value for the salvation of the world. Gumilev's own column on literary criticism (originally printed in *Apollo*) would eventually find a new incarnation in the 1923 book *Letters on Russian Poetry*. With the collaboration of S. Makovsky and V. Ivanov, in 1909 Gumilev implemented his long-contemplated idea of creating a school specifically for poetry. The first lectures on "The Poetic Academy" (later "Society of Proponents of the Artistic Word") took place at the home of Ivanov and were attended and conducted by members of the creative intelligentsia. Among the speakers were the poets I. Annensky, M. Voloshin, Z. Gippius, and E. Dmitrieva, in addition to Professor F. Zelinsky and many others. Though these sessions eventually turned from planned "collegial exchange" into lectures dominated primarily by Ivanov, they provided Gumilev with instructive experience that proved invaluable later in his poetic career.

In December 1909 Gumilev returned to Africa, following an itinerary that included Port Said, Djibouti, Djeda, and Harrar. He traveled on the backs of mules (led by local guides), studied local traditions, and made plans for the ethnographic trip which followed almost immediately in September of 1910. During that expedition, which lasted nearly six months, Gumilev journeyed mostly on foot, reaching Addis Ababa, attending festivities at the Grand Negus' palace, and even participating in a real African hunt.

Introduction

All the while, Gumilev collected Abyssinian songs and cultural artifacts and, of course, wrote poetry. Upon his return Gumilev gave a lecture about his trip at the Poetic Academy, placing special emphasis on the importance of ethnographic work during scientific journeys, including the collection of songs, legends, records of religious dances, and customs. He argued that only by mapping out the "ethnography of the spirit"[12] and documenting people's art can we come to an understanding of a nation's character.

However, important events took place in the short time between the African journeys. In April 1910 Gumilev married Anna Andreyevna Gorenko (with whom he would spend the summer in France) in the same busy month that his third book, *Pearls*, was published. In a stirring review, Bryusov (to whom the volume was dedicated) praised Gumilev's ability to create "countries which live not according to the laws of nature, but rather by the rules established by their author."[13] The world of *Pearls* is like an island with lakes of a mysterious "night" and bubbling waterfalls, with "groves of palm trees and thickets of aloe." "The regal leopard," the "wandering panther," and the "elephant-hermits" "freely roam the forests," and dragons perch comfortably on the rocks. The setting is populated by a myriad of characters both gallant and malevolent. A brave knight, for instance, embraces his death in a fight with a warrior maiden, and a queen awaits her city's conquerors upon a bed erected in the center of the main square. "Sullen Druids" rule among stones while maiden-witches hover by sleepers' windows, casting their spells in the obscurest hours of the night. "Old drinking buddies" plan a trip to China; an amazing raja

---

12. Luknitskaya 114.
13. Valery Bryusov, "Nikolay Gumilev. *Zhemchuga*," *Russkaya Mysl'* 7 (1910):318.

leads his armies to conquer the north and there, amid ice and snow where nothing but deep bear-tracks can be seen, he creates a "kingdom of dreams."

Upon the book's publication, Vyacheslav Ivanov referred to Gumilev as "Bryusov's squire," acknowledging the young poet's right to "receive a tap on the shoulder with the sword,"[14] while Gumilev, for his part, minimized the volume's significance with the label of a mere "exercise."[15] Indeed, the connection between visual arts and poetry, which Gumilev tried to advocate in his first publication, the journal *Sirius*, became clearly evident in *Pearls*. Just as an aspiring artist copies hundreds of masterpieces before his strokes become confident, his eye exact, and his ideas independent, Gumilev reconstructed a wealth of literature in *Pearls* by playfully varying themes of his favorite masters: Bryusov, Balmont, Rabelais, and Knut Hamsun. Nevertheless, in this "sketchbook" of poetry one can already see something of what would characterize Gumilev's style: a scrupulous polishing of the poetic form, a continuous and meticulous tinkering with the word, and a determination to bring the body of the poem to its utmost perfection. According to critic A. Pavlovsky, *Pearls* showed also Gumilev's "pompous, intense, and colorfully excessive 'baroque romanticism' penetrated by a rhetoric of pathos."[16] The highly ornate language of Gumilev's early verse, along with a fondness for epic poetry, storytelling, and even story-painting, connects his work to the ancient poetic tradition shared by the Slavic ballad-singers (*guslyary*), the African griots, the Irish seanchaí, and the medieval minstrels. But perhaps the most obvious characteristic is what many critics called the "foreignness" of Gumilev's poetry, his preoccupation

---

14. V. Ivanov, "*Zhemchuga* N. Gumileva," *Apollon* 7 (1910):38.
15. Luknitskaya 110.
16. Pavlovsky 20.

Introduction

with the "Alien Sky" (the title of his next collection, published in 1912). His love for Gauguinian virgin landscapes, ultramarine skies, faraway lands, and adventures on the edge of death is what made Gumilev so "non-Russian" among the pleiad of poets for whom Russia was always both source and destination. This exotic fascination and restlessness contributed to an image of the poet as a wanderer in a search of a spiritual homeland. However, it could be argued that Gumilev was always a Russian poet merely because he wrote in Russian, bringing portraits of foreign lands to life only with the artistic palette of the Russian language. The importunate legacy of the Russian literary language and the rich heritage of its imagery perhaps made it possible for Gumilev to approach Pushkin with his Russian "all-worldliness" or cosmopolitanism, the ability to comprehend and experience a foreign culture, history, and words as one's own. Critic A. Pavlovsky considered *Pearls* a culminating work in the first portion of Gumilev's poetic path and took it as a sign of both Gumilev's recognition of his own poetic gift and, more vitally, the discovery of his own unique voice.[17]

In 1911 Nikolay Gumilev attempted once more to create something akin to a "Poetic Academy," this time structured around a definite program with himself as leader and lawmaker. On October 20 the first gathering of the "Poets' Guild" (*Цех поэтов*) was held in the apartment of poet Sergey Gorodetsky. The formation of this new poetic school also reflected Gumilev's personal development, as he (along with others) found himself drifting away from the Russian Symbolist movement in search of a new direction. The Poets' Guild was intended to become both the stage for his own mastery of writing and a school of poetic thought, and he welcomed fledgling poets into the fold. The guild functioned

---

17. Pavlovsky 20.

according to its own set of rather unorthodox rules, which made it resemble a medieval institute for enlightenment and growth more than a modern literary society. One such doctrine was the perception of poetry as a craft. Under the direction of Gumilev, Gorodetsky, and the lawyer-historian D. Kuzmin-Karavayev, sessions were led with an element of theatricality designed to create a ceremonial atmosphere and a feeling of connection to the great masters through their historic legacy. Students worked according to Gumilev's technical principles of verse construction, which strove toward an ideal in form and content, a perfect union of body and soul in the creation of "eternal verse." The students not only wrote and revised their poems in an endless search for the perfect form, but also listened to and prepared lectures on world literature, a practice meant to nurture their inspiration and fill, so to speak, their psychic plaster-molds with words of everlasting bronze. Gumilev considered poetry a craft, a skill that must be learned.[18]

He also drew a parallel to childbearing in that both are accomplished only through patience, labor, and pain.[19] While the form of a poem is achieved through a familiarity with acquired words, the essence of the lyric should be born naturally, and only delivered into the world after having been carried, nurtured, suffered over, and slowly molded by its author, in the same way that a flower needs nourishment from the earth in order to grow. Poetry is a craft, a labor, but also an independent creative force. As with any type of art, its technique can be taught, but the required vision is something with which one must be born. Regardless of the tribulations involved, Gumilev saw poetry as the highest spiritual employment of human life: "Poetry transforms a

---

18. Odoevtseva, I., *Na beregakh Nevy* (Moscow: Khudozhestvennaya literatura, 1988), 154.
19. Luknitskaya 147.

INTRODUCTION

poet in the same way that a woman is transformed into a mother: both become creators, both are one step closer to God in this divine function. Truly superb poems are like human souls—eternal. They live for centuries while teaching and rousing people. Among them one can meet guardian angels, wise leaders, tempting devils, and cherished friends. Under their power, people love, fight, and die."[20] The guild also started publication of *Hyperborean*, a literary magazine promulgating their artistic views, which appeared 1912–1913. A year later, a publishing house of the same name was formed, which would go on to print Akhmatova's *Rosary* (1913–16; four editions) and *White Flock* (1917), as well as collections by O. Mandelstam, S. Gorodetsky, G. Ivanov, and M. Lozinsky.

Many aspiring poets were naturally driven away by the "medievalness" of the guild's gatherings, dissuaded by such apparently draconian characteristics as a strict hierarchy and dogmatic rules expected to be followed by all of the initiated. However, the nucleus of this poetic school (composed of Akhmatova, Gorodetsky, Mandelstam, Zenkevich, and Narbut) devised a new poetic direction, a movement which proclaimed it had replaced Symbolism. In his article "The Legacy of Symbolism and Acmeism" (*Apollo*, 1913), Gumilev declared the birth of Acmeism and outlined its basic principles: veracity and realism in the depiction of all physical and psychological aspects of life, precision of words, clarity of images, rejection of the mystical trend so common in waning Symbolism, and, finally, genuine artistic interest towards *all* moments of life whether seemingly insignificant or epically grand. Acmeists held up as their literary models William Shakespeare, who had shown them "the inner world of the human being"; François Rabelais, who had outlined "all of the joys and wisdom of human physiology"; François

---

20. Luknitskaya 148.

Villon, who told of "life, which never doubts itself"; and Théophile Gautier, "who had found for this life suitable garments of the most flawless form." The acknowledgment of the "inherent value" (самоценность) of each aspect and phenomenon of life is the cornerstone of Acmeism. "By feeling ourselves to be 'phenomena' among other 'phenomena' we become participants in the world's rhythm, we receive the impact of the world and, in turn, affect it ourselves."[21] Most pointedly, Acmeism rejects the rebellion and protest so common to previous poetic forms, explaining that "Here, where death exists, for a poet to rebel in the name of reaching a different state of being is as strange as for a captive to break a wall in a room with an open door."[22] He writes:

> All's dust—there's no denying.
> True sculpture, though, lives on,
>   Outvying
> Us humans when we're gone. ("Art," 1912)

A "decisive break away from politics and a pursuit of ascetic hermeticism" is, in Pavlovsky's opinion, what constitutes the foundation of Acmeism.[23] Parallel to the Acmeists' rejection of social reality stands their equally resolute departure from attempts to understand and solidify the deepest truth of every mystery. In the same article, Gumilev wrote: "All the beauty, all the holy meaning of stars resides in the fact that they are so eternally far from this earth, and that no advancement in aviation is capable of bringing them any closer. Childishly wise, painfully sweet is the feeling of one's own ignorance: that's what the unknown is giving us." "Always to keep in mind the incomprehensible"

---

21. N. Gumilev, "Nasledie simvolizma i akmeism," *Apollon* 1 (1913): 43.
22. Gumilev 42.
23. Pavlovsky 31.

Introduction

and resist the temptation to "assault one's thoughts with more or less possible answers"[24] may perhaps be called the personal credo of Gumilev as an artist.

A new collection of poems in 1912 titled *Alien Sky* became a paradigm of the new poetical movement and included not only new poems by Gumilev but also his translations of Gautier, whose poetry he considered an ideal representation of Acmeist principles. Gumilev enjoyed repeating Gautier's lines:

> More pure the art we fashion
> Whose matter will have shown
>   Dispassion—
> Verse, marble, metal, stone. ("Art," 1912)

The *Alien Sky* years of experimentation with rhyme and meter culminated in the development of a uniquely Gumelevian phrasing, characterized by spontaneity, lightness, and intensity of emotion. Favoring the poetic rhythm of the ancient Greek paeans, Gumilev shaped his verse into an almost colloquial narrative, allowing the written text to mimic the quality of a live voice in all its trembling, entreating, joyous, or mournful melody.

Along with the purely Acmeistic objectives to halt the flow of time, capture the aroma, and seize the fleeting emotion, the poetry of *Alien Sky* touches on philosophical questions of human existence and the duality of the world. The image of an "experienced helmsman" who skillfully and steadily guides a ship onto the open sea, confronting the forces of nature and eventually succeeding in the voyage, is a motif that runs throughout many poems in the collection ("At the Sea,"1912; "Rondeau," 1911; "The Discovery of America," 1910; "Pilgrim," 1911). What Gumilev had

---

24. Gumilev 44.

continually demonstrated in his own personal life—by turning his dreams to reality, by overcoming obstacles in love, and by exploring both the corporeal and artistic worlds—his poetry trumpets in a passionate declaration of the power of the human spirit.

Despite the previously mentioned "non-Russianness" of the majority of Gumilev's poems (particularly the African ones), even the foreign sky is only observed through the veil of authentically Russian clouds. Thematically, Gumilev's immersion in the cult of risk (and by extension fatalism), his characters' readiness to die, the love of freedom, and persistence in the attainment of a desired object could be linked to the incontestably Russian poetry of Mikhail Lermontov. The poems dedicated to Anna Akhmatova bear image traces of the Eternal Feminine and the Madonna, while the exalting of self-sacrifice by her eternally devoted knight calls to mind Blok's poems to the "Fair Lady." Additionally, the generally youthful optimism and lightness of the verses recall some of Pushkin's poetry. In his review, M. Kuzmin noted an increased simplicity on Gumilev's part, a "clarity of the author's individual voice" that exemplifies a "youthfully courageous and novel look at the world."[25]

In April 1913 Gumilev (together with his 17-year-old nephew Nikolay) set out on a new expedition, approved and sponsored by the Petersburg Academy of Science. The day prior to the journey, Gumilev fell severely ill, yet even a delirium–inducing fever did not prevent him from departing on time. The poet traveled to unexplored areas of Africa, as he and his companions covered hundreds of miles through barely accessible regions. They made their way with caravans of mules and camels in the mountains, on foot through canyons and deserts, through valleys and across rivers filled

---

25. Pavlovsky 34.

with crocodiles, and even cut through the pristine jungle in order to reach forbiddingly isolated tribal areas. Living much in the way Gumilev had dreamed of as a child, they braved the dangers of fishing for sharks, slept under an open sky, and suffered from malaria and the pangs of hunger. Most extraordinarily, the poet and his entourage were accepted at the country's highest court, and they even had the honor of photographing both Prince Lij Iyasu and Dejazmach Tafari, later to be known as Emperor Haile Selassie I. Near the town of Sheikh Hussein, the explorers visited the tomb of a saint as well as a local cave from which, according to legend, only the righteous could depart unharmed. The venture was recreated in Gumilev's account: "One had to undress ... and crawl through a narrow entrance. If anyone got stuck, he died in terrible torments: no one attempted to extend a hand to him, to give him a piece of bread or a cup of water. ..."[26] Gumilev crept into the cave and returned successfully, an experience which may have resurfaced while he was writing the poem "You and Me" in 1918:

> I won't die on a bed, surrounded
> By dull doctors and notaries—
> Some ravine, in a land unbounded,
> Ivy-cushioned, provides fine ease.

The African trip lasted for six months, from April 10 to September 1, 1913, and covered areas of Djibouti, Dire-Dawa, Harrar, Sheikh-Hussein, and Ginir. Though Gumilev's journals containing detailed descriptions of the trip have

---

26. Polushin, V., *Nikolai Gumilev: Zhizn' rasstrelennogo poeta*, p.68. <http://royallib.ru/read/polushin_vladimir/nikolay_gumilev_gizn_rasstrelyannogo_poeta.html#1366998>

been lost (with the exception of incomplete copies made by Pavel Luknitsky[27]), noteworthy artifacts and photographs (physical mementos of the journey) remain preserved in the African Collection of the Petersburg Museum of Ethnography. The expedition also lives on in Gumilev's poetry, which for its depiction of Abyssinian geography and culture was once called Africa's "Poetic Tour Guide." According to memoirs, Gumilev contemplated including this African cycle in a groundbreaking "poetic geography textbook":[28]

> In between the broad shore of the stormy Red Sea
> And the mystery dark of the sylvan Sudan,
> Four plateaus that converge we in overview see—
> Like a lioness lies Abyssinian land. ("Abyssinia," 1918)

Gumilev was a pioneer as the first European to come to these lands for the purpose of serious scientific study. Over the course of two months he made detailed records of climate, vegetation, wildlife, and landscapes, in addition to the daily rituals, ceremonies, and conditions of life of the tribes he encountered. His observations and impressions of this expedition would also be reflected in the collection of poems, *Tent*, published after the revolution, in 1921.

At the outbreak of the war in 1914, Gumilev participated in demonstrations in support of Serbia. The feeling of patriotism that overtook Russian society, united in its desire

---

27. Gumilev's first biographer and lifelong devotee, who worked with Anna Akhmatova to create a comprehensive portrait of the poet's life, Pavel Luknitsky emulated Gumilev's adventurism and poetic style, and his own collection, *Labors and Days*, became the basis for a new wave of Gumilev-inspired poetry, analysis, and biographical exploration. Some of the surviving entries from "African Journal" were published in the magazine *Ogonyok* #14 (p.19–22), #15 (p.20–22), 1987.

28. Anna Gomer, "Exotizm i geosofiya Nikolaya Gumileva v kontekste evropeiskogo kolonial'nogo diskursa", Nikolay Gumilev: elektronnoe sobranie sochinenii, 12 July, 2013 <http://gumilev.ru/>

to help "brothers in faith," had captured Gumilev's heart. His brave spirit and unquestioning love for his country seemed to have been awaiting an opportunity of such heroic dimensions to come forth. As A. Levinson wrote: "His patriotism was as unconditional as his religious faith was cloudless. I have met no one to whom doubt was more completely alien. ... His mind, dogmatic and willful, was absolutely devoid of any duality." [29] Gumilev's decision to volunteer for the frontlines was momentous and firm:

And then, amid the roaring of the crowd,
Where rumbling ordnance I would soon be meeting,
'Mid sound unceasing of the trumpet proud
A sudden hymn—my fate!—I heard aloud
And ran to where the populace were fleeting—
"Amen, amen, amen" I, meek, repeating.
  ("Iambic Pentameters," 1916)

But once again he was forced to grapple with the injustices of fate, this time in the form of his rejection from the army on account of an eye disease. Nevertheless, he obtained permission to join the military on the condition that he shoot left-handed (using his good left eye to aim), and learned on his own to fight using sword and spear. With a true Gumilevian optimism he never ceased expecting a victorious conclusion to the war: days and nights of grueling conflict served only to liberate the poet's spirit and words. "I have not slept all night, but so great was the excitement of our attack that I felt quite energetic. I think that at the dawn of humankind, people lived in a constant state of anxiety, building and creating feverishly before an early death. I can hardly believe that a person with the luxury of both a daily lunch and nightly sleep could contribute

---

29. A. Levinson, "Gumilev," *Sovremennye zapiski* 9 (1922): 309–315.

anything to the treasury of spiritual culture. Only fasting and vigil, even if involuntary, awaken special, latent powers."[30] Twice Gumilev was decommissioned during the war for health reasons, but he always managed to return to the frontlines:

> Hunger, thirst, he knew, and knew full well—
> Troubled sleep, and travel reft of rest:
> Yet St. George, with twice-effective spell,
> Warding off the bullets touched his breast.
> ("Memory, "1920)

While at the front, Gumilev kept a detailed diary which the newspaper *Birzhevye Novosti* published in its morning edition for almost a year. These entries, which would later be collected and published under the title *Notes of a Cavalryman* (1915–1916), chronicled the everyday labors of war and the routine of a soldier's life. In them, Gumilev describes the places where the soldiers slept and their feelings on the mornings before battle. He records first-hand the intensity of attacks and sudden explosions, and he includes excerpts of conversations that sketch the psychological portraits of his fellow soldiers. By 1917, the swell of patriotism which had helped Russian forces achieve their victories early in the war had all but dissipated. While the country's reserves were depleted, and as widespread famine both at home and at the front began to take on alarming proportions, groups of Social Democrats continuously undermined the authority of the military commanders by disseminating propaganda among solders and peasants alike. The proliferation of their message was so widespread that antiwar leaflets were being read in every

---

30. Evgeny Stepanov, "Poet na voine. Vokrug "Zapisok kavalerista"—1914–1915," *Toronto Slavic Quarterly* 26 (2008): 6 June 2013, http://www.utoronto.ca/tsq/

Introduction

trench. Many of the dissidents' expectations were (at least initially) gratified by the February Revolution, which toppled a 300-year-old dynasty and shifted the center of power to a provisional government. With the Bolsheviks' *coup d'état* in October of the same year, the government signed a peace treaty with Germany that brought the long-sought termination of an unpopular "tsarist" war.

After spending the entire spring confined to a military hospital, Gumilev dreamed of transferring to the allies' southern front, a destination where he sought (and expected to find) order and discipline. Interestingly, his persistent drive toward conflict did not arise merely from his undying thirst for adventure and bottomless appetite for new impressions. To him, war presented a slice of time and space that not only constituted a piece of humanity's history but was instrumental in shaping it. From that standpoint, war becomes spaceless and timeless, equally constant in its destruction and elevation of human life and spirit at any given moment in history. Only in this context did Gumilev truly feel "at home," executing his exalted purpose as a poet by depicting the history of human sorrow and heroism, an assignment which, though simple, captivated him. The same feeling of "timelessness" and dissolution into the universal matrix enveloped him even more distinctly during his journeys, when the sight of ancient lands and the sound of strange tongues created an impression of both witnessing the flow of history and observing the origin of the world.

Y. Toporkov remembers how once, during an inspection, a group of staff officers came under fire and quickly relocated to the security of the trench. Gumilev, however, remained and, with an astonishing calmness, began to light a cigarette, only departing from the dangerous spot after the tobacco had been satisfactorily enkindled.[31] Gumilev subscribed to

---

31. Luknitskaya 184.

the belief that the poet must alienate himself both from the world and from his earthly body, observing and recording the world's evolution as if protected by the high function of his art. Every movement of human thought and soul was of interest to him, but nothing was more revealing and transcendent than the moment of mortal danger. Only in the fleeting moment just prior to death does the human spirit find its highest testing ground, when masks are discarded and armor is shed. What Gumilev confronted in his suicide attempts, his 1909 duel with the poet M. Voloshin,[32] and his descent into the caverns of Abyssinia was the phenomenon of death itself. Countless others have faced similar obstacles. What emotions filled Pushkin's consciousness while he raised the pistol in his final hour? What thoughts occupied the African when pierced by the ochre gaze of a feral hyena? What traversed the mind of Columbus while facing down his mutinous crewmen? In his moments of defying fate, Gumilev joined the universal human experience, perhaps in anticipation of that sudden burst of survival instinct that reconnects all of us to our primal place of origin: nature.

Maybe as a means of cathartically illustrating this point, in 1916, at the very peak of the war, Gumilev published *Quiver*, a collection of poems that critic A. Pavlovsky called a "book of great sorrow, enlightened by the remorse of wisdom."[33] The constant presence of death and the daily witnessing of its hideous work imbue the verses with thoughts of life's transience and the ephemerality of love.

---

32. The culmination of a convoluted disagreement between the two poets, fought beside the Black River, where Pushkin in 1837 had received his fatal wound. Gumilev fired his pistol into the air. But when Voloshin took his turn, the firearm repeatedly jammed, despite his second's subsequent success when aiming at the ground. The duel was declared at an end and both men were put under house arrest. This may have been the last Russian duel of the 20th century.

33. Pavlovsky 42.

INTRODUCTION

While a significant portion of the book consists of Gumilev's "Italian poems," drawn from the memories of his journey to Italy with Anna Akhmatova in 1912, the more prominent "war" and "peace" poems are juxtaposed with great care. To Gumilev's mind, both life and death were paths to the immortality of the spirit. On one hand, the masterworks of human architecture bear silent witness to the years of peace that allowed their construction. Paradoxically, however, the rampant bloodshed and elimination of life in times of war also may summon an individual toward greatness. The poems in *Quiver* glorify conflict as an art, not its violence or its abstract political goals, but the terrible and awe-inspiring beauty of the martial tempest that moves men to forge their own spiritual masterpieces of heroism:

> In these most wondrous days of war,
> To which I bow in deep devotion, [...]
>   ... now when all
> The best of use comes out of hiding,
> And power rises, there will fall
> Our fetters, many years abiding.
> ("Ode to D'Annunzio," 1916)

Similarly, Gumilev explores the interconnectivity of creation and destruction, particularly in their roles as co-producers of the future. Destruction can often scour the tablet clean so that new creations can be made, or leave a half-demolished piece of artwork behind as a temporal memory that stimulates but does not suffocate the imaginings of the succeeding generation. War is idealized in Gumilev's poetry as a type of craft, a task that in principle must be accomplished and in the process of which a human approaches God's likeness as both creator and destroyer. Appropriately, a soldier's profession is portrayed with an agrarian tint, as that of a "harvester of glory" "over fields already wet with blood" ("War," 1914). A fallen defender of the motherland acquires paradise, immortality akin to that of the masterpieces of art:

> Workers, trudging, as in olden story,
> Over fields already wet with blood—
> Deed of sower, harvester of glory—
> Bless them, Lord Almighty: they are good.
>
> Like the hearts of those who yet are plowing,
> Like the hearts of those who pray and grieve,
> Hearts of fighters burn before You, bowing—
> Waxen candles burning. They believe.
> ("War")

At the same time, the preservation of Roman architectural and artistic masterworks (as observed during his years with Akhmatova) through war, famine, and the corroding effects of time once again illustrates Gumilev's faith in creation. Art is immortal, and though the human body is destined to perish, human genius (through stone, metal, heroic deed or words) will glorify the beauty and virility of life through eternity:

> There is a God, there is a world, they live
> Eternal, though our life is grim with grief.
> But we receive the deeps that it can give
> If we but love the world and hymn belief.
> ("Fra Beato Angelico," 1912)

In the lyrics of this collection, *Quiver,* Gumilev achieves an intimate familiarity with death unparalleled in his other works. Death, despite its tragic presence, far from inspiring depression, becomes something epically essential and justified ("Death tells the truth; and life—but stammered lies ..." (Canzonas 1915)). Death is the portal into the infinite,

INTRODUCTION

a proving ground for the true perfection of human creativity. From a plexus woven of conflict, harmony, art, and mortality, *Quiver* articulates Gumilev's ponderings on endlessness and immeasurability, concepts he saw reflected in the Tower of Pisa, the Roman Coliseum, the primitive legends of Abyssinia, and the memorial jewels of the Scythians.

By 1917 Gumilev was still longing for a transfer to the Macedonian front. After meeting with poets G. K. Chesterton, Boris Anrep, and others in London, he traveled to where the Russian Expeditionary Force was stationed in Paris, and upon arrival began serving as *aide-de-camp* at the commissariat of the Provisional Government. While there, he drafted what may well be his most magnificent collection of love poems, *To the Blue Star*, dedicated to Elena du Boucher[34] and published after his death in 1923. Gumilev remained in Europe until the spring of 1918, when Russia's participation in the war officially came to an end with the signing of the Brest-Litovsk Treaty. He had to choose between remaining abroad or returning to Soviet Russia inflamed by civil war. Approaching that crossroads, Gumilev weighed the possibilities and, in the tradition of the Russian fairy tale, followed the stone sign promising certain death, returning to Russia.

The Bolshevik Revolution of 1917 drew varying responses from Russian literary circles. While some saw it as a catastrophe and the end of Russia's greatness, others embraced it with hope and feelings of elation. But the first few years after the revolution (up until approximately 1921) were undeniably marked by relative freedom in the realms of publishing and artistic projects. Among the triumphs of

---

34. A Russian-French émigrée that Gumilev met in Paris, and for whom he made repeated attempts at courtship until her betrothal to an American. His disappointment did not prevent him from making frequent amorous advances to other women on his return to Russia. Nevertheless, some of his most beautiful love poems, including "Why did Columbus Discover America?," were dedicated to Elena.

the period were exciting innovations in cinematography, theatre, advertising, fashion, and street art. In addition, intelligentsia members joined in the creation of literacy schools and of writers' and artists' unions, as well as universities and research centers. A publishing house, World Literature, established in 1918 under the leadership of Maxim Gorky, set the goal of acquainting and enriching a newly literate 20th century nation with the masterpieces of world literature in translation, materials one hoped would act as a catalyst for the Russian people's own future contributions to global culture.

Gumilev actively participated in this literacy project together with some of the key cultural figures of Petrograd,[35] first as an editorial committee member and chair of the French Literature Translating Department, then later as the chief editor of literature in translation. For him, translation was not merely an attempted equivalence of words, but a penetration into the "other" and the joining of two poetic souls. Due to his work with World Literature, the Russian people were offered superb translations of works by Robert Southey, Samuel Taylor Coleridge, Jean Moréas, Antero de Quental, and Giacomo Leopardi. His translations also included Heinrich Heine's *Atta Troll*, the Babylonian *Epic of Gilgamesh*, the tales of Robin Hood, and many other masterworks from the world's literary treasury.

In June 1918 Gumilev began teaching poetic structure at the World Literature press, a position later incorporated into one at the Institute of the Living Word. He went on to lead the poetic group "Sounding Shell" (*Звучащая Раковина*), which found its home in the cold attic of a photo studio on Nevsky Prospect, as well as at the "House for the Arts" on the Moika River, pedagogic endeavors into which he poured the entirety of his soul. The combination of nearly incredible

---

35. That period's "nationalistic" name for St. Petersburg.

Introduction

diligence, poetic talent, versatile erudition, and a critical, unbiased outlook on art made Gumilev a superb teacher, and consequently his lectures at World Literature had the highest attendance rate of any at the time. He also gave lectures at Proletcult, Baltflot, The Cultural-Educational School for Militia, folk clubs, and anywhere else he was invited to speak, remaining loyal to his vocation as a craftsman, taking it as given that the shoemaker does not choose customers, but crafts footwear for whoever requires it. Thus he completely disregarded the frequent illiteracy, ignorance, and rudeness of his audience. N. Otsup wrote that for Gumilev poetry was "a form of religious service."[36] The poet himself once explained:

> I do not spend my time with scantily gifted youths because I want to make them all into poets—it is, of course, unthinkable, as one must be born a poet. I want to help them become human. Don't poems liberate us, as if shaking a load off our shoulders? For the sake of self-healing, writing poetry is a necessity.[37]

Art, in Gumilev's opinion, "teaches people not only how to live well, but how to live beautifully."[38]

Now, in both his work and his behavior, Gumilev seemed to shed the last remnants of the conquistador's armor, becoming hazardously transparent about his beliefs. If all his life had been spent walking beside death, during his last three years in Petrograd he was holding her hand. Poet G. Ivanov remembered that

---

36. Luknitskaya 217.
37. Nikolay Otsup, "N.S.Gumilev", Nikolay Gumilev: elektronnoe sobranie sochinenii, 18 July, 2013 <http://gumilev.ru/>
38. Luknitskaya 215.

Gumilev, coming back from a lecture with his proletarian students, would naturally take off his hat at the sight of a church and earnestly, broadly cross himself [in defiance of the state's secular dogma]. In the past, the poet had kept his political views largely to himself, yet in Soviet Petersburg he began brazenly to announce 'I am a royalist' to strangers and Bolsheviks alike. I remember the dull sound across a worker-filled lecture hall when he read, *'A new pistol from Belgium I offered to him / And my sovereign's portrait, quite fine.'*" [39]

It is possible that Gumilev's open proclamations of royalist sentiments and unwavering religious views were relatively harmless when muted by the sheltering walls of his classroom, where they were perceived by his listeners as eccentricities or products of a theatrical persona. However, in a city under siege by continual civil war, widespread food shortages, and Cocytian frost, Gumilev's persona as a proudly posturing lecturer clad in a long exotic coat, teaching secret spells of a high art to sailors and peasants, seemed petty and laughable to many. K. Chukovsky writes: "Except in very narrow literary circles, where he was respected and loved, no one felt any compassion toward him."[40] But Gumilev believed in the protection offered by the mystical power of the word: "Words would make the sun halt, subjugated— / Make a city drop into the slime" ("Word," 1919). Though the world might seem crumbling all about him, Gumilev published a new collection of poems inspired by French translations of Chinese and Indochinese poetry, a work he titled *Porcelain Pavilion* (1918). As with the title

---

39. O.N.Vysotsky, *Nikolai Gumilev glazami syna* (Moscow: Molodaya gvardiya, 2004) 469.
40. Luknitskaya 217.

Introduction

of his next poetry collection, *Tent*, one cannot fail to note the ephemerality and fragility of these architectural structures conceived for contemplation, relaxation, luxury, and beauty, abodes that offered a tired traveler or a shade-seeking romantic heroine brief protection. The exotic poems found in *Porcelain* are like broken pieces of precious china glittering in the sand after the destruction of the ship carrying them, yet the verses seemed to provide an escape for Gumilev alone.

In the newly renamed city of Petrograd, even more than elsewhere, these were frightening times. Students and workers at public institutions labored in coats and heated their homes using books and furniture for kindling. An ardent collector, Gumilev traded tomes he had brought from his trips to Europe for bags of potatoes, not only to feed his new family (he had married Anna Engelgardt following his divorce from Anna Akhmatova in 1918) but also to help anyone he might happen to meet on his daily walks home. N. Otsup recalls: "We will never forget Petersburg during its time of loneliness and death, when after 9 PM no one dared go outside; when the roar of a car's engine in the middle of the night made us listen with dread, wondering whom they would take next; when there was no need to clean carrion off the streets before the emaciated dogs or even more emaciated people tore it apart. The Petersburg vanishing before our eyes was, to us, as sad and beautiful as the face of a dying loved one."[41] Gumilev, according to his contemporaries, withstood all these adversities with calmness and humility, never losing his capacity for clear thought and compassion, or the desire to continue his work. His brittle "porcelain pavilion" seemed to remain intact because it existed in a parallel dimension of poetry. The poet felt himself to be not only a citizen of a blessed country,

---

41. Luknitskaya 220.

but maybe its ruler and lawmaker. "Art does not care what type of flag waves above the Peter and Paul Fortress. While a man has strength to look at the world and be surprised, while the desire to create lives on in his soul, he is alive."[42]

Writer Korney Chukovsky recalled that once, on his way to see Gumilev, he had fainted on the street from starvation, only to awaken lying on the exotic quilt of the poet's spacious bed. On an antique gold-painted platter which would have belonged more appropriately in a museum, Gumilev brought him a gray "petal" of bread, moving slowly and carefully with the solemnity of a reverent priest. After providing the food, the poet reached for his new poetic script (a tragic play titled *Gondla*), and started reading the first lines, continuing the narrative from memory long after the lights had gone out.[43] The play's prophetic hero, Gondla, is the chosen ruler of Christian Ireland, whose lofty soul shines through his physical deformity—a "swan prince" protected from murder at the hands of the pagan "wolf-people" by his continuous playing of the lute, a motif found in Gumilev's earlier poem, "Magic Violin." Having finally earned the respect and recognition of the "wolf brothers," he nonetheless rejects their proposal to make him their sovereign, offering instead a (voluntary) conversion to Christianity. When they refuse, he sacrifices himself, thereby transforming the "animal people" into Christians through his innocent blood.

In this work (which offers parallels to Gumilev's own life and philosophy), the concept of the redemptive power of art is evident once more, as is the idea that a person who never ceases to create is sheltered within the world of his creation. In a confirmation of Pushkin's description of a poet as "prophet" who comes to earth to "burn men's hearts with the word"("Prophet," 1826), Gumilev saw a poetic

---

42. Luknitskaya 220.
43. Luknitskaya 112.

mission in bringing spiritual rebirth to the world even if it brought death upon himself. A. Amfiteatrov, playwright and historian, said that poetry for Gumilev was not an accidental inspiration ornamenting his life but the defining factor of his entire being. "He didn't like to be called a writer or littérateur. He isolated the word 'poet' into a specially drawn magical circle elevated above the base world, as if on an altar. He was always ... priestly serious—a hierophant. He wrote poetry as if preparing an aromatic offering of spices,"[44] tributes to eternity meant to "christen" the world.

On September 5, 1918 the Union of Soviet Commissars issued a law authorizing the use of the death penalty for all members of "alien classes," a broadly defined demographic which could include bourgeoisie, clergy, wealthy peasantry, former White officers and monarchists, religious believers, and "doubting" intelligentsia. The Red Terror unbound the hands of the more craven elements of society, who immediately initiated a newsprint-driven crusade against "aristocratic writers" in order to strengthen their own careers or, in some cases, to save their lives. It was at this point that, like the eponymous hero of *Gondla,* members of the Russian cultural intelligentsia truly became surrounded by wolves. Hounded by the Soviet press, they were hunted down and arrested, many dying from malnutrition and disease, or outright execution. Then, as if to compound the domestic troubles, the intelligentsia's former colleagues and friends who had emigrated in the wake of the revolution began to accuse them of traitorous collaboration with the Soviets. From the safety of their Parisian and Berlin apartments, they mercilessly berated writers like Gumilev for apparently forsaking their social and political ideas to save their own skins. In a Parisian newspaper article, D.

---

44. Luknitskaya 230.

Merezhkovsky accused the World Literature Publishing House of "shameless profiteering." Though Nikolay Gumilev considered it his duty to protect the honor of writers, he knew that in the existing political and artistic climate any public defense of the intelligentsia's cultural cause could be interpreted by the authorities as a willful rejection of Soviet ideology and thus could further endanger the lives of people already under strict surveillance. Yet in response to attacks from both sides, the poet said:

> Naturally, in a group of experts responsible for the ideological content of our publications there are various beliefs, and it is pure chance that among 16 employees there is not a single member of the Russian Communist Party. However, all 16 of them are unanimous in the opinion that during these difficult and frightening times, salvation of the nation's spiritual culture is possible only through the function we independently perform here. It is not the fault of the publishing house that the work of its employees is done under conditions that would be unimaginable for our foreign colleagues. One can only pass by such a situation in silence, and only those ignorant of their own actions or lacking in self-respect choose to boo and giggle.[45]

Gumilev may, in fact, have been the only poet not to write about the revolution. Neither supporting nor opposing the communist movement, he emphasized the loyalty with which he followed his true vocation as a poet, a troubadour, and a nomad in time and space with his honest and straightforward lyric attempting vigorously to defend the sovereignty of his craft: "You know that I am neither red

---

45. Luknitskaya 231.

Introduction

nor white—/ I am a poet!"[46] He held that poetry did not serve politics: it always stood outside the divisions between social classes and ideological opinions, did not answer to state laws, and did not confirm to state-assigned authority. Furthermore, it was his impression that the Bolsheviks' discrimination was limited to the targeting of unknown factors, and that therefore by means of his political transparency (and thus a kind of nonverbal contract with the authorities) he could maintain his autonomy. Anna Akhmatova believed that during the last years of his life Gumilev had amalgamated his identity with the image of the warrior-poet and thus failed to comprehend the tragedy of his situation. Similarly, O. Mandelstam commented on the sadly absurd light in which the poet saw his dealings with the Bolsheviks as being "like a relationship between foreign enemies who ought to respect each other."[47] Yet according to poet Irina Odoyevtseva, Gumilev, like most poetical souls, had felt terror in the anticipation of a mysterious and quickly approaching end. Once, he impulsively walked into a Petersburg church and ordered a commemoration service for the "senselessly murdered" poet-warrior Mikhail Lermontov. Falling to his knees, he chanted alongside the church's small choir, and later insisted that he had heard his name at one point mistakenly substituted for Lermontov's during the priest's invocations.[48]

At the beginning of 1921 Gumilev was elected chairman of the Petrograd branch of the Russian Union of Poets, previously led by Alexander Blok. He re-initiated meetings of the "Poets' Guild" and organized evenings of poetry and lectures, focusing on such artists as Gautier, Baudelaire, and Pushkin. In March he had assembled the Guild's first

---

46. Luknitskaya 245.
47. Luknitskaya 234.
48. Odoyevtseva, I., *Na beregakh Nevy* (Victor Kamkin, Inc., 1967), 170.

literary journal, *Dragon*. Because of the critical shortage of paper, many poets were selling handwritten manuscripts of their works. Gumilev compiled and illustrated a number of his collections—including *Fantastica, China, French Songs, Persia, Canzonas, Shavings*, and *Fire Column*—for the publishing house Petropolis. At the same time he tried to provide material assistance to writers in the form of food, fuel, and clothing, and even helped find housing. A short business trip to Sebastopol, Rostov, and Moscow in 1921 inspired Gumilev to write a new book, the plan of which he drafted a few months prior to his death. Its title, *The Middle of the Earthly Journey*, coincided chillingly with the brink of his own life. Under cover of night on August 3, 1921 Gumilev was arrested by Soviet authorities. His friends and relatives would later read in the local newspaper that on August 27, 1921 he was executed, having been accused of participating in a counter-revolutionary organization, one of 96 people who were detained or killed in connection with the so-called "V. N. Tagantsev Case." The poet was 35 years old. He had predicted his death with characteristic accuracy—blood on the "dusty, trampled, faded grass" described with oneiric gravity in "Worker" (1916):

> Over the Dvinah, gray-foaming river,
> Whistling by, the bullet he had cast
> Fated aim will seek—foreknown forever—
> Reach my breast, and enter it at last.
>
> I'll be falling—destined—as when dreaming,
> Feel my lifetime in a moment pass—
> Blood upsprung outgush—then see it streaming
> Over dusty, trampled, faded grass.
>
> God, in fullest measure, will reward me
> For my brief and bitter years ...

Introduction

The last three years of Gumilev's life had proven to be the most productive of his journey as a writer. He had published three major collections: *Pyre* (1918), *Tent* (1918), and *Fire Column* (1921), now considered to be the magnum opus of his lyrical career. Alongside these there were also several smaller works, such as the love cycle *To the Blue Star* (1917); the poem "Mik" (1914–1918), the oriental cycle of *Porcelain Pavilion* (1918), and the powerful *Gondla* (1917). Gumilev also authored plays such as *Allah's Child* (1917), *Poisoned Tunic* (1918), *The Tree of Metamorphosis* (1918), and *Rhino Hunting* (1920), as well as making numerous translations. Each of Gumilev's last three books is distinguished by its artistic maturity and its classicism of the poetic word polished to perfection. Behind subtle melancholia, simple solemnity, and wisdom touched by gentle irony is a millennia-old heart, the spirit of a cosmic traveler. In its course, the poet's search turned to the origins of the world and man, to the mystery of the cosmos and the supreme enigma of its inception. "Poem of the Beginning" (first song "Dragon"), the most cosmogonic of all Gumilev's verses, echoes the ancient heroic epics, and restates Gumilev's faith in the power of human will. The human being who creates the Word is capable of conquering evil (the dragon) and turning the wheel of history to begin a new cycle ("Prememory"). Perhaps this was what inspired his son Lev to launch his own theory of passionality.[49]

---

49. One aspect of which is that all significant historical personalities appear due to an excess of an internal (and amoral) "passionality" force, speculated to originate in solar activity or cosmic radiation, which has various environmental effects on the planet's ecosystems. This energy motivates them towards enacting changes that (collectively) shape the direction of their ethnic group's history. Lev also asserted that entire nations are subject to "passionality pushes," which account for their emergence and rapid development. He referred to those like his father as "people of the long will" *(люди длинной воли),* and argued that the

Gumilev once wrote that "Chronologies coexist like waves flowing into one another, a temporal swell into which one can step as if into a present and corporeal sea."[50] This sentiment finds its reflection in the poem "Strayed Streetcar," a story that spans countries and histories, the lives of people and the Neva, Nile and Seine Rivers, all places central to Gumilev's life, and passes into the train station where one can buy a ticket to the "India of the spirit," a destination not existing on any map:

I knew I had strayed and for ages had wandered
In passages, blinded, of space and of time.
Though somewhere were flowing dear rivers, I pondered
The path, now cut off, that I never would find.
 ("Stockholm," 1918)

On one level, a pervading melancholy stems from Gumilev's unsatisfied search for a spiritual land. Yet alongside that subtle anguish, one can feel softly coursing throughout his last poems a quiet joy and contentment inspired by a rediscovery of beauty in life and of the earth, the poet's only cosmic home. The "little golden fingers" in "Starry Horror" (1920) are pointed earthward, to everything that has happened, is happening, and will happen, as the dark, glittering sky inspires people to sing of all they see on the corporeal sphere. Sharply poignant are the lines from "Creativity" that speak of the author's love for this brief terrestrial existence:

      Suddenly, with a sigh,
      I rued the empty day

---

concentration of *"passionarii* personalities" is what characterizes a nation's creative or destructive potential.
50. Pavlovsky 45.

Introduction

> I'd lost—it had passed me by
> On its self-determined way ...

Pinings for an ancient, simpler Russia are woven into Gumilev's last poems with gentle, loving allusions: to Tsarskoye Selo and Pushkin, to the small gray villages in the north, to its major saints, and to the childlike purity of the Russian people. Among these poems, the Russian soul appears most vividly in "Strayed Streetcar" (1919), taking the form of "Mashenka" (an affectionate diminutive of "Maria"), who serves as an embodiment of both the sacred Mother of God and Mother Russia, and for whose health Gumilev prays at the poem's conclusion. The image of Mashenka also embodies the ideal Russian woman, recalling the heroines of Pushkin's "Captain's Daughter" and "Bronze Horseman," a figure both loving and loyal, self-sacrificing and fragile, and always in need of protection. Perhaps Gumilev's young relative Mashenka (Kuzmina-Karavayeva), who had died of tuberculosis at the age of 22, whose gentleness worthy of "Turgenev's maiden" and whose tragic fate he sang of in his poems, served as the prototype for this image. Gumilev saw that the feminine aspect of Russia which he, the knight, was unable to protect, would nonetheless live while he perished under the hooves of the bronze horse or at the hands of the Red executioner. It seems that in the end Gumilev does surrender to his earthly home, accepting Russia's compelling power, which grants her poets such a unique aptitude for brilliant poetry in exchange for their lives, just as the most beautiful and fragrant of flowers pay for the vigor of their blooms with an existence brief as a flash of light:

> Old Russia, wizard-witch relentless,
> You take what you have named your own.
> Flee? Loving novelty ... yet—friendless?
> To live apart from all you've known?
> ("Old Country Estates," 1916)

In "Winged Soul," Kuprin describes the scale and range of Gumilev's writing:

> He wrote verses of an acerbic charm, wafted about with aromas of high hills, the torrid desert, far-off seas, and flowers rare—splendid, resonant, flexible lines, where into a brief and willingly receiving form has entered something far beyond what was openly said. He was the wandering knight or the aristocratic vagrant, in love with all eras, countries, professions, and situations where the human spirit could blossom into bold heroic beauty. When you read his lines you picture the writer with shining eyes, chilled windblown hair, a proud and tender smile on his lips.[51]

Can one truly speak of the untimely death of such a poet, who had proven in his works that people remain, immortal, through their eternally living words and heroic deeds? Gumilev had recognized his mission very early on, and followed its course undeflected throughout his life. He was the pyre, the blazing column, who burned by giving his being to art, his love to the world, and his work to the people, igniting the spark of creation in millions of hearts. His perseverance and bravery proved the potency of human will and the vastness of human capacity, while his poetry praised the optimistic prospects of life and the captivating flicker of the mystery beyond it. His youthful ardor and unquenchable thirst for adventurous discovery demonstrated determination and self-confidence, while a life of straightforward valor and rectitude in the face of danger exemplified an ideal of honor and honesty to strive for. He taught himself to befriend death and told his readers "not

---

51. Luknitskaya 299.

to fear—/ Not fear—and to do what's needed" ("My Readers," 1920). His hopefulness and love of life taught patience and faith:

> And when a woman, with a lovely face,
> Uniquely treasured in the universe,
> Says, "No, I do not love you,"
> I teach them how to smile,
> And go, and not return.
> And when their final hour approaches,
> And an even, red haze overspreads their eyes,
> I will teach them to remember
> All of their cruel, kindly days,
> All of their dear, strange homeland
> And, appearing before the face of God
> With wise and simple word,
> Calmly to await His judgment.

With Gumilev, more than with most, the scale and complexities of the life and work cannot be summed up in a single introduction. The infinitely colorful intricacies of his prose, plays, and extensive literary criticism are things that must be experienced, not merely told of. At the same time, vague areas exist in the story of his family, his loved ones, his turbulent historical era, his arrest and death, his relationships with other writers of the "Silver Age," and the influences that helped to shape his poetry and view of the world.

Though at present Gumilev's bright contribution to the treasury of Russian poetry is becoming widely recognized in his homeland, his lyrics remain largely unmapped territory for western readers. Perhaps now that his poetry is more accessible to that demographic, light may be shed on many of the unclear or mysterious areas in his writing. After all, Gumilev always remained a traveling poet, a bard in search of his spiritual homeland. With this book, the gangplank of Gumilev's poetic ship is lowered, and the captain welcomes all interested readers, discoverers, and adventurers to come aboard.

ACKNOWLEDGMENT

We wish to thank Joshua Kaplan for his assistance in proofreading and copyediting.

Nikolay Gumilev

1. Sonnet

As a conquistador in iron mail
Have I set out, and travel with a smile,
In gladsome garden resting for awhile—
But yet before the pit I sháll not pale.

I face a turbid heaven, murky bale,
And laugh: I wait, continue to maintain
A faith unfailing. For my star will reign:
I'm a conquistador in iron mail.

If it's a harder fate than I may think
To loose the last reluctant fetter-link,
Then let death come: I'll summon it—you'll see!

I'll struggle with it till the destined end.
Perhaps the hand that I when dead extend
Will get the light-blue lily meant for me.

2. Ballad

My friend Lucifer gave me five horses to keep
And a fine golden ruby-set ring so that I
Might descend, if I wished, into cavern-life, deep
As I liked, and might see the young face of the sky.

Horses snorting, hooves beating, competed to see
What a grandeur expanding we'd pass on our fling,
And I felt that the sun was enkindled for me
While it gleamed like the ruby well-set on my ring.

Many star-laden nights, many days bright with fire
I kept wandering, wanting it never to end,
And I laughed when my friends, in their might,
    wouldn't tire
And I laughed at the play of my ring, golden friend.

On the heights of awareness are raving and snow,
But my horses I forced, whip a-whistling, to race:
To the heights of awareness I made my steeds go
And I there viewed a maid with a sorrowing face.

Vocal tone growing faint, I could hear a sweet tune,
Strange the gaze, blending answer and question for
    me:
I surrendered my ring to this maid of the moon
For the wavering shade of her hair streaming free.

And with laughter and glee, and with scorning, of
    course,
There was Lucifer, leading me into his lair,
There was Lucifer, giving me here a sixth horse,
And the name of the steed that he gave me—Despair.

3. Ossian

Clouds vagrant and heavy and gray in the heavens
    are leaden.
Between them we view how the moon mortal-
    wounded can redden:
Cuhoolin, the warrior-hero of Erin's green glory,

Has fall'n by the sword of Swarán, he the ocean-king
    hoary.

Portentous the spell of the gray-headed sibyl, her
    wailing:
The sea, foaming whitely, now towering high, now
    subsiding:
Swarán, in a frenzy, his triumph the thunderclouds
    hailing,
Meets Fingal, the hero of heroes, in wildness abiding.

Advancing, they grapple—on cliff, dewy, slippery,
    sliding,
Each trying to shatter the spine of a bear, of his
    foeman,
While heralding winds with their railing, reverberant
    chiding
Tell tidings of struggle-ravine, of the sibylline omen.

And when I get tired of the tenderest words and
    embraces
And wearied by deeds of routine, unrelenting,
    unresting,
I hear how the air is atremble with curses—the faces
I glance at on hills in their cruelty yet are contesting.

4. Rat

In the lamp, the fire is terrified—
Chamber dimming: it's an eerie place.

Timidly, a child attempts to hide
Underneath pink blankets trimmed with lace.

Is the elf a-coughing, little devil,
Short and hairless, waiting in his lair?
No! it is a rat—and that means evil—
Coming out behind the wardrobe, there ...

By the lamplight with reflection red,
Moving twitchy whiskers, he is trying
Hard to view the girl upon the bed,
Huge-eyed, breathless, under blankets lying.

"Mama, mama!" No, her mama's busy.
(In the kitchen, Vasileessa laughed.)
Burning bright, with bliss and anger dizzy,
Focal rat-eyes' coal-gleam makes you daft.

Scared to lie there, frightened more to stand,
"Bright-wing'd angel!" (Fear has made her numb.)
"Dearest angel, hurry if you can,
Save me from the rat, have mercy, come!"

5. Dawn

Flamy ringlet-coils will slowly pale
While the Serpent, stretching, looks around:
Burning on his throat—the stony mail,
Gem-dominion, lifting off the ground.

What a wonder, frightening and bright!
But—the Peacock none may comprehend:
Blazing eyes a myriad-colored light
To his brilliant golden tail can lend.

At the threshold quietly they've waited:
Came an angel—rustling, rushing wings
Clouds diaphanous dropped unabated,
Falling feathers, paradisal things.

Now, the more they cover all in white,
Snow-heaps grow on vulnerable fields.
Snaky glow must fade, without a fight,
Peacock-fan as well his wonder yields.

What's the moral of the morn's illusion?
What were bird and serpent furnished for—
Melting into mist with fickle fusion?
Never may we glimpse them anymore.

We're like little children left to tremble:
We are frightened by the flight of time.
Comes the dawn, for pray'r we reassemble
Calmly in a marble grot benign.

6. Death

Tender, pale, in ashen dress appearing,
Eyes caressing, and with charming words—
You were once far differently endearing
'Mid the trumpet-battle, clank of swords.

You were fierce and fine and drunken-golden,
Having bared your shining bosom bright—
In the blood-smoke, armies to embolden,
Cutting through a path to heaven-light.

You, Astraea, thirst eternal showing,
Piercingly had gazed at me that night.
Blood was borne along my veins more glowing
And the muscles of my hands gained might.

Though you've changed, I know the one that lured me
Dreaming, heaven seeing in a song.
Of my place in Eden you assured me:
I will meet you there before too long.

7. In the Heavens

Flaring days!—and they're brighter than gold—
And the Great Bear of Night runs away.
Go and lasso her, Prince, grab ahold,
Strap her tight to the saddle, I say!

Strap her tight to the saddle, I say!
Take her off to the tower of blue,
For the capture will brook no delay:
Canis Major will know what to do.

Fatal, doggéd his grip: she'll be caught!
He is brave, he is strong, he is sly.
And his forebears undaunted have fought
With the bears in the ages gone by.

There's no way she will find a release.
She will die in a while: that is best,
So the others may pasture in peace,
Taurus, Capricorn, Aries, the rest.

8. Thoughts

Why do these thoughts keep crouching now around
    me
Like thieves in dark, suburban, wordless night?
All ominous—wild ravens—how they hound me—
And screaming caw Revenge! in raucous might.

My hopes are fled, my dreams evade me, smitten—
My eyes have opened wide with wild affright:
I read, on a transparent tablet written,
Each act, idea, scheme I'd hid from sight.

Because I glanced but tranquilly, serenely,
On those who sailed to meet glad-fancied fate,
Because I kissed her with my lips, so meanly,
Whose own were innocent, inviolate,

Because my slender hands, in pleasure flagrant,
Knew naught of heavy labor at the plow,
Because my wayward melodies and vagrant
Were melancholy, a despondent slough,

For this I hear the call to vengeful violence.
Deluded temple smashed, in blindness mangled,

Thieves come upon me in half-rural silence—
Trapped beggar, in the night will I be strangled.

9. Cross

When card after card told me lie after lie
I felt no success in attempts to get drunk.
Cold stars, 'mid the terror of March in the sky,
Paled one, then another, and fainting had sunk.

In coldness, in madness, my starving heart sank.
I knew that the game was no more than a dream:
"This card—let it cover the whole bloody bank!"
The card proved a loser. That settled my scheme.

I needed fresh air. Snowy dawn. Ah, so tender
The wandering shade on the softness that now ...
Gold cross to my lips I would hold!—in surrender!—
I fell to my knees then, I hardly know how.

"I want to breathe freely, like stars to live purely:
Your rod, Lady Poverty, sister of loss,
I'll take! I will wander, beg bread! I will surely
Bring healing, redeem—with the help of the cross."

A pause ... and at once, 'mid the loud jubilation
All stopped. They were silently rising, bestirred:
I entered the hall in a flaming elation
And onto the card put my cross. Not a word.

Nikolay Gumilev

10. Masquerade

In corridor, hall, once deserted and muffled,
Each masquer today has a costume entrancing.
With flowers entwined and with ribbons beruffled
The parlors are hosting a hurricane dancing.

The moons arm-in-arm with the dragons are
    straying,
Rare vase of Cathay sweeping by unattended.
A torch is enkindled, a lute you hear playing,
A singing, a name that is not comprehended.

The sounds—a mazurka—reverberate loudly.
I felt something sad, and I felt something cheering
When Sodom's own courtesan danced with me
    proudly:
I felt something not unfamiliar, endearing.

I said to my partner, "So brightly bepainted,
Your mask made me think of a tale I have savored
Whenever I heard it. We may be acquainted.
So take off your mask—I would deem myself favored.

For no one need know who you are, still remaining
A stranger to others and nothing revealing:
I'll keep your identity masked, while retaining
The secret that you, Sodom Queen, are concealing."

Evading my glance, though, her worries betraying,
She youthfully laughed with a verve that was
    splendid.

The moons arm-in-arm with the dragons were
      straying,
Rare vase of Cathay sweeping by unattended.

But then, near the window, while, threatening vainly,
The blackening face of the night glided over,
She slid, like a slithering serpent—and plainly
She pulled off her mask—and she glanced, like a
      lover.

So much had I learned in that moment, yet never
Could vanquish my terrible vow. "I'll not fear it,
My queen: I'm your captive, your vassal forever—
And gladly surrender my body, my spirit."

11. After Victory

While my curls are turned golden, the sun rolls
      along:
While the flowers I pluck, with the winds I converse.
As I ought to be childlike and playful, what's wrong?
I enjoy royal favor: what's making me worse?

Near the well-tested bow, the tried quiver yet shakes;
Whisper, whisper I hear from my glittering sword.
It remembers, relentlessly, islands and lakes
And the maritime wars that it waged as a lord.

So then whom, master sword, are you planning to
      smite—
You, aspiring, outdistancing, traveling bow?

Have you maybe forgotten the sway of our might
When the world as a friend to our lordship bowed
    low?

All the waters my ship had respectfully kissed
While with conflict and conquest we honored the
    shore.
Past the end of the world—there's a foe you have
    missed?
Beyond heaven—you're finding one enemy more?!

12. Choice

Though a piler of towers be ravaged,
Though a flier down headlong be hurled
When, submerged in the world-well and savaged,
Gripped in madness he curses the world,

Though the sacker of cities be shaken,
Overturned like a statue of stone,
By the all-seeing Father forsaken,
Left to mourn in his torment alone,

Though the cavern explorer may cower
By the backwater, stagnant, of streams
When he meets a proud panther whose glower
Will outheat all the demons in dreams,

Though you cannot evade what a mortal
Will endure as the payment for breath,

Yet be silent: your right is the portal
Of your dying—of choosing your death.

13. Sly Devil

My devil, best of merrymakers,
A song had made, and cleverly:
"All night the sailor breasted breakers,
Dawn saw him deep beneath the sea.

Ascended wave-walls, taller, vaunted—
Then fell, then foamed and rose again.
More white than foam he saw, undaunted,
His love, above the ocean plain.

He struggled on, he heard her calling:
'I love you, dear, as you love me!'
But," said the devil, "he kept falling.
Dawn saw him deep beneath the sea."

14. Refusal

A princess, or merely a child who was plaintive and
 tender
And sad, as she leaned toward the sighing and
 somnolent ocean ...
Her figure was elegant, flexible, pretty and slender,
And drawn to the silver-pink dawning, the glowing,
 the motion.

The gray will be going. A bird muttered something
    above her.
And now, of a sudden, come dolphins that offer to
    bring her
To visit the turquoise domain of a prince who will
    love her.
They proffer their glittering backs, but she rather
    would linger.

"No, thank you ... " Her crystalline tone—how severe,
    inauspicious,
But clear when she stubbornly clings to the fated
    foreclosure.
A princess, or merely a child feeling sad and
    capricious,
Eyes painfully weary and weak in her lone
    discomposure.

15. Memory

It is noon. With her quietened eyes
(Sparkles dancing—the noon-heat athrobbing)
Flew a bird from afar—we heard cries.
Facing fate, she is silently sobbing.

She was lured by a clever green snare,
And her eyes were enwrapped in a cover—
Blinding fog—she no longer could bear
To do more than keep gliding, and hover ...

As the whimsical whirlwinds lead on,
Unregarding of prayer, resistless,
From the planet forever are gone
Pinions languid and pallid and listless.

You are saddened, I see, in your gaze
Where restrained summer lightnings are hiding ...
I recur to the bird in her maze,
In her martyrdom, silently chiding.

16. Dreams

Past their ravaged and ramshackle dwelling,
Blackened shell of itself, had they straggled:
The old raven was eagerly telling
Dazzling dreams to the beggar bedraggled.

The old raven, atremble, pursuing—
With the shakes unabated—his story
Told of viewing, on towering ruin,
An ineffable vision of glory.

In his flight, in elation unstinting,
And forgetting his wretchedness-dower,
He had turned to a swan, feathers glinting,
And the man, to a prince of great power.

Came the heavy night heaven descending,
An old beggar's salt tears flowing thickly
While a woman, no word comprehending,
Walked by rapidly, crossed herself quickly.

17. Glove

On my hand a glove I'm wearing
That I never shall remove,
For it hides a riddling treasure,
Which to think of lends me pleasure:
It directs me to the deep, my magic glove.

The impression of her fingers
In the mind will never end.
As my ears remember singers,
Lively memory yet lingers
Of her soft elastic glove, my steady friend.

Every person has a treasure
That will lead him to the deep.
So, for me, the glove's a pleasure
Sweet, transcending any measure.
Till next meeting, on my hand the glove I'll keep.

18. I Dreamed

I dreamed that our faces gleamed brightly,
Serenely, right after our dying.
Two coffins gleamed whitely, so whitely,
   So tranquilly lying.

"How long have we *been* here? Tomorrow
Will more be revealed?" As if sleeping,
The heart isn't dealing with sorrow,
   The heart isn't weeping.

Our feelings, grown faint, have expired,
Yet, frozen, our thoughts become clear.
Your lips now, no longer desired,
    Resplendent appear.

All ended: our faces gleamed brightly,
Serenely, right after our dying.
Two coffins gleamed whitely, so whitely,
    So tranquilly lying.

19. Sada-yakko

In a hall, austere, half-darkened,
You were dancing to the singing
Of the violins. I hearkened:
Lilies, butterflies were talking,
Silken-green, to twilight spark and
On the canvas, interlocking,
Shading of the svelte acacias
Lay in decoration gracious.

You appeared a bonbonnière
By a charming étagère
And, like little kittens, neat,
Or like children rapt in play
Were your darling dancing feet
Trembling on the smooth parquet
When like golden fireflies bright
Glowed your name in flowing light.

Seeing, when you'd speak to us,
What was loved and fabulous,
We received the blooms you threw
Of a distant, winning art:
Stirring words one never knew
Roused the finely drunken heart.
We might thank the rising sun
From Japan for having come.

20. Suicide

Gently smiling, then she sighed—
Calm foresaw—one final time
Looked at things that would abide:
Papered walls, and carpets fine—

Into patterned goblet slips
Carefully a crimson pill—
Whimsied, wetting coral lips,
That the wine may work its will.

Next, the living hint of red
Yields the way to tint of white:
Drops the body, twisted, dead,
In a dancer-action light.

Sounds from distant worlds away
Try to reach her quiet heart:
Her transparent bracelet they
Shake, and make it fall it apart.

On the rug, though life is gone,
Dovelike, white, she's trembling yet:
There are gold reflections on
Her envenomed goblet wet.

21. Princess

Under cover of a summer night
Wandering, a youthful princess wept:
In the woods a worker, welcome sight,
Kept the maiden sheltered while she slept.

Helpfully he'd led her to his hut,
Given flatbread with a bitter suet,
Lent her pillow, blanket. These were what
He could hardly spare, and well she knew it.

In a corner then he fell asleep:
Still, the night—in visionary quiet.
Weak, the icon light could barely keep
Vigil over trifles lying by it.

Could it be?—these ragged scraps were only
Wretched refuse, dumped in disarray—
Dried-up, cast-off rabbit paws, a lonely
Peasant's cigarette-end tossed away ...

Why had enigmatic languid fog
Suddenly a morbid torment grown?
Why had whispers from a filthy log
Made the maiden think the hearth was home?

... Early morning, sleepily, next day,
Back the worker brought the princess. But
Wakeful nights of yearning yet she lay
Crying tears of longing for the hut.

22. Cave of Sleep

Where the ancient mage is buried deep,
Where the cave in darkest marble yawns,
Listen! Timid step, more soft than sleep—
Lucifer we'll view before it dawns.

Duller day goes out, its murmur dumb:
Muffled world is like a temple stilled.
Wait! A shadow, Lucifer will come
On a night with many shadows filled.

Ridden there, invisible to all,
We'll be waiting, muter than the tomb—
Silver laughter heard in hollow hall,
Bitter and exhausted sobbing, soon.

Glimmer glimpsed of mad cerulean blue,
Mab the Queen makes lurid legend rise:
We will watch as, wandering, the Jew
Terrifies the orange butterflies.

While the airy lunar sign grows wan,
Falling, and proceeds to her decline,
Mage is made a corpse, all life is gone—
Lucifer, evading, shade malign.

Romantic Flowers

Now Queen Mab we'll see on lunar petal
Rousing to resume her darkling reign:
Gloomy—huge the rod of wood and metal
In his hand, the Jew sets off again—

And, ascending to the altar stone,
Through a window thin, we watch Him come—
Sing a kingly psalm, while on His throne
Flames in golden glow the flaring Sun.

23. In Love with the Devil

What a pale—and handsome—knight is this
    On a black and a galloping steed!
Fleeting bird of legendary bliss
    At so whirling and stirring a speed!

What a baleful, gloomy glance he threw
    At the hues of my beautiful glass!
Why my sudden sad regret and rue
    For the days I had favored, alas!

What has frightened Older Brother so
    That by wavering, glimmering light
Testing armor, shining sword and bow
    And a lance, he's advancing to fight!

Why's the proud astrologer descending
    From his tower to come to our house?
Why his sudden quarrel, strange, unending,
    With my father, so ready to rouse?

Ah! so unrelievedly appalling:
   I'm so young, and I *don't comprehend*—
Sitting, sobbing, wailing, waiting, falling
                Into dreams without end.

24. Lovers

Their spirits fell in love along the waters
In holy groves of naiades, with song
To thrum of strings, contending with the throng
Of winds, the bliss of all the virgin daughters.

High priest was he ... More strange and stern-
      discerning
Than his could beauty rarely have been seen,
Calm eye, stilled lips, tranquillity serene,
And on his brow a blood-red band a-burning.

The priest held rites of magical resistance
When fog arose above the ocean main:
Along the shore in pearly woven chain
The dancing naiads granted their assistance.

To one of these the priest had offered honor—
More lovely she than any fairy tale,
But band of red made blind to beauty's bale
One drunken with the light that gleamed upon her.

The pre-dawn stars, though glimmering, were
      fading—
Forgotten the supreme and priestly vow.

Her lips no longer dared deny him now
And, in her eyes, he saw no more dissuading.

Then, to the seal of slander given over,
They left the holy grove—enchanted night—
And went to dwell where, hearts deprived of might,
By love alone they'd thrive, each ardent lover.

25. Spell

Clad in purple chiton had the mage
Cast unworldly spells. Abundantly
To the queen of lawless mood the sage
Lisped the ruby words of wizardry.

Bold-aroma'd had the burning plants
Opened lands unlimited by words
Where the twilight shadows did their dance,
First resembled fish, then turned to birds.

Lyres unviewed were crying from afar,
Fiery columns floated, flaming waves,
Tribunes, arrogant, well tried in war,
Lowering their eyes: so did their slaves.

High the queen, disturbing hidden things,
Courtesan of all the world might seem:
Hypnotized would be the sober kings
By her satin skin of snowy sheen.

Given over to her potent whim
Open is the mage to lasting harm,
Gazing at her breast, enchanting him,
Or a bracelet on extended arm.

Clad in purple chiton spoke the mage,
Breathing tenderly, a gentle spell:
To the lawless queen he dared presage
Everything her spirit favored well.

Soon the swaying moon began to fall,
Fading as it marked the midnight hour
By the em'rald Nile. The willing queen,
Paling, dropped, for him, a carmine flow'r.

26. Hyena

Above the sluggish Nile with rushes green
Where only birds and butterflies are borne
None at the tomb, forgotten, of the queen,
That captivating malefactor, mourn.

From mist incline deluding fantasies:
The moon's arising, guilty siren she.
While whitish fogs run freely at their ease,
Her lair Hyena's left, yet stealthily.

Her moans are wild and harsh in silent night
And desolate, portentous are her eyes.
Sharp, threatening, her scarring teeth shine white
Near pinkish marble where the monarch lies.

"You, moon, who are in love with the insane,
You stars, accordant in your elegance,
Dark Nile, who over quiet waters reign,
You butterflies, and birds, and silent plants,

Behold my bristling hair, the thrilling gleam
Of eye-shine doubled, each with evil flame!
Who'd not believe I, too, like such a queen
As here the stony sleeper, merit fame?

In her there beat a heart of perfidy:
High-arched and elegant, her brows meant death.
Hyena-queen you find—like her!—in me!
She loved the smell of blood on breezes' breath."

In villages the dogs in terror lie.
The frowning fellaheen take firmer grip
(While, in their houses, little children cry),
Each one, of pitiless and limber whip.

27. Ship

"Can you see what is hid in her eyes—
In their fading, yet glimmering embers?"
"There's a ship that is sunken: it lies
In the ocean, where no one remembers.

More majestic and braver than she
Never vessel was viewed on the water—
Trembling waves—heaving powerfully,
Swelling sails, and the winds made them tauter.

Flying fish, their subaqueous haunt
Fleeing eagerly into the air,
Curving, twisting, their beauty would vaunt—
Bending, flexible, emerald-fair.

From a cliff you were calling. You waited
With a hope that your might would create
An enkindled desire unabated
In a sailor made blind to his fate.

No one ever will learn of this story,
Of the struggle he waged before dying,
Who aspired to a passionate glory,
Nor will find where the vessel is lying—

Or why slender and elegant fingers
Sunder water with pearl of their gleams,
Like the swallows when melody lingers,
Or like soaring and summoning dreams.

Only he that is ever abiding
With you yet would remember, with sighs.
Ah, the sepulcher blue that you're hiding
In the soft-clouded mist of your eyes!"

28. Jaguar

Starry, I had sparkled in the sky
In a dream I'd strangely dreamed of late:
Life, though—lottery for such as I—
Lent an evil draw that made my fate.

Romantic Flowers

To a jaguar suddenly I turned.
Kindled—endless devilish desires:
In my heart a flaming menace burned,
Muscles trembled, madness-flashing fires.

I approached a human dwelling soon
By an empty field lit gloomily.
Seeking food by meager midnight moon—
Now my heav'n-extended destiny.

Unawaited, in a coppice dark,
Was the image of a maiden seen:
'Twould impart a brilliant regal spark,
Gait of deer, demeanor of a queen.

"Happy apparition, fairest bride …"
Shaking, shamed, I thought—and dared not move.
"Stay right there!"—she wouldn't be denied—
Tenderly she looked at me with love.

Still, I stood—her terror to allay—
Powerless. Her sign had fettered me.
Like a jackal, I became the prey
Which the dogs attacked, and savagely.

She, beyond the coppice, went her way—
Light, what gentle steps, the precious girl.
Lunar rays upon her pendants play:
Stars converse with jewelry of pearl.

Nikolay Gumilev

29. Horror

Down endless corridors I went,
The silence hiding like a foe
While statues glared with grave intent
From lofty alcoves—watched me go.

In fantasy all objects froze,
In twilight, gray, of silent hall
Sound—omen pendulum—arose:
Loud echo—every footstep-fall.

And where the gray was deeply dark
Perturbed my agitated gaze
A barely stirring shape that—hark!—
High-rising pillars hid in haze.

I, lost in lonely vast arena,
Felt fastened talons at my breast:
I saw the head of a hyena
On splendid maiden shoulders rest.

A sharpened muzzle blood exuded—
Completely empty gaping eyne—
A whisper, cruel, hoarse, intruded:
"You chose—you came here—you are mine!"

Time speeded up as fear accreted:
The twilight seemed solidified—
The horror boundlessly repeated
In countless mirrors multiplied.

ROMANTIC FLOWERS

30. Beyond the Grave

Mighty rise the tow'ring sepulchers
In a hidden cave below the earth—
Fiery dreams are they of Lucifer's—
Where the well-formed prostitutes come forth.

You may die in praise or in disgrace:
Either way, old bony dolor-man
Death will come and stare you in the face:
Boring, slow, he does the best he can.

Corridors and corridors—no end—
Tower after tower you will pass:
Usual routine ... you'll comprehend
With your shiny bulging eyes of glass.

Fallen down to meet your sepulcher,
Dreaming of a temple in the sky,
You will see a prostitute, with her
Pearly teeth well sharpened. There you'll lie.

She will nestle up for her delight.
You will have no room to move or cry—
Every kiss malign will drip with spite:
There, for all eternity, you'll lie.

31. Lion's Bride

Priest proclaimed, and men, complying,
Knifed my mother. But, for me,

God resplendent, wilding Lion,
Waits on meadow heavenly.

Fearing naught, why hide in wasteland
From a threat, or enemy?
I've put on a scarlet waistband,
Amber, pearls, and finery.

Loud I shout: "Sun-Beast! Light-giver!
Hear my grief impórtuning,
Roar forlorn. Come, wounds deliver
To a human victim, king!

Clasped in heavy paws, to coma
Lapsing, never rising more,
Let me sense the harsh aroma,
Dark and love-drunk, I adore.

Sweeter, herbs, than incense burning:
Quiet, I, on wedding night,
Bloody gaze awaiting, yearning,
Of the golden bridegroom bright."

32. Soul Gardens

The gardens of my soul are decorated
Where freshened breezes, mildly wafting, blow,
Where golden sand, with blackest marble mated,
To blue, translucent pools will lead below;

Romantic Flowers

Where birds of pink, a dawn on water, wander.
Strange climbing dreamlike plants appear beneath:
And—what on mysteries will make one ponder—
A maiden wears, august, a priestess' wreath.

Her eyes, like pure gray steel, reflect the light.
Her lips are known to have been kissed by none;
Her brow—an eastern lily—shining white.
She utters not a word to anyone.

Her cheeks are pink—rare pearls come from the
 south;
Their hidden wealth—a treasure undivined.
While pious prayers issue from her mouth,
Her hands caress each other, intertwined,

While at her feet two night-black panthers lie:
How soft the fur metallic tints would lave.
From rosy caverned mysteries he'd fly—
Flamingo gliding on the azure wave.

I will deny the world of hurried lines,
My dreams—to the eternal dedicated.
Sirocco, devilish, let rise betimes ...
The gardens of my soul are decorated.

33. Contagion

Nearing Cairo comes a ship with breezy
Banners of the Prophet grandly sailing.

Guessing where the sailors come from—easy:
   From the east they're hailing.

Shouts the captain 'mid the busy bustle:
Guttural, abrasive, harsh the greeting.
Faces dark are seen where mainsails rustle,
   Bright red fezzes fleeting.

   The children rush in, pushing on.
   (Their calves have come ambling and straying.)
   They came at the rising of dawn
      To watch: it's like playing.

Storks on rooftop sit, observing,
Stretching their necks in calm collective—
   Their perches serving
   For broad perspective.

   The storks are ethereal mages,
They grasp the matter seeming hidden:
They can tell why a red spot rages
   On a beggar unbidden.

The storks—they shout above the houses
But none will heed their grimly message:
What came, with fragrance, with silken blouses,
   To town? A plague, a presage.

34. Sindbad's Eagle

Trailing Sindbad, avid Master Sailor,
I doubloons had gained in alien lands:
Seas unknown I roamed, horizon-hailer,
Patches flaming where the light expands.

Many times to Sindbad turned my thought:
One fond fancy moved me most of all:
Sweet the dream—to Baghdad I'd been brought,
Walking shore-sands of that port of call.

Having carried Sindbad, proud and rich,
Now the eagle, feathers made of flame,
Lifted, tossed me onto boulders which
Cold enwound, a chill I'd never tame.

When my robe with running blood was stained
Dreams of ruin had my spirit crowded:
Like a youth by passion crazed, unfeigned,
For a maiden rich in silks enshrouded,

Quiet I perceived on far horizon,
Like a feast of shining impotence—
I'd perturbed the bird, that, hurt, arising,
Spread his wings on high and hastened thence.

35. Giraffe

Today, I can see that your eyes are uncommonly sad—
Your arms are exceedingly slender, embracing your knees.
So listen, then: far, far away on the shore of Lake Chad,
    The limber giraffe roams at ease.

A gracious and elegant litheness is native to him:
His hide is embellished with patterns of magical make,
Alike in variety strange to the moon-shapes that skim
And shimmer and shatter and sway on the waves of a lake.

When viewed from afar he's a colorful ship-sail made taut,
His running so fluent, the arrowy flight of a bird.
I'm sure, when at sunset he hides in marmoreal grot,
A sign comes to birth of whose like never human has heard.

I've tales entertaining of nations' mysterious ways,
Black maidens young passionate fighters would die to attain:
But you have inhaled for too long heavy, burdensome haze ...
You've lost all your lightness, believing in nothing but rain.

ROMANTIC FLOWERS

So how can I tell you of tropical garden-life glad,
Aromas of herbs unimagined—tall, elegant trees ...
Why weep? Listen ... far, far away, on the shore of
 Lake Chad,
   The limber giraffe roams at ease.

36. Rhinoceros

See the monkeys, shrieking, playing,
On the long lianas swaying
That so low are drooping, drooping?
Hear the rustle of their feet?
It's the rhino sweeping, swooping,
Plunging through the clearing, preying
On the slow, with rage replete.

See the general confusion—
Hear the pounding? No delusion
If the buffalo despotic
Sinks more deeply in the muck!
You who love the strange, exotic,
Do not seek for aid, collusion:
Run, and hide, and pray for luck!

Lift your arms up high, with singing
Say goodbye, while hope is ringing.
Looks to rosy fog a-fleeting
Lead afar your thinking—and—
Hid feluccas hear the greeting,
Through the waters quickly winging,
Coming from the promised land!

NIKOLAY GUMILEV

37. Lake Chad

Immemorial baobabs stand
By the hidden Lake Chad, looking on,
While, majestic, the Arabs command
Rapid, sculptured feluccas at dawn,
And along the lake's lush, woody banks,
'Mid the hills, below pedestal green,
As they bow to strange gods, giving thanks,
Are the ebony priestesses seen.

Once, I was a mighty, lordly leader's wife,
    Daughter of Lake Chad, with all his powers,
And throughout the time when winter rains were rife
    Kept the rites at the appointed hours.
For a hundred miles around, the people said,
    Never was a woman more resplendent,
Bracelets hanging from my arms, and garlanded
    With an amber necklace, jeweled pendant.

    Elegant, the warrior's mien,
    Lips red, skin pale, gaze serene,
    Leader ready to insist.
    Doors had opened in the heart:
    When it whispers to depart,
    We don't struggle, won't resist.
    Then he said no lucky lad
    Maiden more alluring had
    Ever viewed in France, at home,
    And that, at the dawn of day

Romantic Flowers

On a Berber steed, away
We would hasten, we would roam.

Then my husband, armed with arrow,
Swam across the twilit lakes—
Trampling thickets, made his way,
Felt, as through the woods he raced,
Torment that to hear would harrow,
Leaping narrows, breasting brakes,
But became, one scorching day,
Cold, a corpse now shamed, disgraced.

On a camel unstoppable riding,
In my thick-folded furry wraps hiding,
Silken shawls wound luxuriantly,
Like a bird to the north I was borne,
Broke my fan made of feathers and horn,
Drunk with visions of what was to be.

Like a withered figtree, dead, neglected,
One whose leaves have flown, blown all away,
I, a boring mistress, lie rejected—
Thing cast off, abandoned, in Marseilles.
Left to feed myself on meager leavings—
Forced to entertain, amid my grievings,
Laughing sailors when their goal is gained,
Timid, with my troubles overridden,
Gaze that fades with every hour I live.
Die? But there, 'mid unknown fields, well hidden—
There my husband waits—and won't forgive.

Nikolay Gumilev

38. Pompey and the Pirates

From the festive-red stern gently gliding
Waft the fragrances into the hold
Where, in danger, the pirates are hiding
Though they're threatening-seeming and bold.

Fear concealed by a firm resolution,
Now they're boasting, and now they turn pale:
Voices low, they demand execution:
Pompey's head—it must fall, without fail.

Many days they've been serving in slavery,
Now submissive, now rising in ire.
To ascend to the tent requires bravery—
To the stern, carmine-ardent as fire.

Of a sudden, a summons is sounded.
Pompey orders: "Get *up*, dogs! Look spry!"
—By a dove-flock is Pompey surrounded—
"You are letting my goblet get dry!"

They're subdued by the mood of the weather—
That's the end to piratical vaunts ...
Flowers, wine they'll supply him, together—
Pomegranates—whatever he wants.

39. Founders

Remus and Romulus climbed a mountain.
Seeing before them a hillock wild,

Romulus said, "We will build a city."
"Sunlike," said Remus. And then he smiled.

Romulus claimed, "By the constellation
Honor was granted us from of old."
Remus replied with determination,
"That is all past. Look ahead. Be bold."

"Here, by the circus, we'll build our villa:
All will be welcome, from hills and plains,"
Romulus added. Said Remus, "Still a
Need for close burial vaults remains."

40. Manlius

Toppled, Manlius! Rome's glory
Must of course remain the same—
Indestructible her story
As Tarpeian cliff might claim.

Rome—a heaving sea, affrighted:
Wailings penetrate the night.
Yet—a smile, serenely lighted,
From the one deprived of might!

Why, as when a noontime cloud
Is illumined by a ray,
Comes now Marius, made proud,
Sword new-bloodied? What to say?

Nikolay Gumilev

41. Games

Hail the consul—the people are gladdened!
Three whole days—and the games—not yet finished!
And the tigers are wild, and they're maddened—
And the boas breathe ire undiminished.

And the elephants, bears—what a wonder!
Fighters drunken with blood, and untiring!
And the bison hooves, thudding like thunder,
Even Rome hardly tires of admiring.

Alemannic, the captive delivered,
Who'd been wounded within the arena.
Haze and winds, when he conjured them, quivered:
With his murder-eyes dire—a hyena!

So we welcomed this fight: he'd be giving
All his best, he was brave, he was daring.
Tear, you beasts, the hot body, still living!
Drink the blood, neither flinching nor caring!

Holding hard to the handrail, strong, oaken,
He was howling!—and, wildly surprising—
They replied with a roar when he'd spoken—
Every wolf, every bear, every bison.

All the serpents, subjected, were sprawling:
To their knees all the elephants falling,
With their bloody trunks—bellowing, bawling—
Stopped to listen to what he'd be calling!

Romantic Flowers

Consul!—gods!—though we love to watch gamely,
Never seen—such a weird apparition:
Hungry tigers the dust licking tamely
From the feet of a healing magician.

42. To the Emperor

Phantom of force never known unto men,
You're to the fates an unchangeable law,
Emperor. How, from a moribund fen,
Dare I to laud you in suppliant awe?

Woe! Not a tribune, no senator I,
Only a singer, a vagrant, and poor.
Why with a wreath do you favor me, why?
Fragile, my anthem will die, not endure.

Locked to me all are the gates of the rich:
Meager and scant are my narrative rhymes.
Only the shepherds, the animals which
Live on the hills, come and listen betimes.

Torn is my chiton, skin wrinkled and dry.
Vision and singing—they're faded and weak.
Yet when you summon I humbly comply:
Emperor, I am the slave that you seek.

NIKOLAY GUMILEV

43. Caracalla

Emperor, with stature of an eagle,
Curly, perfect beard of blackest hue,
Ah, you would be veritably regal
If you'd once become another you!

Tender feeling curiously pensive
Shadow strict on kingly lips allows,
Yet what wild rebellion apprehensive
Had been hiding in your knitted brows!

Images of Roman strength effusive,
Julius, Augustus, Pompey, too—
They're a strangely paling shade elusive
Covering the quiet eyes of you.

Visions darken, rest, of martial planners
In crepuscular ancestral vaults—
Yet before the steps of lordly manors
Rapid Tiber water never halts.

Neither do your dire ambitions dwindle:
Everywhere outspreading camps of troops
In Jerusalem infernos kindle,
Vanquishing the Paphian rebel groups.

Yet, what good are triumphs in the twilight
If descending shadows darken all
When, like gold-on-black-niello highlight,
Feet of dancers glimmer in the hall?

Romantic Flowers

Passionate as youthful tiger-temptress,
Tenderly, as swan on water sleeps,
In the bedroom darkenened waits the empress,
For the ruler who his counsel keeps.

Where, above your park, in glimmer-rebus,
Star aspersions are delirium,
There you may have seen nocturnal Phoebus
Wandering among the gardens come.

By oneiric arrows penetrated,
Curiosity has made him cold.
Now, like you, he views, unsubjugated,
Crocodiles of darkened em'rald old.

As capricious cameos enameled
Quietly abandoned gardens wait
Where, from palm-branch onto plants untrammeled,
Dangle snakes, rare fruit to contemplate.

Restive plants behold disordered visions:
Dream the floating fogs across the night.
Flit the butterflies, like swift elisions,
'Mid the dark their pearly wings of white.

Mystery can Nature feel arising:
Youthful, bright, in love, descending soon,
With unsounding step comes down, emprising,
Wrapped in cloud of quietude, the moon.

Of the summer lunar music hidden
Otherworldly is the hush on high,
Yet more frightening and more forbidden
Hidden things you tell her in reply.

Later you, within your temple golden,
Slowly, gravely, as would fit a king,
Diffidently, humbly, unbeholden,
Come to greet the day's awakening.

44. Mariner Pausanias ...

Mariner Pausanias
From the distant shores of Nile
Into Rome imported has
Fabric of the highest class,
Doeskin—and a crocodile.

That was in the era bad
Known for Caracalla's jags:
God of merry and of mad,
He with chains adorned the sad
Crowds upon his royal crags.

Guileless-gold, immersed in woes,
Sun is covered utterly:
Purple-clad the monarch goes
Into waters where he knows
One the crocodile can see.

In the galleries agaze,
Bearded, crazed carousers stand:
Charming courtesans who praise
Venus' gentle strength will raise,
Marble-white, a slender hand.

And, as in a legend old,
Harmony-defiler, soon
Glides along the vessel-hold
Crocodile, the green and gold,
On a silver-sheen pontoon.

45. Neoromantic Tale

Rose a mountain great in fame,
High, with towered castle crowned,
As in a capricious frame
Girdled with a river 'round.

Lived therein a gladsome pair:
Young, in childhood-realm fantastic
Dwelt the prince. With whitened hair,
Wise, the steward—stiff, bombastic.

In the handsome Hall of Bold
Interjection might be found
Lassos, javelins untold,
Meant for doe and boar that bound.

Well got-up and proud-appearing,
Goes the prince to hunt some game:
Yet the steward's interfering:
You can hear him, loud, exclaim:

"Once, on highway magical,
Wild, in Velledd, woe betiding,
I beheld a cannibal
On a rushing rhino riding.

Dark, blood-hungry as he was,
Dire in gaze—my heart was frore,
And the huge rhinoceros
Parted mountains with his roar.

On, as if he'd never heard,
Rode the prince aglow, and yet
Now his falcon, royal bird,
Shakes, by hidden fear beset.

Oh! a people-eaters' dwelling!
On the rock-edge you descry
Trophies of his triumph telling:
Half-consumed cadavers lie.

Creatures never seen before,
Many-spotted boas lour:
Yet the steward, with his lore,
Burns some herbs with magic power.

Romantic Flowers

Barely has the altar cooled
When the cannibal abhorred
Tries to rouse himself but, fooled,
Frightened, cannot find his sword.

Horror all his courage draining,
Anguish passing comprehension,
Loud he'll blast the trumpet, straining
To awake the beast's attention.

Yet he leaves the horn behind,
Trusted friend, 'mid trees to fade
Where, determined, dauntless, find
Dogs their prize, impatient made.

Comes the youthful prince unruffled
And the host, by terror tossed,
'Mid this gloom of sobbing, muffled,
Funds himself now lassoed, lost.

They've confined the cannibal
(That was only right and just)
Safe behind the highest wall
In the tow'r of dark and dust.

People say he's growing mild,
Likes to make amazing faces,
Telling an emboldened child
Fairy tales of ancient places.

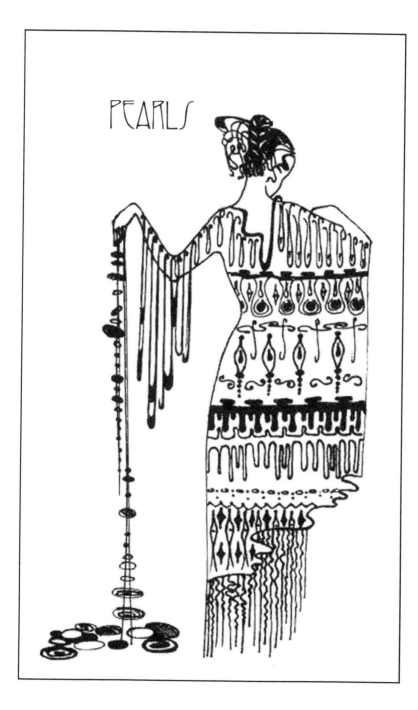

Nikolay Gumilev

46. Magic Violin
to Valery Bryusov

Little boy, you look so happy, and so brightly you are
    smiling,
Love your luck! And just enjoy it, though it poison
    worlds away:
You don't know—don't know the terrors that your
    violin beguiling
May begin again to wake when the musician starts
    to play!

Yes, the one who once had taken it in hands that
    were commanding
Soon would feel forever vanish placid light within the
    eyes,
For the tone can summon spirits who, with hellish
    understanding,
Join the wolves that, rabid, roam where the
    musician's travel lies.

One will sing, lament forever to the strings, the dolor-
    makers:
One will strike and struggle, turn and twist the wild,
    demented bow
In the daylight, stirred by whirlwind, 'mid the
    maelstrom, under breakers,
In the flaring of the sunset and the dawn's
    enkindling glow.

Pearls

You will tire, slow down, the singing for a moment
    still, defeated,
Now unable to cry out, to stir, to sigh, to beg for rest:
Then will come the howling wolves, blood-hungry,
    frenzied, fierce, breath fetid,
And their teeth will fasten, grab your throat, their
    paws attack your breast.

You will know how mocked have always been
    musicians skilled in singing:
In your eyes will gleam a long belated, yet a sovran
    fear—
And a mortal cold your body will surround as
    garment clinging,
And your fiancée will sob, the dark possess your
    friend most dear.

Boy, away! You won't discover either gaiety or
    treasure!
Yet I see that you are laughing—radiant, playful is
    your gaze.
Well, take up your magic violin, outstare, if that's
    your pleasure,
Ogre eyes, and die the dreadful glory-death of one
    who plays!

47. Descendants of Cain

He didn't lie—that stern and somber devil
We call the Morning Star—with luring prods;

"Eat of the fruit, and you shall be as gods,
You need not fear from heaven any evil."

All paths had tempted youthful strength primeval:
Man's work, forbidden latterly, belauds;
The damsel amber fruit no more defauds,
Nor virgin promised unicorn-retrieval.

But why are we so bent, and limp, and weak?
Why yet appear unpardoned in a pique?
Why does the horror of our ancient straying

Become so clear whenever someone's hand
Is playing with two sticks or grassblades—and
A cross the pairs are all at once portraying?

48. Rock

for A. I. Gumileva

Rock wrathful, staring—watch it flare!
Those deep, odd cracks—they're more than marks.
Beneath the moss—a gleam, a glare:
Don't hope to see mere firefly sparks!

A druid-gloom of ancient ages,
Of somber king a sibyl grim,
To work revenge in envy-rages
From sea-abyss had summoned him.

Pearls

He issues, black, and fearful, lours—
Reclining now along the shore.
At nighttime he'll be smashing towers,
On random foes pent anger pour.

Across the fields of desolation
He flies, on hedge to lie and wait:
Through rifts—a seething conflagration—
Impelled ahead—relentless fate.

No eye, mostly likely, will detect him
On this nocturnal, hidden flight:
Take care your steps do not deflect him,
Collision rile an ireful might.

Resentment, burning, woe betiding,
Mute frenzy threatens, cannot flag:
He moveless then remains, abiding
As quiet cliff or jagged crag.

Wherever you're concealed when sleeping,
You cannot steal away from him.
He'll seek you out while flying, leaping
Upon your chest—capricious, grim.

You'll glimpse unfading flamelets gleaming,
Amazed, and utter anguished moans
To hear the rockfall, worse-than-dreaming
The clatter of your crackling bones.

With hot blood drunken, satiated,
He leaves a house by dawnlight, hushed—
What horrid corpse, forgotten, weighted—
Collapsed—the dog a bull had crushed!

Then, crossing fields and meads of clover
He'll wearied sink in ocean flood
Where skillful tides can wash him over
And clean him from the crusted blood.

49. Possessed

The moon, round shield, in heaven glides,
Who long ago a slaughtered champion
Had left. The beating heart betides
An aching doom in lunar lampion.

Past frowning woods and meadow haze,
Undaunted by the ocean's warning,
Lance ready, wanders all the ways
My monster-woe through night and morning.

It is in vain I take my horse
And seize the reins with hand aquiver
By frenzied lash the beast to force
Across a thawed and flooded river.

In somber swamp, war viciously,
By neither side decided, rages:
He holds the balance over me
Who well in twilight battle wages.

Pearls

A darkness rushes through the eyes ...
In frenzied, full-speed gallop racing,
From saddle toppled, I'll arise
To roam through murk all forms effacing.

How fearsome is that coup de grâce!
Deep-bruised by heavy armor-braces,
I'll comfortless bewail my loss
Whom riddling fortune daily faces.

I'll recognize that muffled walk
In fickle fog, in mist approaching,
Yet, as before, my wits to mock,
The Unknown goes—no queries broaching.

Come morning, I'll awake alone.
Girls, cutting short their springtime play,
Will whisper: "Torment made him moan,
Led by a shifting shape astray."

50. Duel

Your scutcheon: guileless lily whiteness—
In mine are blooms of crimson hue.
Close battle—wailing horns—the brightness
Of golden war-shield glimmers, too.

I'm summoned forth to fight a duel
By hand on kettledrum, tambour:
'Mid smiling garden paths, I'm cruel—
Unguarded tiger—gloomy Moor.

Nikolay Gumilev

War-damsel of an ancient grandeur
As in the lay the minstrel sings—
Unrivaled lance on sea or land, your
High valor's been the pride of kings.

Now we have started, now have halted:
The trembling troops look on to see
Whom victory will have exalted—
Smooth steel or granite, you or me?

I fell—more jubilant than lightning
The shining knife-blade drank its fill.
You thought my moans a bliss, not fright'ning,
My shivers that would not be still.

Now off you go in martial glory,
Crowd-hymned, by fortune-favor kissed—
But you'll return, to end the story,
Alone in spring, encloaked in mist.

Beside the haze-ravine appearing,
In golden helmet, crowned with fame,
You'll find my stiffened body. Nearing,
You'll bend the knee, and then exclaim:

"I love you! Do you hear me, cherished
Beloved? Open eyes! Cry, 'Yes!'
As you were slain by me and perished,
I now am yours in faithfulness."

PEARLS

The tone of sobbing hasn't vanished:
Distinct, your rustling silk I hear.
But through the mist, no longer banished,
The lupine ravener draws near.

51. Portrait of a Man
picture in the Louvre, by an unknown hand

Each eye a lake of Underworld—they're hidden
In chamber long forsaken of a king:
Distinguished by a sign on high, he's chidden,
Nor speaks of God—indeed, of anything.

The lips are like a purple wound unhealing,
Incised with blade by vilest venom nourished;
Sealed early, saddened, they recall the feeling
Of unexampled pleasure when they flourished.

The hands, with pallid marble-moonlight laden,
Hold all the horror of old maledictions:
They once had stroked a black magician-maiden
And known of sanguinary crucifixions.

At every age he knew a fortune frightful,
By dream of poet and of killer kindled.
Perhaps, when he was born into a night full
Of ills, a bloody comet melted, dwindled.

Within that spirit unnamed dolors burgeon:
Within that soul are injuries, infections—

Yet not for all the gardens of the Virgin
Or Venus would he trade his recollections.

That spite—not the contempt of a blasphemer:
That skin of satin—tender as a flower.
He yet can smile, he yet can laugh, that schemer,
But weeping ... weeping is beyond his power.

52. Forest Fire

Cloudy smoke the winds are driving—
Pack-horse-black and corpulent:
After it, relentless, riving
Air, the glaring flame unspent.

Rare and strange the light-shafts rearing,
Dark brown poplar trunks between:
Blazes, rosy-pink appearing
Mad, on maddened field are seen.

Maize-field blazes—with appalling
Sharp and acrid pitchy smell,
Hissing, flaring, tree-trunks falling
Meet the rising fiery swell.

Trampling, crushing—din of thunder—
Wailing, bellow, squeal, and roar:
Boding death—a quiet under-
Tone of streams that boil and pour.

PEARLS

Elephants, protection seeking,
Run—the lion from his lair
Leapt! The date-fed ape-male-shrieking,
Penetrating, rends the air.

Lightfoot lion comes, eye livid,
Side by side with bristly boar:
White-toothed terror!—ire less vivid:
Now is not the time of war.

Next, from smoky thicket soaring,
Pours in wave a force of flame:
Singeing, rushing, rearing, roaring—
How may we these nightmares name?

Hear him crack his whip? The Devil
Underneath the roof of hell
Drives the roiling mass of evil
From the underworld pell-mell.

To escape the suffocation,
Running, heart-beat feeling burst,
Blinded by the conflagration,
Bloodied by the fire-purgation,
Human beings perish first.

53. Queen

Curls ring your brow—they're molded bronzes—
Sharp, sparkling light within your eyes:

Nikolay Gumilev

Contémplative Tibetan bonzes
Made bonfires in your honor rise.

When Timur, by resentment harried,
Quelled nations on the battlefield,
You, through the Gobi Desert carried,
He let repose upon a shield.

You Agra Fortress entered singing,
More light than Adam's Lilith sweet:
Your happy onagers made ringing
Bright tones with gaily gold-shod feet.

The evening earth seemed barely breathing
And ev'n the bloom-bed scarcely sighed.
Above them, green canal enwreathing,
Black beetles fluttered far and wide.

In column-shade I watched, expecting
Your face, that diamond of the east:
I waited, patient, genuflecting
In pale pink vestment of a priest.

The painted bow was bent and ready:
With hardy freedom long loved well,
I knew my muscle-strength was steady
And that my marksmanship would tell.

Thought tried to rise—of laud that hallows
Triumphal princely pageantry—

Pearls

A dance 'mid undergrowth of aloes—
Gay long-gone days—their venery—

But carven, stern, your lips' compression
Hid torment, though you made no sound:
I saw a god in your expression—
I dropped my bow upon the ground.

The crowd attacked me, shouting, screaming.
You, lazily, did not demur
But smiled upon the steely, gleaming
Axe of the executioner.

54. Comrade

Someone is passing by, quite closely:
I feel a chill inside my chest.
Now every night that looms morosely
Strange face I view. I loved it best.

Old comrade-huntsman, mighty master
Of hounds, you rise from haunted night,
Snow-leopardlike but lither, faster
Than tiger—elephántine might.

And I remember all: how *could* I
Forget that sword for ruin borne—
The power of your arms? Nor would I
Neglect your bow of aurochs horn.

Our friend the wolf would never tire:
He roamed, then slept beside me. Song
I played at evening on the lyre—
And he, my helper, moaned along.

What happened? Whose the lethal power
That wilding garden-life erased?
A wounded hawk—my friend—the flower
Of manhood, passion now embraced.

Entangled memories—blood, terror
Can yoke the soul that nothing saves:
Night, fallen heroes, ocean-farer—
Dead comrade's body on the waves.

Have you, 'mid serried ages straying,
Now left death's grove of gnarly oak?
Nets, bow, in darkened palm displaying,
You've folded in a carmine cloak …

Hope arrived—it will leave us never:
Dreams reply to our heart-demands.
Soon will I stroll with you, as ever,
Over the fields of unknown lands.

55. In the Library

O yellowed, faded leaves that lie
In evening libraries necrotic
Where thinkers purity descry
When drunk on dust, a wild narcotic!

Pearls

Behold the fateful problem posed:
How then evade this troubling vision?
I've come upon a flow'r enclosed
In Gilles de Rais' court trial decision.

Reticulated, pale, and sere,
With frail and secret-strange aroma,
'Twas placed, indubitably, here
By someone in a lover's coma.

Still from an ardent woman's kiss
The cheeks were warm, touched by a jewel.
But now the eyes were dulling: this
A new thought suited, coldly cruel.

A vision rising up from hell,
Chant passionate, had filled that spirit:
Love's gift, a flow'r with fragrant smell,
Was pressed into the crime book near it.

The gaze in late nocturnal shade—
What was it dully contemplating?
Who, in the dark-confined arcade,
A cry had uttered, supplicating?

Love's riddles lie beneath a flood,
Oblivious, of long-dead ages.
'Tis very clear to me that blood
Had left a spot on blotted pages.

Ah, thorns are part of bridal wreaths,
Life's mournful ills an evil burden ...
We know one reader, though, who seethes,
Time-tireless, yet deprived of guerdon.

My dreams are pure. But love bereaves.
Dead killer, why your vile purloinings?
O agéd yellow faded leaves,
Chagrin-creating bindings, joinings!

56. On the Way

Time for amusement—now past,
Flower not blossoming twice.
Shadow the mountain had cast
Fell on our path in a trice.

It is a region of tears,
Cliff-giants climb at our sides.
Now a bare crag-face appears
Yon, where the dragon abides.

Knife-boned and ridgy the spine,
Fiery sirocco the breath:
Him would the people define
Well by the epithet "Death."

Should we surrender our plan?
Turn our stout vessel around?

Manage—as well as we can—
Scanty, intractable ground?

Better go forward than fall!
Now is the time to be bold.
Better blind Nothing-at-all,
Brighter than yesterday-gold!

Take out your treasure-sword: kind,
Stainless the naiades' blade.
Riant, we'll finally find
Gardens that never will fade.

57. Semiramis
to the bright memory of I. F. Annensky

My fortune, high sovrans with envy convulsing,
    Had brought even gods to the ground.
With marble-cold pillars in heaven-hot pulsing
    My garden is girdled 'round.

I've groves holding wells for the rose-petaled water,
    Blue mosses in delicate rings,
Each dancing-girl servant—Terpsichorë-daughter,
    And mages—the element-kings.

All's joyful and blandishing, intimate, shining,
    Half hiding the joy of heights—
But yet I am frightened by lunar declining,
    The bending, the boding nights.

In twilit affright from a gaze without pardon,
    From moon-nets cast around,
I'll throw myself over this high-walled garden
    Sev'n hundred cubits down.

58. Old Conquistador

Deep 'mid unknown barren mountains roaming,
Hazy desert heaven yet withstanding,
Came the old conquistador while homing
Condors glided, snowy height commanding.

He eight days had wandered, near starvation.
Then his horse had died. Below the only
Hanging ledge he made his habitation,
Not to leave the much-loved body lonely.

There, beneath a withered fig-tree shelter,
Singing old romances of Castilla,
Of beloveds, battles helter-skelter,
He could see a crossbow, a mantilla.

He remained as ever, bold, unbested,
Undismayed by fear, not caring whether
Death arrived. That Warrior suggested:
Might we play a bone-dice game together?

PEARLS

59. Barbarians

The country was sobbing, the gods knowing nothing
 of pity.
The queen placed her couch in the popular square,
 for the ruder
Barbarian hosts had intended attacking the city:
The queen was prepared, wholly naked, to face the
 intruder.

The trumpets of heralds were blaring, the banners
 were flying
Like late autumn leaves flying past her and pungent-
 erotic:
Smooth silks in luxuriant heaps with each other
 were vying,
Adorned by the gold-molten brush of the climate
 exotic.

The queen like a panther appears of unpeopled
 dominions,
A savage abysm each eye, wide-affrighting, exciting,
Below pearly net rose her breast and, like fluttering
 pinions,
Gem-bracelets were trembling, her legs and dark
 arms brightly lighting.

Now silvery, lutelike, her clear proclamation
 proceeded:
"Make haste, all you heroes, your bow and your sling
 boldly bearing!

A woman you never will find so unsheltered,
    unheeded,
Whose moans are more sweet and more tempting to
    fighters uncaring.

Make haste, all you heroes, bronze-armored, whom
    zealotry musters:
Let sharp-pointed nails drink their fill of corporeal
    sadness!
Much finer to you than the purple of vineyard-spring
    clusters
Your hearts overflowing with frenzy, with pity, with
    madness.

I've waited so long to admire you, strong fighters
    unfawning:
Come freely, then—full-blooming breasts are
    awaiting your pleasure.
I've dreamed of—and wondered at—tower-tall camps
    in the dawning:
His trump when the herald shall sound, do not spare
    to hunt treasure!"

The slaves to the herald have offered on bronzen-
    made platter
The silvery horn, well adorned with an ivory casing:
But now the barbarians, frowning, show something's
    the matter—
The love for their snow-land abandoned's the feeling
    they're facing.

Cold sky, barren dunes they remember, the resonant
 ringing
Of birds' happy chirping in undergrowth eager to
 flower,
Blue eyes of a northerly queen, of the skald apt in
 singing,
To harp, northern ballads of womanly grandeur and
 power.

The square yet is seething and sparkling with people.
 Heat searing,
The sky of the south has a fire-fan. But, forced to set
 forth and
Mouth foaming, the horse of the sullen commander
 is rearing—
With pride and contempt he's returning his men to
 the northland.

60. Soldier of Agamemnon

Turbid and troubled, my soul thinks of one
 Thing—and one only—the dread
Question: why live when proud Atreus' son
 Died on a petal-strown bed?

All that we fancied we always had known,
 Fear and desiring and sighs,
Mirrored shone back in the Atreid's own
 Calm imperturbable eyes.

Might unexampled in muscle we saw,
  Languor in bend of the knees,
Cloudy-bright body—maecenal the law
  Known by unspoken degrees.

Now, what am *I*? Just a fragment of pain,
  Javelin fallen in grass.
Leader of peoples, he'll rise not again,
  Wise Agamemnon, alas!

Deeply transparent, the dawn-greeting lake
  Showed an admonishing face:
How to go on, for his memory's sake?
  Heavy—the shame, the disgrace.

61. Androgyne

With humble entreaties we harry your hearing,
Divinity, wonder we marvel to see:
We know you are here. We await your appearing,
Believe in your triumph that soon is to be.

Dear friend, I know well there is much you
    surrender:
Yourself most of all you are offering—yes!
To god that's above, your sweet body you render,
Your tender and elegant body we bless.

Then hasten, dear! Naked, we each, like a spirit,
The promise will keep that we made with a sigh:

To whisper the name long forgotten, then hear it—
To hear with a shiver the longed-for reply.

I see you delay—you're embarrassed—why
    frightened?
Let two of us die for his singular fame
If yet from the bed of mad heedlessness, brightened,
The Androgyne rise, like a phoenix in flame!

The air filled with roses, we're each like a vision:
The pilgrim returns, to his fatherland near—
Believe? The delights we enjoy no derision
Of lashing contempt will require us to fear!

62. Eagle

The rapid eagle upward, Throneward flew,
Through stellar vestibule to the Transcendent:
What clarity, that cleaving of the blue!
His dark brown feathers glossy shone, resplendent.

Where had he dwelt before? Perhaps a king
Enchained him in the royal bestiary,
Acquainted with the goddess-maiden Spring,
In love with some young pensive prince unwary.

Or maybe, in a wicked-wizard-den,
Perceiving sky through narrow window bright'ning,
By lofty prospect charmed, he dreamed—and then
His heart had turned to heat, his love to lightning.

No matter. In the play of heaven-lights,
The azure splendor was to him a token
Of Endless Upward, new-revealed. Three nights,
Three days he flew. With bliss that heart was
      broken—

He perished! To the earth he couldn't fall
But was at one with planet-motion 'round him.
Abysses yawned below him, but for all
Its work, too weak, no gravitation found him.

In heaven's vaulted hall each rending ray
Was of a coldness calm and never-ending;
Beyond corruption, upward went his way
Emboldening, with mortal will unbending.

In boundless blue he more than once felt break
A universe, heard angel-trump resounding!
He'd victim be of none. Make no mistake:
Though he'd attain a grave, there'd be no grounding.

63. Submission

Only the weary are worthy, entreaties to bring:
Only a lover, to step through the meadow in spring.

Stellar the heaven, and tranquil the sadness below:
Quietly heard, the *So be it*—in mist let it flow.

That is submission—then come, gentle being, bow
 down,
Palest of maidens a-weeping, black veil and black
 gown.

Saddened—my region, unspeaking—bemuffled in
 leaves:
Here see the finest retreat for a spirit that grieves.

Here are but hummock turned rusty, a moistened
 ravine—
Yet it's for these I reject a chimerical dream.

Am I in love—or grown merely and mortally tired?
Fortunate I, that the lights of mine eyes have
 despired.

Quiet, I feel how the swell in the grasses went by—
Quiet, I'll listen and weep and the bittern will cry.

64. Knight with Chain

I again may hear the wailing horn to summon me to
 war—
I, who subjugated cities, am again conquistador.

Fettered slave, I lived in jail humiliated, withering,
In oblivion ungrateful of the higher might of spring.

But she came, advancing lightly on the rubies of the
    flowers—
She, the rival, steel to shatter, with its vainly
    chaining powers.

Now again I roam the cliffs, and drink of brook in
    wood and field—
In the breathing of the balmy ocean sea my wounds
    have healed.

Yet, when now I walk renewed amid an altered
    universe,
There is nothing I would fain forget—and nothing I
    would curse.

That I every hero-feat and every height and plain
    might feel
To my radiant silver helmet will I weld my chain of
    steel.

65. Christ

He is walking on a pearly
Path by gardens near the shore.
Superficial folk are surly:
Simple tasks will matter more.

"Shepherd, fisherman, a treasure!
I would summon you to higher
Pasture waiting for your pleasure:
Nets a different skill require.

Is a sheep or fish more worthy
Than the spirit of a man?
Trade in skiey goods, not earthy
As mere wordly merchant can.

Not a hut in Galilea
Will you have, but—better far—
Higher paradise will be a
Brighter guide than any star.

Though the sun will hurry, surely,
To its long-appointed end,
You will joy in heaven, purely,
With your tender Father-Friend."

What a choice! A wonder-leap—and
Hope undreamed of will arise:
They will leave the fish, the sheep—and
Join the seeker of the skies.

66. Marquis de Carabas
to S. Auslender

The woods at eve are light and singing—
And glad are blackened field and plain.
My fate, today, to me was bringing,
Behind the threshing-barn, a crane.

I look at snow-clumps melting, streaming—
Pink summer-lightning, glowing yet:

Nikolay Gumilev

My cat will catch a fish, then teeming
Bright birds entice to waiting net.

He knows the tracks of ferret, hare—
The reed-gaps near the river—and
The magpie eggs he'll savor where
They're tasty, nicely hatched in sand.

When dark the coppice all has swallowed
And fog lets fall her drops of dew,
I doze. The damp-nosed friend who followed
Is rubbing me—begins to mew:

"I'm glad to serve you, sir. For you
I challenge all the world to witness:
Marquis de Carabas—yes, true!—
Of ancient race, of blood so blue—
Let no one doubt your noble fitness.

The woodland game, the pines that grow
On mountains rich in gold, in copper,
Broad yellow cornfields in a row,
The fish with underwater glow—
They're yours by right of birth—quite proper!

Why in some burrow do you sleep,
And play the winsome child capricious?
Why don't you live at court, and keep
A lapdog, parakeet, and heap
On silver platter snacks delicious?"

My learnèd cat, my cat devoted,
Has heaved a sigh of sympathy.
With sharpened claws, he, furry-coated,
Combs out in pique a stubborn flea.

Beneath a yew tree I awaken
(Of restful roots I'm very fond)—
In lazy mood, with aim well taken,
Toss pebbles toward the misty pond.

How nice and firm they are, how agile—
They on the water skip and skate!
I love each bough and grassblade fragile:
'Tis there I have my marquisate.

67. Trip to China
for S. Sudeikin

Pure is the vibrant and vivid air:
Oxen have filled the granary.
Lambs have been killed, which the cooks prepare:
Wine in the dipper gleams merrily.

What is afflicting our heart, our liver?
Why do we suffer?—and why not *live*?
Even the loveliest girl can't give her
Lover more than she has to give.

Well have we known how sorrow rends,
Cherished the heavens we've thrown away:

Still we believe in the sea, my friends—
China, then! Why don't we go—today?

There—just imagine! Good fortune's waiting,
Think of the cockatoo—shrilling shriek!
Think of the passions we'll each be sating—
Sweet little thing under teahouse teak.

We'll be facing the pink foam gleaming:
Copper lions won't terrify.
Won't it be fine, 'mid the palm-trees dreaming?
Palm-wine's the key, so our mood stays high.

All those weeks will be one big feastday—
We'll compete as we drain the cask:
Are you acquainted in the least way
With strong drink, Rabelais, I ask?

Big as a barrel of sparkling Tokay,
You'll be a fright to the Chinese eyes.
Cover your wisdom with your cloak, eh?
Wind green ivy around your thighs!

Be our captain! We all implore you!
We'll take the oars, give *you* the staff:
Only, to China let's go—before you
Change your mind. And at death—let's laugh!

PEARLS

68. Testament

By delights of my life yet enchanted,
I'm reluctant to melt into gloom
Or return—should my death wish be granted—
To my homeland, a somnolent doom.

By the roseate lake that assuages
All my pain in the evening, I ask:
Let the younger and mightier mages
Make a pyre of sweet cypress their task—

In obedience bent, laying gently
The cadaver well wrapped. When in place
I'll appear to gaze 'round me intently
With a half-hidden smile on my face.

And when dark-golden light touches clearly,
From the sky, the marmoreal piers,
May the pondering torch drop austerely
Aromatic and resinous tears.

With a soft woodland flute piping sadly
And a loud-sounding gong fore and aft,
I will tremblingly travel, but gladly,
On the fire-wafting funeral raft.

Like a wood-elf, a spell madly casting,
Wilding life will erupt once again:
Crimson kisses in martyrdom lasting—
All my body will quiver in pain.

And until what no mortal can master
Grants me heaven or nil on the pyre
I will gutter out—brighter, and faster—
With the soul-drunken life of the fire.

69. Lakes

My fortune I dashed in a blasphemy bold,
    No anguish—and penitence? Needless.
Yet clearly, at night, I am feeling the cold
    Of night's giant lakes, deep and heedless.

On mournful, dark waves are the nenuphars gliding
    More still than my calm meditations—
Awaking forgotten enchantment, unchiding,
    Are silver-white yews' divinations.

The bends in the pathway look soft by the light of
    The moon, but I'm gasping for air:
The barren fields watched are untouched by the sight of
    My hand-clenching pain, unaware.

That something will shortly appear I am certain:
    A tragedy's peripeteia—
Sad maiden, white bird, just before the last curtain—
    Or strange, tender tale of things higher.

And then a new sun, hazy heaven unending,
    And shadows to dragonflies changing!

Proud swans of old legend, their stately necks
    bending,
  White stairs will descend, bravely ranging.

But memory fades, thinking fails. I, made weaker
    And wingless, at water extending
Must gaze, hear the waves babble powerless, bleaker
    Decrees of a bleak reprehending.

I wake. As before, I am confident speaking:
    The night-vacillations have gone.
The harsh and the splendor mundane of our seeking
    Go on—rest, and labor—go on.

70. Rendezvous

Today you'll come to me again,
    Tonight I'll comprehend
Why strange to me is moonlight when
    I'm home without my friend.

You'll swiftly come, quite pale, and soon
    Arrive, and shed your cloak.
Is it not so the swelling moon
    From grove will rise of oak?

Ensorceled by the lunar light,
    Enspelled the more by you,
'Tis glad I'll be in silent night,
    With fate, with blackness too.

A wood-beast thus, before the flow'rs
    In spring begin to bloom,
Can hear soft rustling of the hours
    And look upon the moon.

Mute, stealing into deep ravine,
    Awaking hidden dream,
His lightfoot step to blend will seem
    With moving lunar beam.

Like him, I would remain discreet,
    In anguished love's delight,
And with foreboding, too, I'll meet
    With you, my lunar might.

Though, moment past, you won't be there,
    And night to day decline,
Yet, deified in moonlit air,
    My soul will bear your sign.

Whoever bodies will unite
    Will separate them too.
Forever, though, is lunar-bright
    My midnight love of you!

71. Remember the palace ...

Remember the palace of giants,
The silvery fish in the pond,
The avenue plantains—defiance
Of tall rocky towers beyond?

Pearls

The horse rearing up, great and golden,
How startling his play, unforewarned;
White ladle with patterns of olden
And delicate carving adorned?

Remember how cloud-gaps, enframing,
Showed cornice-like forms that we found,
Where grape-gathered stars in their flaming,
Precipitant, fell to the ground?

Agree, if you can—without paling—
We'd best come to terms with the change:
Our bravery, strength, unavailing—
To dreams we will ever be strange.

Though aging our frames, they are gracious:
Our names, even, mem'ries unlade—
But boredom—so fatal, rapacious—
Our souls cannot ever evade.

We aren't yet oblivious of dreamland,
Sweet season we lived, you and I,
The time when our love was supreme and
When still we were able to fly!

72. Antiquity

Within wild wood-bounds of the park,
The bittern and the booming frogs
'Mid grassy rustle in the dark
Resume their evening dialogues.

A house, unpainted, antiquated,
With vaguely floating fog is rife;
The halls, loud-sounding, decorated
With paintings—former peasant life.

I think of sorrow, ancient ruth ...
When grandpa laid out solitaire,
Each aunt with pleasant, hand-picked youth
In contradances liked to pair.

My homeless heart—how discontented!—
That now the legacy must be
Such languid, boring, tired, tormented
Un-Golden Age antiquity.

Far better seek a looming slope
Where snow on moonlit crag may lie,
Where blue-gray clouds—or black—dash hope—
And avalanches groan and sigh.

73. He had sworn ...

He had sworn by holy omen
At the Virgin Mary's altar
To be faithful to that woman
Who her gaze would not let falter.

Wholly was that oath forgotten—
While he squandered tender gazes ...
Died at night in battle foughten,
He's in Heaven's hall of praises.

"Did you not, by sacred omen,
At My own most holy altar
Swear devotion to that woman
Who her gaze would not let falter?

You must go. Such harvest rotten
Can't be counted worth the bother.
One who left his vow forgotten
Dies unknown to God the Father."

Sad but firm, our stubborn yeoman
Fell before Madonna's altar.
"I have never met a woman
Who her gaze would not let falter."

74. Gates of Paradise

Not with seven seals of diamond brightness
Locked is Heaven, longed-for promised land:
No enticement here, no dazzle-lightness.
That, the people cannot understand.

There's a door within a wall, neglected—
Rocks and moss—forgotten—nothing more.
Keys on belt, a beggar—unexpected
Guest—before that old, decrepit door.

All can see the knights in armor riding,
Silver-jingle hear, and trumpet-wail.
None espy the watchman there abiding,
None the bright apostle Peter hail.

"At the place of God's sarcophagus,
Or upon Mt. Tabor's holy ground,
Heaven-gates will open unto us.
That is where the promised hour will sound."—

Thus the people dream, and cannot see.
Wailing blares the trumpet past the door.
Ragged beggar-shirt rent wretchedly,
At the gate stands Peter, pale and poor.

75. Backwaters
to N. V. Annensky

The sun declines in the west
Past hills of the promised land.
Still backwaters put on their best,
Dark blue, and a fragrance command.

Sleepily quivers the rush.
A bat is flying... Hush!
A fish splashed in the pond.
Seeking their homes beyond
Are all who have a home—
    With shutters of blue,
    Comfy easychairs, too,
A tea-table cozy, a tome.

I stay alone outdoors
To watch the backwater sleep,
Where in daytime it's good to wade deep,

And at evening to weep,
Because I love you, Lord.

76. Kangaroo
a girl's morning

Sleep appealed not to my tender feeling.
Waking early, puzzled what to do,
Went to breathe the freshened air, so healing—
See him, sweetly tamed, my kangaroo.

Pitchy needles from the pine he'd kept—
Silly! Guess he wanted them to chew.
Funny, all his jumping—how he leapt!
Funnier, that oddly loud halloo.

He is clumsy when he tries to pet me.
When he does, I want to stroke him, too.
This, I know, a fine reward will get me:
Dark brown eyes, their triumph shining through.

Afterward, still half-asleep and moping,
On the bench my dream I tried to view:
When—when will he come?—the one I'm hoping
Soon to see, my longed-for lover true!

Thoughts intrude, distinctly, outlined clearly
As a shadow cast of leafage blue:
How I'd like a friend to pet!—and dearly
Love him, like my loving kangaroo.

77. Maestro

for L. N. Sverchkov

Scent, red coat, and braided laces,
Maestro waves in hall ancestral,
Scatttering before our faces
Chords afloat in rays orchestral.

Tones are sweeping, never stopping,
Maybe giants, maybe visions,
Rushing round the hall, they're dropping
Diamonds in their fierce collisions.

They descend to see the fishes
That are dancing in the basin,
Then, to maiden smile auspicious,
Quiet glide and halt the racing.

Temple-towers now they're making
Set in azure paradises;
Next the ladies' shoulders taking
Pleasure stroking: guile entices.

Whirling back, with happy quiver,
Homage—praise in hall ancestral—
To the maestro will deliver
Chords afloat in rays orchestral.

PEARLS

78. Don Juan

I simply, haughtily, will dream of this:
To grab the oar, to mount the horse, to while
Away the time, my boredom to beguile,
Unnumbered waiting maiden mouths to kiss,

With vows devout in later age a Chris-
tian to become, be cloistral-meek, and pile
The ashes on my head!—in humble style
To feel the cross, O heavy burden-bliss!

And yet, 'mid orgies once, more dead than quick,
Sane suddenly, and pale, a lunatic
In rare remission of a mental smother,

I would remember: useless, barely human,
I never had a child with any woman
And as for men, there's none I call my brother.

79. Parrot

From far Antilles captured by a mage
To lead my parrot life within a cell—
To hear the steady cough, the stricken bell,
With paper, globe, retort around my cage—

I feel, in hours of wizardry—when rage
A whirling voice, a dagger eye—a swell
Of boldness bristle every feather! Well
And fiercely then I fight, in spite of age,

To counter ghostly owls. Yet hardly here
Will come a gold-cloaked, gambling buccaneer
To play at cards or boast his lady love—

And when remembered boats appear to me
Within the sunlit quiet of a cove,
I know how galling is all secrecy.

80. Book Reader

I've been a reader, and I'd hoped to find
My peaceful paradise in meek reflection.
I loved them all, strange roadways of the mind,
Where there's no need for hope or recollection.

To glide unwearied on the streams of lines—
Impatient, enter chapter-strait or sound,
Observing how the foaming current winds,
And then—to hear the roaring tide-wave bound!

But in the evening ... I was frightened soon—
Saw shades behind the bookshelves, icon-case:
A pendulum, more moveless than the moon,
Above the quagmire-glimmer—still—in space!

81. I can never ...

I can never help flowers to grow.
By their beauty awhile am I sated,

Pearls

In a couple of days they'll be faded,
I can never help flowers to grow.

And the birds—they will never survive.
Bristle first, if but mutely and madly—
Ball of down the next morning, quite sadly ...
No, the birds—they will never survive.

Only books, eight elongated rows,
Keeping silent, those tomes—they are heavy,
The collectors of lassitude's levy,
Gleaming teeth, eight elongated rows.

And the bookman who sold them to me—
I remember him, humpbacked and slouching,
Near the churchyard of curses a-crouching,
That's the bookman who sold them to me.

82. It Wasn't the First Time

Well, it wasn't the first time, it won't be the last,
    In our struggle, unyielding, unspoken:
Though you've given up now, as you've done in the
        past,
    You'll surrender, humility's token.

There's no need for surprise, my inimical friend—
    As with darkness your loving is tainted
If the moaning of love will be groans at the end,
    If the kisses with blood will be painted.

83. Prayer

Frenzied Sun, threatening, force on fear battening!
    Sent from a god in space running—
        Face of mad mystery:

Burn it up, Sun—what is happening—
    In the name of what's coming—
        But have mercy on history!

84. Groves of palm ...

Groves of palm and undergrowth of aloe,
Stream of color silvery but matt,
Light blue heaven never turning sallow—
Radiant!—why not content with that?

Tell me, heart, what further's worth the reaching?
Happiness—a lie, a fairy tale?
Why, bedazzled by some alien teaching,
Meek surrender, all to no avail?

Is it some new poison you are craving?
Why not live as do the thriving reeds?
Why in vain consume yourself in raving?
Noisome edens cannot suit your needs.

PEARLS

85. Evening

Another day I've wasted, right?
Magnificent and ineffective.
Come, solace of the shade of night:
My turbid spirit hide from sight
In pearly chásuble protective.

You came! You always chase away
Ill-boding raven-melancholy.
O night, whose might-commanding sway
None can protest, rebellious, may
Your sandal-step allay my folly!

Descended stellar quiet when
The moon-gleam showed your bracelet shining.
My dreams have made me learn again:
The promised land returns to men,
Lost gladness back, an end to pining.

86–89. Beatrice

1

Muse, if you cannot make merry,
Pour out your grief, be unsparing,
Telling of great Alighieri,
Singing of Dante, his daring.

Wearisome fauns, you're absurd—
Best were your melodies mended.
Beatrice—haven't you heard?—
Heaven has left—and descended.

Strange the white rose-bloom appearing
Cool, in the peace of the garden ...
Is there a threat to be fearing?
Or an entreaty for pardon?

Once lived a sinner, unholy,
Sunk in concealment and scheming:
Beatrice taught him the role he
Ought to perform in his dreaming.

Strangely, his fancy indulgent,
Seeming caprice when emerging,
Turned into current refulgent,
Fervent and tidelike and surging.

Muse, of your gift be not chary:
Aided by blest amoretti,
Help me to sing Alighieri
And Gabriele Rossetti.

2

My garden—yours: one flowering—one sad.
So come to me! In sadness, and yet splendid,
Enchant, as with a hazy veil extended,
My gardens far, where gladness can't be had.

Pearls

You, whitest petal of a Persian rose,
Take part in this—my garden where I languish—
That there may be no sudden shock of anguish,
But moving melody of pliant pose,

That there be borne, to every terrace edge,
The name of Beatrice, the mind-inspiring,
That not the maenads', but the maidens' choiring
To hymn your lips may have the privilege.

3

Pray forgive me—enough of the sting of repentance,
Of the pain of despair, of the torment of shame!
I've abandoned what fatally lured—independence:
Newly humbled, your servant, I worship your name.

Far too long were we lost, in abysms awhirling,
Where the breakers that hurt us in iron embrace,
With their glimmering beast-backs high-lifting and
    hurling,
Onto rock tossed the victim with grief-hidden face.

As a steed after battle runs free of its tether,
So have vanished the wisps of the clouds of the
    storm.
If you want, let us offer a prayer together
On the crackling sand of gold islands reborn.

4

I'll not curse you, nor chide you indeed—
I am sad with the sadness of parting:
But your hands I would kiss, that would lead
Me away—a new life may be starting ...

All's accomplished—the dreams I had made
When a boy, to strange love-mind awoken:
I have seen the dire dagger's bright blade
In that so-much-loved hand lying open.

Deadly trembling you give me, great fear,
Not the shakes of pale passion, elating.
You will take me forever, my dear,
To the isles of a joy unabating.

90.–92. Return of Odysseus

1 On the Shore

My heart—with honeycombs high-piled—
Becomes a hive where bees are toiling.
Yet I must fight with whirlpools wild—
Bubbling, gurgling, foaming, boiling.

The trireme with her pointed prow
In frenzied tempest I impórtune:
I hasten to my homeland now
The storm-cloud rising bodes ill-fortune.

Pearls

I'll enter the expansive hall,
Delight my heart with longed-for greeting,
Forget the years—how black that pall!—
I spent with Pallas—woes accreting.

But who is here that, like a hawk,
I see above my spirit hover,
Who—bitter fate that makes me balk—
To bleak abyss would hand me over?

The boat-cracks—wide—alarmingly:
Sea-churning whirlwind-force amazes!
The shores that had been promised me
Now hide behind the heaven-hazes.

I answer, apprehensively,
To quiet croon across the water,
"No, nothing shall dissever me
From Zeus' divine almighty daughter."

2 Slaughter of Suitors

Over the city the moon, newly narrow,
Brightly has knifed through the dark of the west.
Aimed from the threshold, Odysseus' arrow
Rapidly entered Antinoüs' chest.

Fog filled the eyes of the suppliant lover,
Dashed is the cup from Antinoüs' hands:
Lightly he's trembling. That story is over—
Finest young fighter of all the Greek lands.

Others arise, in a panic that harrows,
Timidly groping for shield and for sword—
Vainly! Unfailing, the steel of the arrows!
Angry, sardonic the calm of the word:

"Princely, you pride of the Ithacan nation!
That is the way you are greeting your king?
Hecatombs you in a fane-desecration
Offer—a seal on the shame that you bring!

You, by the kettledrums' beating emboldened,
Wasted what favor from heaven instills:
Corpulent bull, long-horned ram, and the golden
Wine of the warmth of the Cypriot hills.

You poor Penelope faithlessly flattered;
Lecherous slave-girls you fondled by night:
Better than death when your sword will be
      shattered—
Mortal the waters' dark, desolate might!

What could you claim? 'As the ocean entombed him,
Now he can never return to his home:
Eyeless, the fishes no doubt have consumed him
Years ago, miles ago, under the foam.'

Well? Aren't you eager to make me some offers?
Give me a palace? A rich regal crown?
I would reject all Atlántean coffers,
All of the cities the sea'd ever drown!

PEARLS

Arrows with wings have melodious voices,
Brightly symmetric the knife-bladed fire!
All of you princes will pay for your choices—
Quickly prepare for your grave on a pyre.

You there, Eurymachus, fat, undeveloped—
You are more pale than a white marble wall:
Scared! How he struggles—a gadfly, enveloped!
That's how a captured new concubine falls!

You too, Antinomus! What's your thought? Tell us!
He's a real elephant—big, bulky boy!
Might have been one of the heroes of Hellas
Had he decided to join us at Troy!

Tigers and does, equal fortune disarming,
Never again will ascend from their bed.
Look at that covering! Garment of carmine?
Or is it blood overflowing the dead?

Now that the suitors have met their subdual,
Good lad Telemachus, travel with me:
Worshipers, we, of a god who is cruel,
God of much trouble, dark ways—you will see.

Lure of the distant! We'll crave it, unsated—
Golden horizon, much finer than home.
We'll be re-greeting the palms long awaited,
Waters' loud gurgling below Pontic foam.

Ev'n should her bed be unspotted, there's danger
Some of her dreams, and her thoughts ... We will see.
Purer than purest white seamew, and stranger,
Darker than lightning, her beauty to me ... "

3 Odysseus at Laertes' House

Yet one more debt without demur
I'm paying as my fate's requiring:
I'm not a wolf or murderer
But honor's watchman never tiring.

The features of your wrinkled face,
Laertes, that I'm greeting, kneeling,
Life's whirlwind never will erase
From memory, and thought, and feeling.

I look: green gardens decorate
Each hill and cliff and slope surrounding—
Ripe fruit, so prime and roseate,
And freshly sprouting mint abounding!

With tears of deep humility,
I force my heart to feel rejoicing:
Hut—field, where streams flow limpidly,
To you I bow, deep pleasure voicing.

It is most sweet, though painful, too
(For I believe in gods and silence)

Pearls

On goatskin here to sit with you,
Far from disturbance and from violence.

But what to me in farm or field
The gift of Graces, rosy daughters,
When I can see the diamond shield
Of Pallas raised above the waters?

Old man, O most beloved sight,
We part one final time. I kiss you.
I throw myself below the night
Of thunderclouds. I'll sorely miss you.

But when by Zeus' almighty hand
My last black lot will be selected,
When death I face in dolor and
Am thrown to earth, by fate rejected,

I'll then recall no day of strife,
No feast in flame and smoke that smothers
Or cold caresses that my wife
Had shared—alas!—with many others,

But you alone, your myrtle wreath—
Your bluest heaven-eyes that know me:
I'll "Father" say, blest word bequeath,
Face Erebus' abode below me.

NIKOLAY GUMILEV

93–96. Captains

1

On the northerly seas, late and early,
On the verdant-curved swell of the waves,
'Tween the cliffsides basaltic and pearly,
Rustle ship-sails that whitewater laves,

And each captain on quick-wingéd vessel,
Islands finding as far as the pole,
Never maelstrom will fear that may wrestle
With a ship, or perfidial shoal.

Not in dust of historical charters—
Steeped in sea-salt, that mariner-soul!—
On the tattered old map in his quarters
With a pin he'll be noting his goal.

On the deck thinks the venturing Viking
Of the last-sighted harbor en route:
With a staff he'll be angrily striking
Bits of foam from a Hessian-made boot.

If a mutinous cabal he faces,
With a pistol he'll threaten the roughs,
Rip the gun from his belt—from their laces
Getting gold, or from Brábantine cuffs.

Let the sea keep dementedly raging
And the wave-crest climb high; he won't quail!

Pearls

He'll be firm, every terror assuaging,
And will never dismantle the sail.

To no coward such muscle was given,
So alert, such a confident gaze:
The feluccas, soon ravished and riven,
Of the foeman his frigates amaze.

With an iron harpoon well directed,
He the whale can predictably reach
And the lighthouse he'll then have detected
'Mid the stars that illumine the beach.

2

You paladins, all, of the Green Panorama,
Who skilled with a compass to vessels lend wing:
Gonsalvo and Cook, La Perouse and da Gama,
You, dreamer Columbus, O Genoese king!—

You, Prince Senegambi, and Hanno of Tunis,
And mighty Ulysses, and Sindbad! Your story
In dithyramb chant, below heavens' bright blueness,
Gray waves overreaching the green promontory!

And you, filibustering hounds, proudly royal,
Who, hiding your gold in your harbor, have laughed:
You faith-seeking vagabond Arabs, and loyal—
Though always the first to escape on a raft!

Whoever has dared to desire and will bristle
To think of the wearying land of his sires,
Who bravely will laugh and will brazenly whistle
At Elders' advice, while their zeal never tires!

How strange and how sweet is the dream we are seeing:
We treasure and cherish and whisper your names
And suddenly guess what narcosis unfleeing
You felt from the ocean no peace ever tames.

It seems, in the world, as before, there are regions
Where never the foot of a human has been—
With tropical coppices, giants in legions—
Where pearls in the calm of the water are seen.

On spice-laden trees with their fragrant delirium
Speak intricate leaves: "Your adventure renew!
We've ruby-gold bees, roses redder, the Tyrian,
Than ever a purple-robed emperor knew!"

A dwarf and a bird for a nest are contending;
The maidens' soft faces in profile appeal.
Star-guardians numberless over us bending—
Unending, our world, the unreachable real!

3

Past the parted cliff no sooner
Do they glimpse the royal fort

Pearls

Than the sailors on the schooner
Haste, elated, to the port.

Picking up his tavern-cider,
Talkative a granddad tells:
What a hydra—glad we spied her!
Crossbows hit their target well.

Tanned mulattas tell your fortune,
Chant their ballads unafraid;
Soon your palate will impórtune
Fragrant platters freshly made.

In the tavern spit-bespattered,
From the sunset-hour to dawn
Wavy-haired, the gamblers tattered
Cards lay down, the fools lead on.

Fun to stroll, in any season
On the docks along the port,
Picking fights, without a reason,
With the soldiers from the fort,

Or, to fine and stately stranger
Brazenly exclaim, "Two sous!"
Nose-hooped baby ape? No danger!
It's a price they can't refuse!

In a fevered game enticing,
Clasp in hand an amulet—

All your wealth, in frantic dicing,
Wasted on a final bet.

But, euphoria dispelling,
Quelling all the drunken din,
"Time to go!" the captain, yelling
Through the megaphone, calls in.

4

Yet in the world far different regions
In horrifying moonlight languish,
Unwinnable by valiant legions,
Their effort recompensed with anguish.

There waves are glimmering and splashing—
Unintermittent dance unsleeping—
With jumps abrupt and upward lashing
The Flying Dutchman's craft is leaping.

No reef or shoal confronts him ever,
But, sign of sadness, devil weather,
St. Elmo's fires flame out forever,
Aspersed along each mast and tether.

The captain, over sea-gulf sliding,
With one hand clasps a hat and, pressing,
The bloodied steering wheel he's guiding,
The wind's direction barely guessing.

PEARLS

His friends are pale; the terrifying
Death-menace ever more aggressive:
They have the fading face of dying,
Impassible and inexpressive.

If, in the clarity of morning,
Some swimmers come in ocean's ruction,
They'll seem to hear a voice of warning
Presaging vainly their destruction.

For bands and gangs of rowdy fighters,
Full many tales are put together;
But grisliest of spirit-smiters
To hearers in the howling weather—

The tale that in a land outlying,
Past Capricorn, a far-off sailor,
Whose face with that of Cain is vying,
A ship sails, fated—none will hail her.

97. Adam's Dream

Grown weary from dancing and song, Adam slept,
Unwisely, yet peace he was needing, desiring.
The great Tree of Knowledge above him, stars firing
The sky, shade of lilac had lazily crept
On meadows whereover his spirit was flying,
But ill-boding dreams had arrived—and were trying.

Behind him, angelic, the fulgurant sword
That pricks without mercy himself and his lady;
From paradise driven by trouble they'd made, he
And Eve had to flee from the wrath of the Lord.
Like beasts without shelter they'll make a rude
    dwelling,
With slingshot and club helpless prey for food felling.

Abode of hard labor and illness ... But here
With Eve he felt oneness—a love, though belated.
For her, joy and trouble of motherhood waited;
For him, the stern spade, so a town might appear,
By work for an Other devotion expressing
With grief-knitted brows, and lips palely
    compressing.

Yes, both are transformed ... Mouths look grim and
    in pain,
Their gazes don't gleam—random laugh—things
    aren't funny.
While Abel is gathering olives and honey,
Wild boars lure the hunter, the powerful Cain.
Contesting, sons challenge a fatherly chiding:
The younger is dead, and the elder in hiding.

Sore troubled, their father investigates here.
His soul had been drowning in ease, dissipation;
He's hopefully seeking a fane of salvation.
Starts ever again—he is stubborn, severe—

Pearls

Tries horse-riding, plowing, and farming, and
    fighting,
And God has protected his vineyard from blighting.

He dammed up a river, controlling the roar;
Some balance he needs 'mid the troubled world's
    newness:
His falconlike thinking cuts through to the blueness;
Refractory land grants amenable ore.
He finds in calm reading a cure for things odious:
Religions' deep secrets, and poems melodious.

In magical nights, on magnificent moss,
The sylphs from on high have come down for
    embraces;
Most helpful as well, healing injury-traces,
The stellar and element-souls banish loss.
To sun-flashing height from the watery dark
Blue dolphins have drawn Adam's light-gliding bark.

He loves entertaining and dangerous games:
To seek in the ocean strange lands undiscovered,
To wander where wolves have made clearings
    uncovered,
Encounter ravines that a hillscape enframes,
Where mountain-goats now on the paths are
    descending,
Red roses their blooms aromatic down-bending.

When blocks of hard marble for carving are hewn,
He loves the sharp grinding of chisel-incising;

The virginal cold of dawn's rose-fingered rising,
A young, oval face with the beauty of noon—
A canvas, these treats in perfection portraying,
Seems brighter than life, all its radiance out-raying.

But Adam to heaven his face, riven, rent,
Turns, hopeless, for help. Eyes yet blind and
    blaspheming,
The sky appears empty and blank, while, bright-
    seeming,
There glimmers before him the many-starred tent.
On calm, holy nights, meekly peaceful, austere,
Knees bending, he dreams of a God not yet here.

He daily awaits, coming in from afar,
Thoughts—radiant guests long awaited with
    gladness,
And with them, though stellar their glitter, a sadness
Of thoughts yet unknown, nameless passions' bright
    star:
Of downfall in dreams and of horror in art
Foreboding made Adam feel hurt in the heart.

And mild-mannered Eve, the gods' plaything and toy,
Now seeming a child, then a wild summer
    lightning—
A tigress appearing, with energy fright'ning!
Her shimmering pearls tell of strength to destroy:
Foreknower of passion, of storm, ardent carmine,
Of deadliest joy, of misfortune disarming.

PEARLS

So gold will entice and embolden the gaze,
While hiding dire forces despite a fine seeming,
Arousing the weak, newly prone to blaspheming,
And brothers their goblets of venom to raise.
Unable to lessen their greed overreaching,
Vain, frenzied lament is the lesson they're teaching.

He struggles with Eve. He is serpentine, sly.
She's bound in his net, in seductive wild jumbles:
A lecheress, moaning in meaningless mumbles ...
Yet—suddenly—saint! with her eyes lifted high.
Now moon-maiden virgin, now crude, bacchanalian,
But always and everywhere alien, so alien!

He's finally wearied—yes, mortally tired!
He's sated with laughing, and weeping unending;
When swan-flocks fly over, their pinions unbending,
He hears not their calling, all vigor expired.
To Death on the cliff he is praying austerely
(The deity folk overwearied love dearly):

"Beneficent one, will you hear my desire?
On sea and on plain, from your heavenly portal
Asperse, in your mercy, a dew that is mortal;
Quell heart that is dawning with life's final fire.
Enough of my struggle with lunatic fear.
Of dust I was made. Make me *dust* again—hear!"

And, slowly enkindling with bright crimson tail,
A comet comes down with an eerie blue lightning;

To Adam the feeling is painful, heart-tight'ning—
His head is still hurt, as by hard-pounding hail:
A whirlwind full-flaming his frailness had shaken.
He shudders and shouts! ... and again he'll awaken.

Here's Tigris—agleam, spreading foam, on his right,
While leftward he sees green Euphrates' wave racing,
With silvery glimmer the valley embracing,
Where playful dark sandbars are hiding from sight.
Eve calls from her garden, her joy failing never:
"You slept—and awoke! I am happy forever!"

NIKOLAY GUMILEV

I

98. Guardian Angel

"Why," he whispers, "willful be?
    And why so plaintive, sad?
Gloom at losing youth, so free—
    And bliss you may have had?

Surely surges unretreating,
    Darkened waves that rove,
Well are worth the briefest meeting
    With your lady love.

Heartache lightens when the sky her
    Bluer light displays:
Lighter yet when you espy her
    Own heart-lifting gaze!

To object to silence loudly,
    Madly, brings no blame,
But to leave his queen so proudly
    Is—to vassal—shame."

In the quiet night, intently,
    And in morning clear,
He will speak—so eloquently—
    For his sister dear.

ALIEN SKY

99. Two Roses

Near Eden's gate, in heaven-fashion,
Two splendid roses had their birth.
A rose, though, is an emblemed passion;
And passion is the child of earth.

One, like a maiden by her lover
Glimpsed unawares, may faintly blush;
Under the other's purple cover
The darker fires of ardor rush.

The Threshold of Our Knowledge they
Reveal. Had Heaven planned, indeed,
That passion's secret might convey
A tie to Heaven's hidden creed?

100. To a Girl

It's really not appealing—
Your hands aweary, crossed,
Deep modesty revealing—
Ashamed, embarrassed, lost.

So Turgéniev-like—tranquil—yet formless—
You are gentle, yet haughty, my girl,
Quiet, placid, autumnal, but stormless,
On the walkway where leaves are awhirl.

You must calculate, reckon, and measure
Or you'll never believe, lacking heart.
For you fear to go hunting for treasure
If the path isn't marked on your chart.

It can't matter to you, as you languish,
That a mad mountain hunter will run
And in joy-drunken fathomless anguish
Let an arrow loose, aimed at the sun!

101. At Sea

Dusk—and the snaky waves are bending,
Their flaming crests already gone,
Not over-eagerly extending
To boldened shores to which they're drawn.

Alone now, from a distance roaming,
A bow-wave, trusting fogs that mock,
Is wildly borne, insanely foaming,
Upon the glossy, lustrous rock.

It whoops and roars, with shattered motion
To heaven tossing tattered foam ...
But the lateen-sailed bark, on ocean
Afloat, enjoys a dark-red home.

Glad, too, the helmsman, navigating,
Inhaling dampened breezes which
Swell and, from ropes, invigorating,
Acrid, the strong tart smell of pitch.

Alien Sky

102. Doubt

A quiet evening hour. And I'm alone,
Thinking of you, my only, only one.

I take a book, and there, on reading "she"—
Again my soul is stirred, but turbidly.

I throw myself upon the squeaking bed:
The pillow burns ... No sleep. I wait, instead.

I, stealthy, prise the windows open soon:
I see the misty meadow, and the moon.

I heard a "yes" anigh the flower-bed.
I never will forget the "yes" you said.

But new awareness came—and startled me:
That wasn't really you—could never be.

I know that "yes," that trembling—near the pine
That kiss—that dream of spring. You are not mine.

103. Dream
morning chat

Tell me what you saw while dreaming
That has made you look so bright!
    —Willows, streaming
      Lunar light.

Nothing more, quite sure? Alone a
Landscape painted by an elf?
    —Desdemona
    And myself.

Look at me—your mood is mellow ...
Near the grove, what could you scan?
    —Saw Othello,
    Handsome man.

He—two women's wish-requiter?
One's enough for both of you?
    —He's a fighter,
    Poet, too.

Of what beauties sung in haste and
Undiscovered did he tell?
    —Sang of wasteland,
    Dreamland-spell.

And you listened to his groan, a
Sadness hiding tenderly?
    —Desdemona,
    But not me.

104. Fragment

Jesus proclaimed it: "Bessed are the wretched.
Enviable the beggar—blind man—cripple:
Above the stars will be their habitation,
For I will make them chevaliers of heaven—
They will be called most glorious of the glorious ... "

Alien Sky

Fine, I accept it! What about the others—
Whose thought endured to keep us living, breathing,
Whose names we hear today, an eager summons?
How can they fitly pay for all their splendor?
How shall the Will to Balance weigh against them?
Would you imagine Beatrice a harlot—
Deaf-mute, perhaps, the noble Wolfgang Goethe?
Or Byron as the village fool? O horror!

105. That Other One

I, chidden, sit in expectation,
Not of a wife, whose greeting cheers,
For trusting, earnest conversation
Of long-gone things in former years—

Nor yet a mistress I'm awaiting:
Mere languor, whispering abrupt—
These tire me, as do palpitating
Ardors, and torments that erupt.

A comrade I'm awaiting, ages
Ago marked out—for him to sigh
Because in me a yearning rages
For what is silent, what is high.

How criminal!—what is eternal
He left, acquiring for an hour
So daringly the chains diurnal
Of dreams that bind us by their power.

106. Eternal Things

In corridors of closed-in days
With heavy sky our leaden fate,
I live in minutes, ages praise,
For Sabbath of all Sabbaths wait,

An end to grief, the anxious task,
The fumbling spirit's blunderings ...
Come soon, belated day, I ask,
When I will know the stranger things!

A spirit new will I acquire
And grasp whatever mocked me once,
Along the golden way aspire
That leads from worms to golden suns.

And he that journeyed at my side
In thunders, humble quietude,
Who would my slight delights deride
But, kind to wine, would prove no prude,

Who taught me struggle, silence, crowned
With wisdom, worldly halidom,
Will rest the shepherd's crook, turn 'round,
And tell me simply, "We have come."

ALIEN SKY

107. Constantinople

Still by the harbor they bawl in choric
Shouts, bold sailors, and call for wine—
Over Stamboul's tired tide Bosphoric,
The full moon—watch it, lambent, shine.

Into the bay, by the sailors, mocking,
The faithless wife will soon be hurled—
Wife who was far too beauteous, walking
Below the full-moon light unfurled.

She ever loved best her own wild dreaming,
Chatting in cluster of thickest reeds,
Guide of the fortune-teller scheming,
All that the pasha never needs.

Her father is sad, but understanding:
He asks her husband, "Soon, it seems?"
Eyes adamant, cast down, commanding,
The youngest daughter, musing, dreams:

"So many, many—down in the boundless
Bay, those other lovers, how
Interwoven, languid, and soundless:
What luck to be among them now!"

108. Contemporaries

By the window I sat, with my *Iliad* closed.
On my lips the last word of the legend yet hovered
As the gradual light, lunar, lantern-like, rose,
By the guard's tardy shadow at times partly covered.

I had often directed a querying stare,
Had encountered, in answer, full many bold gazes—
An Odysseus hid in a cruise-bureau lair,
Agamemnon in tavern, 'mid billiard-room blazes.

So would far-off Siberian blizzard-moan grow
Where in moon-tinted ice lay a mastodon frozen
With a mute, muffled anguish a-moving the snow,
The horizon—burnt bloody, the color well chosen.

I'm depressed by the book, and the moon made me
    sad,
And perhaps the whole hero-idea is needless ...
Look!—the kids from the high school—a lass and her
    lad,
Like a Daphnis and Chloë, so tender and heedless.

109. Sonnet

I'm truly sick—my heart feels fogged—I brood.
It's dreary, boring—people and their stories.
I see in dreams old kingdoms' diamond glories,
A yataghan—broad, heavy—drenched in blood.

Alien Sky

I see—can't be a mere delusive mood—
My slant-eyed Tartar forebear—wild outlawry—
A savage Hun ... A strange contagion—gory—
Comes, age-old, down within my nature rude.

I'm quiet, tired—walls widen, slow in motion—
With shreds of foam arose a growing ocean ...
By granite, sunset-washed, the water—stilled:

And then, with light blue cupolas, a city
With jasmine garden blossom, vivid, pretty—
We fought there ... Yes! Oh, yes!! And I was killed.

110. One Evening

As the lilies, in vases, showed a languor's last
    blighting,
In the red of the sunset, with the evening light-blue,
And we shared our opinions of Leconte de Lisle's
    writing
And felt sad for the coldness of the man, I and you,

As the silky-smooth pages, more than once, we
    would open
And "Not that!" we would whisper—all was peaceful
    and clear—
And it flashed through our thinking: all the languors
    soft-spoken
Were like stars, the bright nomads that arise once a
    year.

And so canorous, chanting, in the soul resurrected
Were the old solar meters, when the evening came on:
We could see, from our armchairs, what a world
    unsuspected!—
And the face of the Creole, with the soul of a swan.

111. She

I know a woman: silence, chillness—
Aweary, shunting word aside—
Lively the mystery, the stillness,
Of her encircling iris wide.

Her soul is ever open, eager
For bronzen melody in verse
But looks unhearing on the meager
Life of the lower universe.

Inaudible, unstirred, unflurried,
She is not pretty, to be sure:
Her step is limber and unhurried,
And all my joy resides in her.

And when I thirst for headstrong fleetness,
Am brave and proud, to her I come
To learn the lore of painful sweetness,
Her languor, her delirium.

In hours of torment—shining, sprightly—
She holds the lightning in her hand.
Her dreams are shadows outlined brightly
On paradisal fiery sand.

112. Life

At the time when, like a banner, hazy dawn can be
    seen below,
Dull in gaze, and dead in heart, to toss yourself from
    a high rock jut
Or, in dungeon cell, to feel your freedom—freedom
    that eagles know—
Or to find an unawaited peace in savage's smoky hut!

Yes, I know. Life's emblem's not the poet language
    has glorified,
Nor the warrior with hardened heart, the farmer who
    plows the lands,
But the prince with wan ironic smile who lies on a
    lion hide
And forgets about the toys he holds in delicate tired
    white hands.

113. From a Snakehole

    From a snakehole, deep down,
    Near the fair Kíev town
I acquired—not a wife—a spell flinger!
    She loved fun—that I knew—
    And liked willfulness, too,
Singing sweetly—and oh, what a singer ...

    If you'd call, she would frown;
    Hug—she'd put your hands down,
And at moonview she'd pine and she'd languish.

And she'd stare, and she'd groan,
As if hardly alone,
As if drowning would end all her anguish.

"As a Christian," I'd say,
"I have not got all day
To uncover your whims' hidden fountain.
Take your languor away
To the Dnieper," I'd say,
"Or the top of the wicked Bald Mountain."

She'd be quiet, shrink back,
And pretend to a lack
Of all will—looking wretched, though blamable,
Like a bird in a trap,
Or a birch lacking sap
In a swamp cursed by God and unshamable.

II

Dedicated to Anna Akhmatova

114. I Thought, I Believed ...
for Sergei Makovsky

I thought, I believed—now I saw: the unloosable knot.
The fate my creator had made I must face; I was
    banished.
Self-satisfied, smirking, the buyer surveys what he'd
    bought.
I'm sold! I'm no longer divine! And the merchant has
    vanished.

Alien Sky

Behind, like a mountain in flight, I see Yesterday
    push.
Ahead of me waits, like a gaping abyss, bleak
    Tomorrow.
I walk ... But I wait for the flying mount headlong to
    rush—
Collapse in the pit. All my travel's in vain, like my
    sorrow.

If I, through my will, should subdue all my foes in a
    rage,
Or, say, inspiration would come in the night to me,
    flying,
Of if I should secrets unearth, or be poet or mage
Or sovereign lord!—all the harder my falling—and
    dying.

A vision I lately had seen, that my heart felt no pain:
A porcelain bell it became in Cathayan pagoda—
A medley of tints—ringing welcome, again and again,
In skies of enamel, to mimic the cranes' long-drawn
    coda.

A maiden most gentle, in red silken garment that
    gleams
With flowers depicted, and dragons, and wasps
    floating brightly—
She only beholds, with bound feet, without thoughts,
    without dreams,
Attentively listening: bells ring so lightly—so lightly ...

115. Dazzling Dreams

I sink into my easy chair
To be from lighting shielded there.
A long, long time will I be crying
And bring those evenings back again
When "yesterday" meant yet no pain,
No debts, no fetters on me lying:

A promontory by the sea,
A solitary cypress tree,
The virtues of Hussein the kindly,
The slow, long legends he would tell
When eyes no more could make out well
The tree, or pool—we listened blindly.

Again great Baghdad's glorified,
Again old Sindbad wanders wide,
With demons instigating quarrels—
From Egypt, from the warm Red Sea
Again depart the ships for me,
To Basra bringing treats, not morals.

To merchants—profit and esteem.
But riches aren't their deeper dream
On barren plain or stormy ocean:
Secret of secrets, Great Bird Roc,
Was not your isle the sought-for dock,
The guiding star of all their motion?

Alien Sky

The sailors traveled, led by you,
To caves of wolf and genie, too
(Who cherished yet an ancient rancor).
They crossed the bridges hanging free
And passed through dark-red shrubbery
Near Hároun-al-Rasheed's dropped anchor.

I, too, your energy would hail
And, meek submissive pilgrim, sail
To seek a life of peace and virtue
In hope that I would meet Hussein
In gardens damp with dew, with rain
By Smyrna's banks, where naught will hurt you.

But when ... Good Lord, how pure they seem,
And how tormenting every dream!
Again to wounds my heart is open!
I'll sink into my easy chair
And, from the lighting shielded there,
Lament Levant—my heart is broken.

116. Rhodes
to the memory of M. A. Kurmina-Karavayeva

Stony walls, taller poplars in flower
In the solar-seared Rhodian fields
Which the quiet of eve will embower:
Such the landscape a sailor-eye yields.

Nikolay Gumilev

With cathedrals, a citadel, steeple,
Bridge and bastion, church-orders of old,
And the simple attire of the people
To contrást with their crosses of gold,

Here's a place of few strugglers for glory:
Humble people whom none may reprove,
To their Father alone feudatory,
To his Heaven devote their hearts' love.

But in valleys with old-fashioned manors,
Amid cypress and rose-tree and peace,
How to speak of the Bride of Brides' banners
That to battle might mark a surcease!

For our burden's a very great burden;
Fate has found a fine task for the brave:
Not to seek for ourselves any guerdon
But all glory to heap on our grave.

Slogging on through the death-bearing ditches,
We'll discern where a river was born—
The machines, with their loud-sounding pitches,
Piercing all the great clouds of the storm.

People's look shows them endlessly harried:
From their sighs, muffled cries want to leap—
While we wither, in offices buried,
Before books in a dust-covered heap.

ALIEN SKY

We must penetrate hazes unending,
While the rosy aroma retreats:
Fighting nature, space, time, we're contending
To win back battered Rhodian streets.

Will the grandchildren, eaglets a-nesting,
Ask, in wistful confusion, some day:
"Where are all the strong-handed now resting?
Burning spirit, warm heart—where are *they*?"

117. Pilgrim

With walking-stick in Áhmed-Ógly's hand,
He leaves the overpopulated city
To walk upon the loose and shifting sand—
Slow, awkward every motion, more's the pity.
"Oh, Ahmed, Ahmed! you're misguided—and
Deluded—serving silly whims though pretty,
To put yourself in peril of your life
And be abandoned by a witless wife."

"I heard last night the call of Allah, saying,
'Come, Ahmed Ogly, rise! and, in My name,
Go forward fearless, being bold in praying,
The praise of your Creator to proclaim,
Where sandhills heap from reddish whirlwinds'
    playing,
Where tufted eagles come that none can tame,
Where horses over Bedouin corpses neigh,
There, to Medina, Mecca, find your way.'"

"You're lying, Ahmed Ogly. Only one
True Prophet Allah summoned—inspiration
God gave his envoy, from the tear-vale come,
To fly to a corruptless habitation.
But he was handsome—he was tall and young—
His steed well-blest for godly elevation,
And you—quite bald, and on a donkey sitting—
Can *not* be Allah's envoy. 'Tisn't fitting."

He doesn't listen. Stubbornly, severely
He goes, he groans, with anger in his grin:
Although he wears a tattered robe, a nearly
Brand-new one, gold-sewn lilac, is within
His bag; beneath one arm an oak staff, queerly
Old-fashioned, like another arm or shin—
A turban, too, as Shiite rule requires;
And coins stitched tight in sandals, thief-defiers.

Last night a jackal howled below the hill
When some odd shadow floated by, some stranger:
Today he heard a laughter hard and shrill—
Three ragged men—and yet he felt no danger.
But thief or beast or *sháitan* never will
Molest the pilgrim mild, a harmless ranger.
He sees, at nighttime—maybe from the moon—
In great amaze a dream descending soon.

The thorn-tree and the thistle disappearing
Are what he hopes to view now, every night,
As when to Baghdad or to Basra nearing:

Alien Sky

A palace, elegant, will rise to sight,
The Sea of Reeds, a-seething, breakers rearing,
Extends the purple-ruddy waves' delight;
A wondrous leaf-green or a dark-blue shoal
He sees, week after week—his nearing goal.

The road is rough, and Ahmed's very old.
The midnight mists are penetrating, chilling—
He falls down wordless, strengthless—he is rolled
Around in shabby robe—old age is filling
Him with a tiredness in a town of gold
Where in the evening plantains whisper. Thrilling
The ear, the tall, black-bearded muezzin's tales
Portray the lovely houris of the vales.

Ahmed falls down, but to his soul unsleeping
Allah has not for nothing given wings:
Azrael takes him into angel keeping,
As if he were a boy whom passion wrings,
And leads him by the path of joy unsleeping,
Of demon, prophet, star, celestial things.
As much as any mortal man can do
Has Ahmed done. He will see Mecca, too.

118. To the Cruel One

"O fascinating, cruel lady, surely
The holy name of friend's a joke to you?
It seems that, on your moonlike body, purely
A woman-touching's all you'd not eschew—

The touch of lips embarrassed in their passion,
The loving looks of eyes that don't demand?
Surely, in unclear dreams, in some vague fashion,
Your childlike laugh was a tormenting brand?

A man's love is a true Promethean fire:
Yes, it demands, and in demanding, gives.
The glad beloved feels her pow'r expire
As, bush a-burning, flamed in word, she lives.

"I love you, so forget your dream!" In silence
She, barely trembling, downward cast her eyes.
I heard the thrumming of a lyre, the violence,
The thunder of the piercing eagle-cries:

By marble cliff arose fair Sappho's eagle
To soar in triumph—and the loveliness
Of Lesbos' unwalled vineyard, richly regal,
Had shut blaspheming lips that would transgress.

119. Love

A lyricist, bold, without knocking,
Brash, boyish, invading my home,
Declared, with a blatancy shocking,
True sorrow was his—his alone.

He slammed my book shut, in a whimsy:
He pouted, looked down from above
While tapping a slipper, quite flimsy,
And whispered, "There's no one I love."

ALIEN SKY

How dared he put on heavy fragrance
And play with his rings? What burlesque!
With flow'rs in a scatter—what flagrance!—
To spread on my bed and my desk.

I left, trying hard not to mind him,
While yet he obsessively talked—
His walking-stick dragging behind him,
A racket he made as he walked.

Since then I have felt a bit crazy,
Scarce dare to return to my home,
But tell all my friends of the lazy
And shamelessly voluble drone.

120. Ballade

You lovers, under woe beclouding skies,
You thoughtful ladies, gentler than a rose,
In what strange ways you're led by tearful sighs!
What victory, what triumph over those
Who left that legacy do you suppose
Will ever come? Who—what—will lend you calm?
Where is the healing and the breathing balm?
What final loss might bring before your eyes
What weary hearts can feel without a qualm—
The radiance of a rosy paradise?

Come, see what I have found: my song is light!
As in a strange delirium long past,

A mighty arm took mine and—far from sight
To great Andromeda was flying fast
Bronze-armored Perseus, with aid, at last!
Though false far temple blazed, like fiery blades,
Where once I prayed to words and phantom shades,
Yet hail, my homeland, gladdening the eyes!
You lovers, test your fate, where light unlades
The radiance of a rosy paradise!

Throughout my land a tranquil river flows:
In field and grove are foods of rich delight.
The stork will catch the snake where cattail grows;
Made drunk with gum-trees' noon-aroma's might,
Red bears may somersault in frisky fight.
I'm young, an Adam in a youthful world:
I smile at bird and fruit and blossom furled.
At eve will come, in gentle, playful wise,
The infant Christ upon the water, swirled
In radiance of a rosy paradise.

Envoi

To you, my dear, I give this little song.
I always knew you'd not be gone for long.
You, with your look that loves or that denies,
Know there awaits us (and you won't be wrong)
The radiance of a rosy paradise.

Alien Sky

121. Animal Tamer

My Chinese parasol so pretty, ...
My shoes that I have rubbed with chalk.
             Anna Akhmatova

Testing a resolute manner of walking,
Nearer I come to the dearly loved gate.
There, behind bars, ever patiently wait
Colorful animals, captured and balking.

Though they may snarl, they're afraid of my lash.
Might they be sneaky and sly when they scurry?
Maybe they won't—little reason to worry
Since I am young and they fear I'll be rash.

Maybe ... More often I see something violent—
See it and know it's a feverish dream—
Beast that won't eat, only strangely will gleam
Golden all over, six-wingéd and silent,

Long and attentively staring at me,
Watching, alert, every gesture I'm making,
Fellows forgetting, no interest taking,
Hungry, a one-minded predator he.

If I should die in the fighters' arena—
If it should happen—one thing I can see:
Quickly he'll come and he'll bite through my knee—
Quickly, invisibly—none could be meaner.

Nikolay Gumilev

Fanny, your flowers have lost their bright stain:
You, on a rope though, seem happy to balance—
Meanwhile, my beast, near your bedchamber-
    valance,
Dozes, devoted, a faithful Great Dane.

122. Poisoned

"Virgin snowdrift your skin might resemble:
You are strangely, dissuadingly white!
Would you tell me, pray, why do you tremble
As you hand me my cordial tonight?"

She has turned away, sadly if lithely,
But I know, as I've known all the while.
Yet I smilingly drink—I drink blithely—
All the wine she had poured with a smile.

And when, afterward, light is relinquished
And the nightmares come up to the bed,
In whose stranglehold life is extinguished,
Dark and dizziness enter my head ...

I'll approach her, I'll tell her, "My dearest,
I have seen an astonishing dream:
By a golden horizon, the clearest
Thing I saw was a boundless ravine.

I will never again become cruel:
Go, be happy—yes, even with *him*.

Alien Sky

It is far that I'll travel, and you will
Understand—I'm not sad, I'm not grim.

Now from paradise—chill of that heaven—
A vague day-ending whiteness allures.
It's—don't weep, my love!—sweet to me, even,
To have known that the venom was yours.

123. By the Hearth

Shadows glided in. By the hearth's cold stone
Hands on chest enfolded, he stayed alone.

Moveless eyes a distant direction keep:
Bitterly he'll speak—of depression deep.

"I have fathomed depths of an unknown land
Eighty endless days in a caravan.

Mountain range, a forest, and often, too,
Cities in the distance I'd dimly view.

From the towns, at times, in the dead of night,
Wailing, far away, would the camp affright.

Ditches digging, forests we'd chop for wood:
Later, lions came to the camp for food.

Coward? Slacker? None were among us, none:
Right between the eyes they were shot, each one.

I unearthed a fane of antiquity;
There's a local river that's named for me.

In a lake-land, five noble tribes in awe
Made me king and chief, and my word was law.

Now I'm weak, weighed down by the might of sleep.
Soul has taken ill, and the illness deep.

I have known—have known what a thing is fear—
These four walls a tomb, I am buried here.

Even silver gunlight, a splashing wave,
Barely break the chain of a daylight grave ... "

Hearing him triumphantly, eyes agleam,
In a corner dark is a female seen.

124. Margaret

In the pub you hear Valentine brag of his sister,
    How endearing her face and her mind.
It appears many men find it hard to resist her
    Though a ring on her finger you'll find.

Seems that Margaret's hidden a casket of jewels
    In the ivy right under her room.
And the red-coated scoffer who breaks all the rules
    Gives her plenty more jewelry soon.

Though the window's not easy to reach in her
    dwelling,
  Yet the scoffer can bring his own ladder;
And though loudly the students in lyrics are telling
  Of her honor, it cannot much matter:

For the rubies are bright, and the April breeze warm,
  And one wants to forget about ... what?
Martha, loving, must look at the purse—to her harm!
  The aroma of brimstone is hot.

Reckless Valentine, why not forget your disgrace?
Things will happen—all kinds—on a crazed April
    night!
Rigoletto—the hunchback—much trouble would face:
His own daughter made fun of him—proud she was
    right.

Now you're summoning Faust to a duel—in vain!
For a virginal shame all bravado has stilled.
But the scoffer in ragged red cloak—ah! *he* came:
  You will find him—and you will be killed.

125. The Ragged One

At the rumbling Pullmans gawking,
  Following the thread
Rails have made, I spy while walking
  Yellow skies, and red.

Ragged, in the halls of stations
    Roaming, I'm afraid
They'll expel, in their impatience,
    Folk they think low-grade.

For the hundredth time returning,
    Briskly darts her gaze—
Well-remembered lady turning
    Toward me, eyes ablaze.

What would all my love have meant to
    Her, so distant, proud?
Yet—such blue-eyed beauty, sent to
    Me amid that crowd!

I will tell my friend the story,
    Lightly, teasingly,
Some warm hour when misty glory
    Spreads along the lea.

With a smile of grim derision
    He will shout, "Go on!
Trash romances bleared your vision:
    Now you're *too* far gone!"

126. Generals of Turkestan

Below the ballrooms' measured light,
Amid the mild commotion, muffled,
It's odd, along the walls—the sight
Of tall old generals, unruffled.

Alien Sky

Receptive tone and forthright gaze,
Their eyebrow arches clearly graying—
These tell us nothing of the days
They lived through in their youthful straying.

It might appear, in whirlwinds past,
Each dignitary and each dandy
Forgot his legend wouldn't last,
However fragrant, hallowed, handy.

Forgotten, former boring days,
Alarms at night: "To arms! Get ready!"
The salt-marsh, the miasmal haze,
The camel-walking, slow and steady—

The fields trudged through so wearily—
The company—the tragic dying—
And Chu-Kuduk, and Kinderley;
The Russian flag at Khiva flying.

Have they forgot? No! Memories
Return at any time, insistent—
The tears well up in tranquil eyes—
To memory made unresistant.

"How do you feel?" "Pained leg—no fun."
"Podagra?" "No, a shot went through it."
The heartache—bright remembered sun
Of Turkestan won't quite undo it ...

Amid the prints of Greuze, Watteau,
The easy chairs and ottomans,
Not one (some friends have told me so)
Of all these aged veterans

Would make a secret of the cot,
Decrepit, frail, that he had used
On treks: yet living, unforgot,
Heart-moving pictures, not refused.

127–130. Abyssinian Songs

1 Military

Rhinos—they've been trampling on the sorghum,
Monkeys grabbing fruit from all the fig-trees;
Worse, though, than the monkeys and the rhinos
Are the hordes of white, Italian vagrants.

First their flag was waving over Hárrar,
City of Makkonen's doughty people;
Then the ancient Aksum was awakened,
And in Tigre howled the wild hyenas.

On plateaus, in woods, amid the mountains,
Now the savage murderers are running.
Cutthroats! Hunt for blood where you can find it—
Soon you'll drink your fill of what you wanted.

Clamber—quick—from *this* bush up to *that* one!
Serpents trailing your unwary victim—
Jump from highest cliff, leap down! leap headlong!
Leopards gave you tutelage in leaping.

Alien Sky

He that can in battle grab the rifles—
Get the most, hack down the most Italians,
Will be called the soldier of all soldiers,
Ride the whitest of the steeds of Negus.

2 Five Bulls

Having served, five years, a wealthy man—
Taking care of horses in the fields—
I at length received, for my reward,
Bulls to plow well suited—five of them.

One a lion quickly ripped apart—
In the grass, the traces barely seen.
That is how I learned to guard the kraal,
Where a watch-fire is required at night.

Then the second bull went mad and ran
When a buzzing wasp had stung it hard—
Roaming through the undergrowth five days,
Yet I couldn't find it anywhere.

Then, as two more bulls were at their trough,
Came a neighbor, poured some henbane in.
Soon the bulls were flound'ring on the ground,
And their dark blue tongues were lolling out.

Well, the last I slaughtered for a feast—
It was right, I thought, to celebrate
When the neighbor's house burned—how he'd
    howled!
Being bound, of course he couldn't move.

NIKOLAY GUMILEV

3 Slave Woman

Comes the morning, the birds all scatter,
Gazelles run off to the fields:
The European has left his tent,
Waving his long, thin whip.

He sits down under the palm-tree,
With his face wrapped up in a veil.
He puts down his bottle of whiskey—
Starts lashing the idle slaves.

We have to clean his equipment;
We have to take care of the mules
And to eat salt beef, in the evening,
That has rotted during the day.

Praise to our Boss-European!
He carries long-range guns,
And he has—what a supersharp saber!
What a painfully lashing whip!

Praise to our Boss-European!
He's brave but a little naïve.
He's got such a tender body,
A stab with a knife will be sweet!

4 Maidens of Zanzibar

Once a poor Abyssinian
Heard that up north, in Cairo,
Maidens of Zanzibar, dancers,
Will sell their love, for money.

Alien Sky

He had been weary awhile,
Of the women, fat, in Hábesh,
The evil ones, sly, in Somalia,
And the dayworkers, dirty, in Kaffa.

The poor Abyssinian journeyed,
On his one lone mule, riding slowly,
Crossed plains, and woods, and mountains,
Far, far away to the northland.

Then brigands fell upon him;
He left four dead, escaping
To the forest, thick, of Senaar.
His mule—by an elephant trampled.

New moon twenty times had appeared
Before he arrived in Cairo
And remembered he had no money
And returned to where he started.

III

From Théophile Gautier

131. On the Seashore

The moon had let fall from her hands
(Distracted it seemed she might be)
The most cloudy and pink of her fans
On the light-blue carpet of sea.

She inclines ... To retrieve it she's tried
With her silvery fingers thin:
But in vain! For away it will glide
In a wave-carried rapid spin.

Then, Moon, I'd have come to your aid—
Would have leapt into waters blue—
If you'd lowered yourself, dear Maid,
Or if I'd have been raised to you.

132. Art

More pure the art we fashion
Whose matter will have shown
        Dispassion—
Verse, marble, metal, stone.

Companion gleaming sweetly,
Constraint from me dispel:
        And meetly
Cothurni fasten well.

All easy means denying,
No one-size-fitting-all
        Complying
With gods' and beggars' hall.

Materials obeying
The lightly guided hand?
        Dismaying!
Let high be your command.

Alien Sky

To Paros' marbles loyal,
The priceless take to heart,
        A royal
Residing place of art.

A holy shrine amazing!
In bronze of Syracuse
          The gazing
Of high aspiring Muse.

An agate-line inclining
Has made a brother dear,
        Divining
Apollo will appear.

You, artist-heart umtrammeled,
No aquarelle need haunt.
          Enameled
Ecclesiastic font!

Marine your verdant siren
With smile on lip I see
         Environ
Odd creatures' heraldry.

A three-tiered radiance framing
Madonna, Savior-face
        In flaming
Of cross's Latin grace.

All's dust—there's no denying.
True art alone lives on,
      Outvying
Us humans when we're gone.

Upon the simple medals
'Mid elegance of rings
      Unsettles
The gaze of unnamed kings.

A god that yet will perish
A poem will surpass.
      We cherish
Lines mightier than brass.

The struggle, form-outpouring,
Will aid the swelling dream
      In storing
The more than mortal theme.

133. Anacreontic Ditty

You'd like it if I'd braver be?
Then do not scare away my love:
She'll come, in shape a graceful dove,
In ruddy heav'n of modesty.

A dove along the avenue
May seem to view an enemy:
More tender, will my love from you
Run off—don't walk too pressingly.

Alien Sky

More mute than sculptured Mercury,
Be stiller than the trembling beech—
Descending from the wood you'll see
A winged friend who'll greeting reach.

As touch of a caressing wave
You of his breath may feel the might;
The air will quiv'ring pinions lave
In sparkle-skies of blinding white.

Onto your shoulder will your dove
Fly tamely down; her flight allures,
That from the goblet pink her love—
The treasure-taste—may soon be yours.

134. Rondeau

You, child, with look of duchess high—
Though dove, yet falcon-like in sway—
You love me not, and yet will I
Appear before your gates today.

And there I'll stand, and gladly strum
The strings, while leaning on a tree,
Till sudden will the vision come—
Your candle-lighted brow—to me.

Guitars of others I'll forbid
To sound—I won't allow them there—
Your nook is mine. To rivals hid,
Unshakably I say: Don't dare.

I'll seize the ears of him, soon cowed,
Who, cad, might come in reach of me
Should couplet, muffled or aloud,
He chant beneath your balcony.

My blade, quite drunkard-like, will swish:
You're fond of red? You're talking tough?
The novel color might you wish
Of pomegranate on your cuff?

Blood's dull in veins—when life is violent
No more will it be still and bored:
The night is black, the night is silent—
Home, coward! This you can't afford.

Off, bully! Bravery unstinting
Though you may show, 'twill be your loss—
Your brow my dagger's carven printing
Will feel—a sharply riven cross.

Then let them come—they'll soon be broken:
As rabid mongrels though they roar,
Upon my belt, for trophy-token
I'll hang their noses by the score.

Across the gutter-ditch that used to
Besmirch your silken stocking-hem,
The handsome brigands that refused to
Obey—I'll make a bridge of them.

ALIEN SKY

And if a shroud for me be fated
Of two big sheets, I, warrior-liege,
Will burst Inferno, fortress-gated,
And there I Satan will besiege.

Unspeaking door, and window bolted,
You yet may to my voice reply.
Stabbed bull, I'll paw the earth—and, jolted,
You'll hear a wailing canine cry.

A nail upon this wooden siding
I'd like to find, and end my path.
Why live?—when heart and brain are hiding
The plague of loving and of wrath!

135. Hippopotamus

The hippo, with distended belly,
Resides amid the Javan weeds.
When in the pit the monsters yell he
Must dwell in nightmare no one heeds.

The hissing boa, slopeward crawling—
From tiger-throat the roaring deep—
The buffalo with snort appalling—
The hippo will but graze, or sleep.

Of assagai he's never wary
Nor will he tremble at a spear.
The bullet of the mercenary
Flies by his armor, and his ear.

I, like the hippo, live defiant—
In armor clad from shrine held dear,
Quite undeterred and triumph-riant
Through wilds advance denying fear.

IV

Narrative Poems

136. Prodigal Son

1

This home—it is one of a kind, simply peerless!
With books and with incense, with prayers and
    flowers!
What's lacking, though, Father, has rendered me
    cheerless:
Far better in battle to try out my powers.

For why was I born and brought up, all afire,
Now handsome and mighty, health superabundant?
To barter my victory cries for a choir?
Crowd-roars for doxologies, glorias redundant?

No longer a boy, I will not be deceived—
Mere altered directions for thurible-waving
Are meekness and pride. But St. Peter, aggrieved,
To John wouldn't bow—for *this* Daniel, no "saving."

Alien Sky

Allow me, I'll try to increase all your chattels ...
Your tears for the "sinner" just make me indignant!
Both freedom and friendship I'll strengthen in
      battles,
Teach kisses to firebrands who'll soon feel benignant.

The world opens up to me now—a renewal!
I'll act as a prince in God's name! 'Tisn't sorrow
But happiness! Hymn of free blood! Don't be cruel,
Dear Father—farewell, then! *Today*—not tomorrow!

2

How pink through the portico shines the horizon!
The galleons are gay on the Tiber-tide flaming!
Bring dancing girls here, with the eventide rising,
From Tyre, Sidon, Smyrna—great Venus' fire
      claiming!

Bring flowers and wine, and bring fragrances, henna!
I celebrate happiness here in the city.
But where are my comrades—Petronius, Cinna?
Ah! *here* they are—*here* they are! Come, comrades
      witty,

Come quickly, your couches are ready. The roses
Are ruddy as maiden-cheek. Yet, I'm a quester:
You well may remember, my mission disposes
Me here to correct all the errors that fester.

But out in the world—whose iniquity's proven
As Roman philosophy's good at explaining—
I see but one vice—of the sloppy, the sloven:
One virtue—of elegant boredom—is reigning.

Morose, old Petronius? That Syracusan
Sweet vintage will heat you, or hang me tomorrow!
You, Cinna, are laughing? You won't be refusing
The narrow-skulled slanty-eyed slave? Out with
    sorrow!

3

I dragged the dead meat to the reedy fen distant;
I put a big trough in the stall for the mules.
I'm hungry, boss—help! Hunger's made me insistent:
Allow me—that trough! Let me drink! Bend the
    rules!!

Beyond that big rick there is hay, heaped and
    spoiling;
The bulls will not eat it, the horses reject it.
I'm kissing your knees! Let me please, for my toiling,
Sleep *there,* though I know I've no right to expect it.

Exhaustion is bad for a worker too eager;
The eyes become blinded by sweat flowing steady.
If only one day just to rest ... It's so meager ...
Don't hit me, boss, *please*! Where's the work? I am
    ready.

Alien Sky

The oranges—ah!—they are ripe in my father's
Fine orchards, red gold of a noon that is boundless:
Fair maids, chanting lovesongs, whom nobody
    bothers,
Will pick them—in basket be throwing them—
    soundless.

And there will keep vigil, his son well recalling,
A gray-bearded man—he is old, but yet stately ...
He grieves ... I'll admit, "Yes, my guilt is appalling—
My guilt before God, before *you*. I've sinned greatly."

        4

In bitter heart's dolor we find what is sweeter—
The garden! I dare not go near it, I'm frightened ...
I ran there and played with my fox, a pet fleeter
Than I was, by far, at age three—when hope
    brightened.

Oh yes, I've grown up—for my daring paid dearly:
Presentiment's torment, bereavement's deep biting;
Yet this—little creature—first playmate, now merely
A shadow, revives, young affection requiting.

Proud arches arise by the plot where I gardened;
My ancestors' hearth is that home in the gloaming.
It seems so grown up after many years, hardened,
While I—first a rogue, then a beggar—was roaming.

There's feasting—and tables with platters are laden—
The smoking calves roasting, the dough that is
    glowing;
My sister comes out, with a marvelous maiden
Rose-laden, in white—to a wedding she's going.

Behind them—my father, my father so lordly ...
Again must I go—is my roving not ended?
He knows me—he guessed—he's approaching—
    comes toward me:
The feast—and the bride—it's for *me* they're
    intended?!

137. The Discovery of America

Canto One

Drunken is the heart with breezes blowing.
Hear the hidden whisper: "Leave it all!"
Sky unclouded—time that we were going.
Now we pass the door, the bushweeds tall ...
Through the mead, aroma'd ocean flowing
Tells of wilding clime past port of call.

Wingéd-footed, Muse, are you and I—
Willows glimpsing as we pass them by
On the highway—love the squeaky wheel—
White the sail, the water wide! I feel
Holy is the road, austere and high.
Never a regret, nor sham ordeal.

Alien Sky

Sluggards we—but one divine devotion—
Make a trail transforming every motion!
Then is living more than boring notion,
Dull subsisting. Come alive again!
Sinew-net, or blood-rose where each vein
Branches, road-world did the Lord ordain!

Joyful, raging, punishing and playing,
Blood astream, a-chant in every vein.
There's no end to promising, betraying,
There's no end to happy changing. Staying
Still won't help. They'll drive you on again:
Love and Hunger, double whip of pain.

Beast in forest plunders for a ration.
Crabs climb up the bank on stellar nights.
Hawks may glide at leisure in the heights.
All are slaves of Hunger and of Passion,
All the hunters—in whatever fashion—
Love or Hunger blesses them or blights.

Bloody, gladdening, and unawaited
Are the sadness, happiness related
Here on earth, enchanted savagely!
Lust for glory is predestinated
(Being best of all) for royalty—
So the bolder boats will go to sea.

Yes, dear Muse, we'll soon be feeling old
Sitting here together now at night.

You betray nostalgia for the height.
If you will, we both may set our sight
On the land of coral, nard, and gold
Caravels of admirals can hold.

See? Atop the city banners waft …
Joy, when we were children, sun rays lent us.
Now, from belfries, ringing tones aloft
Herald joy again, but naught portentous.
Over port, like heaving moanings oft,
Comes the greeting, raucous roar—momentous.

Where's Columbus? Passerby, declare!
"In a cell a chart he must prepare
With Fray Juan. But maps—the more's the shame—
All are liars. We had best beware—
Sailing on the ocean's not a game
Even for some captains I could name."

Sprinkled view on patterned windowpane
Gold and purple of the end of day:
Sleep and waking blend in twilight ray,
As in magic cave, or woodland fane
Quiet as a moveless weathervane
"Once upon a time," as legends say.

In a hauberk, jeweled, Christopher;
Prior, festively bedecked, we see;
And, behind them, now catch sight of *her*
Swifter gaze than blazing meteor,

Alien Sky

With predictable inconstancy—
Muse of Distant Travel—patron, she.

Strange and proud, yet broken, phrases fail:
"Journey to the south? Did Díaz sail ... ?"
"Aye, but who survived to tell the tale?"
" ... In the Land of Great Mongolia where
Lies an island ... " "But the sea is bare—"
"Hadn't Marco Polo traveled there ... ?"

Now a tower flag is flapping, freed.
There's a knocking at the door, a sign ...
But the friends don't care, a fight indeed!
Ebbing tide? But no one pays it heed.
All those plans and functions to define,
All those problems yet unremedied!

Only when a fog descended on
Gardens, cool, at night, a quiet came.
Now to lead the Admiral to fame
Like a child a mother yet could tame,
Muse upon a tested strength has drawn.
From his working table he is gone.

Canto Two

Twenty days the caravels have sailed,
Bursting through the coming breaking waves—
Twenty days the chart and mapping failed—
Compass now the only guide that saves—

While the best show fear in faces paled,
Sleeping rarely—nightmare-terror raves.

No one now on board the boat whose tackle
Turns to lands where holy tabernacle
Beckons can the mind from fears unshackle,
Every thought by emptiness oppressed
When the depth by plummet-gauge they test,
Mend the sails' rent canvas heavy-stressed.

Calculations of astrologers
Made with care for anxious voyageurs
Lead to a discouraging conclusion—
Stated briefly: "All is but illusion."
Wind-whipped waves from leftward! Sailors' fright
Claims the gypsy prophecies were right.

Prelates' pulpit promises were vain,
Those rewards the men would never see.
Never knightly armor they would gain,
India's golden gardens in the rain,
Kingdoms in default of salary,
Praised by poets—all was vanity ...

All had vanished as a dream. A host
Rose of omens no one could dismiss.
Glory gone, a doom—how dismal, this!
Came the evening like a flaming ghost
Vilely vengeful to the uttermost—
Light in fiery, watery abyss.

Alien Sky

Threatened with an axe Columbus was—
Mad José—his dreadful manias.
Warded off, José, now in the hold
Sobs ... But the commander made no fuss.
Turbid thoughts of terrors manifold
Rule the rebel, cowering in cold.

Sitting on a hawser, whispering,
Are the sailors—truly wanting to
Shout aloud: "It's foolish what we do,
Following the bloody sun—we're through!
Sunset—black abyss—will quickly bring
Solar hate to souls!—Curst mortal sting!"

Yet Columbus put all thought aside
Of the rebels. Lazy, drunken, he
Rests on captain-bridge—in lover-pride
Dreaming, distant, 'mid the breakers' glee
Sees the Muse of Distant Travel stride,
Sweet her summons, mild her melody.

Now the mariners are tranquil. Thus
When a cowherd, calm, impervious,
Guides the bulls, approaching a ravine,
Feet might pound and stamp, obstreperous,
Heart and mind quite mad with horrid spleen—
Yet submission still will supervene.

Neither toward a town, nor toward a lance
Wielded by a cruel picador,

Nikolay Gumilev

Driving on his timid sailor-corps
Does the cold Columbus dart a glance—
Rather, to a place of strange romance,
Herbs and lakes—a world worth waiting for.

If the old astrologer looks bright
When a new-found comet he discerns,
If a youth, to his supreme delight,
Finds a hidden bloom emerge to sight,
If a bard no higher guerdon earns
Than poetic grace for which he yearns,

If it is the richest gift to find
Undiscovered depth within the mind,
Leaving conscious plummet-gauge behind,
Older than the sun yet bold and young,
Heaven past the tone of human tongue,
Revelation ever newly sprung,

Our Columbus' visage is more bright
Than a bridegroom's on the wedding night!
He envisions, with the spirit-eye,
Worlds no wisdom known could prophesy,
Worlds that 'mid the light-blue depth had lain
Where the east met west on azure plain.

Curst by God, cold water of the sea!
Reefs that no one ever gave a name!
Yet—replying to his dream—there came
Nearer—to the sailors' wild acclaim—
Tree and herb and flower bounteously,
And—in air—loud bird-chirp fresh and free.

Alien Sky

Canto Three

Motionless with wonder—"Land, it's land!"—
Now the flag repairman bit the thread.
Dazed, another, cupping chin in hand,
Doesn't even dare to move his head.
Wanton winds above the riggings, and
Caravels glide on with sail outspread.

Who's the man that called, like raucous kite,
Having spotted from the topmost height
'Mid the sea an isle approach our sight?
One thing we'll assuredly avow:
Helmsman, knight, or pirate perched on prow—
He's Columbus' younger brother now!

What by chart and map he'd understood,
Faded pages, plans—he newly could,
Prompted also by prophetic dream,
Bright at noon behold with joy supreme.
He, his comrade, all are bright-eyed birds,
Muse, like you and me ... Muse, mark my words.—

Like a leaping child on trampoline,
I'm so happpy ... No, I really, no ...
Comic long-beaked crane, an indigene—
Lone on high white cliff how gladly seen—
Traced in sky the outline of a bow.
Here's the bank ... We're on the *shore!!*—let's go!

Vested in a white antiquity,
Now the padre reads the liturgy,
With petition, "Lord, do not forsake
Us, poor sinners." Vocal vibrancy,
Bronze-bright Latin richness, can partake
Of the life the wilding breezes make.

It appeared that dream-delirium
Gave us once before this hidden clearing.
Scampering, again the monkeys come,
With the serpentine lianas, from
Where the thistle blooms. Like sinners fearing
Fire, shrill cockatoos invade our hearing ...

Blissfully so rent our breast asunder
Bloom-aromas never known before,
Every step so thrilled us to the core,
From the bush the selfsame joyful roar
Uttered now as then with smiling wonder:
Copper-naked people's vocal thunder.

There was one who didn't welcome in
This our world of dreaming, hearing, feeling,
Though, at first, a pious paladin,
Still he prayed to God, devoutly kneeling,
Though he kissed the grassy reeds within
Valleys, even dust, for grace appealing.

Weathered sailor, shirtless he'd appear,
Shiny copper ring upon his ear.
Neck-tan, coral necklace we discerned,
But his lips (how deep their hidden fear!)

Alien Sky

Nothing spoke, though bright the eyes that burned!
Then his face away Columbus turned.

Weary, sad, this enigmatic man—
He had walked on ocean as on ground,
Moved men's souls—though gunshots popped
 around.
Far away from homes, from friends, they ran
Hoping savage realms unmapped to scan ...
What's he telling? Muse, explain, expound!

"Though I carried out endeavors high,
Darkness of the crypt my soul devours.
You, Great God Who gave me strength, if I
Merit grace, what most would gratify
Now my soul would be no pleasing pow'rs,
But the gift of scorn and pain that scours!

Proud the wineskin filled with strength of wine,
Yet when empty, it will prove benign
If we set aside the relic. Fine!
I'm a shell without a pearl, a strong
Current by a dam banked up too long.
Flowing with no use, to flow is wrong."

Let the rabble in the public place
Burst with boorish laughter in his face,
Monk show spite; the fighter—if he can—
Hate the sage—defeated charlatan!
Him the Muse of Distant Travel left,
Like her other lovers, quite bereft.

Quietly I closed my eyes for woe.
Beating heart—a taut-drawn string—so fast,
Yet resilient—and no more aghast.
For in dream a voice from out the past
Spoke in lover-whisper: "Mourn not so
Him they called Columbus ... Let us go!"

V

Don Juan in Egypt

a one-act play in verse

Dramatis Personae:

Don Juan
Leporello
American Man
American Woman (his daughter)

Setting: Interior of a temple on the banks of the Nile
Time: the present

Don Juan:
(issuing from a deep crack between two slabs)

Where *am* I? Strange delirium!
I'll bet three ducats—yes!—I'm sure!
I see again the earthly sun,
With calm caress, with comfort pure.
But what has happened since I last
With Dona Anna laughed and played?—
And when the dead Commander grasped
My hand (his pow'r could not be stayed!)

Alien Sky

Down, down we flew, and reached the deep,
Each like a weak and wounded bird,
And there was Satan on a steep,
Through carmine lightning viewed and heard.
My cowed Commander soon they laid
On fires for torments that appall.
I deftly hid myself in shade
To wait in subterranean hall.
When Satan showed by mocking smile
And wearied gaze that torment bores,
To rise I made an earnest trial
By stairways and through corridors.
I sweated from the sulphur heat—
With chill I shivered ... Years went by—
Till finally I saw retreat
To darker shade the spirits wry.
Well, good Don Juan, a happy chance
Confirmed the charlatan was right
Who told you simply, "Learn, advance,
And you'll escape and find the light."

   (He turns to the exit)

Free, free at last! Through wave-made mist
A boat comes—I detect a sail.
Much time's gone by since I have kissed
A lovely female cheek. All hail!
There is a boat, there is a man,
And—sitting with him—sister, bride ...
Hail earth! An Eden here I scan,
A place where love-delights abide!

Enter Leporello in a tourist suit, followed by the
American man and woman

Hey, Leporello!

Leporello:

     Friend—my own!
Odd series of events! You're here!
How glad I am!

Don Juan:

    You're not alone?

Leporello:
(quietly)

Ah, no! You must be still, I fear.

Don Juan:

Be quiet? Why?

Leporello:
(quietly)

     I will explain
It all, quite soon ...
 (embraces him, speaks loudly)
      Ah, friend!

Don Juan:

        Go, fool!

Leporello:

You're driving me away?

Alien Sky

Don Juan:
                    That's plain.

Leporello:
(to the American man and woman)

His manners were not learned at school.

Don Juan:

Manners? You lout!

Leporello:
(continuing to embrace him, speaking quietly)

                    Be quiet! Oh!
Don't hit me!
   (loudly)
                    Ha, ha! *I'm* not frightened!
(to the Americans)
He's still the same as years ago:
Likable, reckless, unenlightened!

American man:
(quietly, to Leporello)

Tell me, who *is* he? What's his name?

Don Juan:
(quietly, to Leporello)

Are these your friends? Who might they be?

American woman:
(quietly, to Leporello, pointing to Don Juan)

He's cute! And why d'you think he came?

Leporello:
(quietly, addressing them all in turn)

I'll tell you; just wait patiently.
    (loudly, striking a pose)
I was his secretary. We
Went roaming through Madrid, Seville,
But then I unaccountably
Lost sight of him, for good or ill.
O lazy days of careless youth!
They flee, they're unreliable;
So window lights go out, in truth,
When taverns are no longer full.

Don Juan:

Well, not for all.

Leporello:
(conciliatingly)
                    At least, for me.
In Salamanca I'd been taught
At college: indisputably
I wine and women soon forgot,
Plain water drank, consumed stale bread,
Slept on a mattress made of straw;
The dissertations that I read
Would make your eyeballs red and raw.
My fate was not the lot absurd
Of some Don Juans that I could name;
I was professor; afterward
Dean of the college I became.

American man:
(respectfully)

We know.

Leporello:

          To pupils, strict I'd be—
Distrusting vague utopias,
But, learning Egyptology,
Won European fame—no fuss.

American woman:

Back at Chicago's ballroom dances
I heard that.

Don Juan:

          Work paid off for you!

Leporello:

And now I'm ready for romances—
And ready to get married, too.
   (introducing the American woman)
Miss Poker, who's so debonair
And graceful, is my bride-to-be.
And Mr. Poker, millionaire—
Chicago stockyard-trader, see?
   (introducing Don Juan)
My friends, may I present Don Juan,
My friend in carefree days of youth;
He's often known to "tie one on"—
He's rough—but kind—and that's the truth.

American man:

Mr. Don Juan, you'll get to know
Us better, and we'll get along.
Say, what's the time? My watch is slow.
Is yours correct? I *know* mine's wrong.
 (pointing to the American woman)
Behold my only daughter. She
Has traveled freely; she is jolly,
And she resembles perfectly
My late lamented wife, poor Polly.
And on this southern journey, I
Can not forget my sadness yet.
But you, young friend, undoubtedly
Are still unmarried, I would bet.

 Don Juan
 (approaching the American woman)

Señora!

American woman:

   Miss!

 Don Juan:
 (insistent)

   Señora!

American woman:
(as before)

     Miss!
Señora I refuse to be!

 Don Juan:

Alien Sky

Let's take a walk right after this.

American woman:

Are you Don Juan?! And wasn't he—

Don Juan:

Yes, wasn't he!

American woman:

         And, since those days,
Just *now* you have returned to view?

Don Juan:

Quite right. That old Commander lays
A heavy hand! I've dreamt of you.

American woman:

Not true!

Don Juan:
(dreamily)

        A haze enwraps the earth,
The dreamy Nile's blue estuary.
I'm lying in the lower berth—
You're sitting by the sail so airy—
Or: dawn is only barely seen
In chilly city; fountains rush—
You whisper, "Silent and serene—
There's Don Juan's grave! You see? Now, hush!"

Leporello:
(suspiciously)

Whom are you speaking of?

Don Juan:

                       The one
You left, remember?

American woman:

                       Go, begone.

American man:
(looking at the monument)

Strange metal plate! The script is dim!
   (Leporello goes off to join him)

American woman:

I can't believe you! But—go on.

Don Juan:

I lie? You don't believe me yet!
Your shoulders, though, are white as cream—
More soft than candles, I will bet,
For I have kissed them in a dream.
That breast! The cloth protecting it
Is gentle, yet how envious
Of those blue veins, light, delicate,
Capricious, a delight to us!
Believe me: I would love to lie
If only not to suffer so:
I could be cold, I might be sly,
Yet still your eyes would warmly glow.

Alien Sky

American woman:

Your face—it is so dear to me!
The Mozart music made me rave.
Madrid, as well, I've eagerly
Examined on a map I have.

American man:
(to Leporello, pointing to the sarcophagus)

Inform me, please, my learned friend:
Who's buried here?

Leporello:

                    Seti the Third.
(to himself, looking at Don Juan and at the
    American woman)
My love is lost! It is the end!

American woman:

His name—?

Leporello:

                Why, Seti, as you heard.

American man:

Hm! Hm!

Leporello:
(wants to leave)
      Now!

American woman:

> Wait—please tell me how
You know this quite uncommon name?

Leporello:

This sign's so clear, you must allow,
Not knowing it would bring me shame.

American woman:

Well, well, all right ... And this one on
The pedestal, with pug-dog snout?

Leporello:

Oh, that is Thoth, the moon's own son,
From Cheops' time, or thereabout.
Of course!—You'll note the bulbous brow—
The crown is low and sloping, too.
The fifth Psammetichus might now—
That style changed later on, it's true ...
The fourth Psammetichus, today,
Resembles Seti, I would say,
And here ...
   (exits with the American man)

Don Juan:
(to the American woman)

> Is he your fiancé?

American woman:

Who?

Don Juan:

Alien Sky

    Leporello.

American woman:

              Go away!
I'm rich, he's famous—that you know—
A scholar, sávant, knows his stuff;
He offers no surprises, though:
Well-combed, well-tamed, and never rough.
And I'm too young for him, you see,
But strength and youth and bravery
In our Chicago parlors we
Encounter quite infrequently ...

    Don Juan:

A lackey, just a servant, he—
In coarse-made coat of livery
Or robe that makes him proud to see—
In purple robe a Dean to be!
Afraid there's something he won't know,
Still craving the respect of all,
Defending fame won long ago,
A fawning dog, his wiles appall.
Quite deaf and blind to nature's life!
Mere scroll-moth bred in reveries,
He'll put you in a crypt that's rife
With worn-out words and enmities.
You'll change your whims and vagaries:
Your blood is warm and flaming still.

    American woman:

Don't speak of love! I beg you! Please!

Don Juan:

Not speak? No?—Yes!! I will! I will!
Angel of comfort and of grief,
I know you're special; I'll stand *by* it!

American woman:

Be silent, give me some relief.

(Pause)
Why are you suddenly so quiet?

Don Juan:
(seizing her by the hand)

I love you!

Leporello:
(to the American man, while looking askance at Don Juan)

          Just one word—right here.
I'll tell you things about Don Juan;
One thing, it seems to me, is clear:
Sooner or later he'll get on
The job: in high society
He's well received without demur.
He speaks quite well: why shouldn't he
Become an adjunct lecturer?
But maybe he's too lively for
A scientific sanctuary;
He might prefer a fine outdoor
Task to the work of antiquary.
I think he might be very apt

Alien Sky

In leading long savannah treks:
On horseback, armed, he won't be trapped
But save his own and others' necks.
That he'd be useful as a guide
And lecturer I'd never question.
I know that you'll be satisfied;
I'll tell him soon of my suggestion.

    (*American man* mutters something incoherent)

    Don Juan:
    (to the American woman)

I love you! Yes! We'll go! Let's go!
You know how, when the dragonflies
Sound in the skies, the roses grow
More lovely for two lovers' sighs?
You know how strange the meadows seem
In milky, half-transparent mist
When your dear lover, in a dream,
Leads you, delighted, to a tryst?
Victory-bringing love aspires
To crown us with a wreath ere long,
Turning our loving into fires
And frenzied bubbling into song.
My horse succeeds beyond success—
More white than snow, and great in story.
From lonely woe to eagerness—
The hoofbeats sound a pounding glory!
I've been in hell, in Satan's face
I've gazed, and now I've, glad, returned.

I've met you in this magic place,

Supernal one, for whom I've yearned,
So that you might—O sweetest hour!—
Become my queen and captive, too.
I'm drunk, I love you; lovers' power
Makes drunken gods of me and you.
My journey to the world below
My eye endowed with depth for aye.
How sweetly to the sea we'll go;
The boat will bear us far away.
Let's go, let's go!

American woman:

                No, no, I, I—
Yes—yes—I will! Ah, sweet desire!

Don Juan:
(embracing her)

I'll teach you bliss eternally,
And die upon your funeral pyre.

(He leaves)

Leporello:
(looking around)

But where's Miss Poker, where is Juan?

American man:

The next hall down, I have no doubt.

Leporello:
(holding his hands to his head)

While I was yawning, they've moved on.
I'm scatterbrained! A stupid lout!

Alien Sky

American man:

Where?

Leporello

      To some shining meadow glad,
Or to a forest border shady.
Ta-ta! I see the shepherd lad
Caress the darling shepherd-lady.

American man:

You've gone insane!

Leporello:

            No, not at all.

American man:

Let's go.

Leporello:

      But won't you want your swords?
You may be looking for a fall.
The wiles of Juan transcend mere words.

American man:

But here I saw the two of them
Five minutes past, not more ... Oh, golly!
   (Covers his face with his hands)
When the Last Judgment comes to men,
What will I answer to poor Polly?
This is an awful place, I think!

Leporello:

I well remember, "Leporello,
Sleep, if you want, or go and drink,
Only don't bother me, good fellow."
I was so happy, stuffed and drunk,
I liked my life, I carried on ...
A dean indeed! How low I've sunk—
Better to serve the great Don Juan!

Nikolay Gumilev

For Tatyana Viktorovna Adamovich

139. In Memory of Annensky

Unprecedented, canorous, fantastic,
   He sang and summoned others on—
Of Tsárskoye Seló enthusiastic
   Disciples dubbed him Final Swan.

On certain days when, shy as I was worried,
   I went into that office high,
I found him waiting, kindly, calm, unflurried—
   The graying bard—respectful, I.

A dozen strange and captivating phrases
   He'd let fall lightly, as by chance,
Into my dreams, into the unnamed places
   That waited. Widened, that expanse ...

The growing dark made object-forms surrender—
   Faint lily-fragrance faded, too,
As, agitating, ominous, yet tender,
   The verse-declaiming voice came through.

A pain unnamed, heard crying in the verses—
   Resounding bronze—then whirlwinds rise:
Euripides, in might, a light disperses
   To blinded hearers' burning eyes.

... I heard a rumor there had been a certain
   Bench he preferred when in the park;
There, on the red-gold avenue, the curtain
   He'd view descending—blue, and dark.

There twilight is both beauteous and alarming
   With gleaming line in misty blue ...
A woman, deerlike, fearful of some harming
   She can't define, comes up to you—

She'll stare, and sing, and cry amid her chanting—
   And then, again, she'll sing, or cry.
She cannot understand what spirit panting
   Would, keening, seek in moan, in sigh.

There's water streaming, gurgling through the sluices—
   The raw aroma from the lawn—
A lone, sad muse whom heaven help refuses—
   In Tsarskoye Seló, no Swan.

140. War
to M. M. Chichagov

Like a dog, in chained frustration straining,
Yelp machine guns, yapping in the wood:
Shrapnel's humming—beelike, bent on gaining
Bright-red honey, other shining food.

Now—"Hurrah!" As if it were the singing
Reapers love at end of tiring day—
One might hear calm worker-blisses ringing,
On the mildest eve, above the hay.

Truly it is bright, and it is holy—
High majestic labor of the war.
Seraphs, hovering, transforming wholly
Sunlit shoulders of each warrior.

Workers, trudging, as in olden story,
Over fields already wet with blood—
Deed of sower, harvester of glory—
Bless them, Lord Almighty: they are good.

Like the hearts of those who yet are plowing,
Like the hearts of those who pray and grieve,
Hearts of fighters burn before You, bowing—
Waxen candles burning. They believe.

Most of all—the soldiers You've protected,
Give the royal hour of strength, of bliss,
To the one who'll say to the subjected,
"Take, please—take, from me, a brother-kiss."

141. Venice

Late. In the tower the giants
Loudly have struck. It is three.
Night. In the heart—a defiance:
Traveler, vigilant be!

Naiad-parading, the city,
In her diaphanal past:
Lacelike arcades looking pretty—
Water-face coldened, englassed.

Curtains of witchery cover
Gondolas black, where at night
Flamelets on lake-waves will hover,
Myriad bees made of light.

Quiver

High on a column, a lion
Vaunting an eye-lighting spark—
Wing'd, he might seem to be flying,
Clasping the Gospel of Mark.

Where the ecclesial spaces
Daily mosaic displayed,
Watch how the doves, running races,
Bill, coo, and dive—unafraid.

Is it a prank? We are leery.
Magic of waters dark-blue?
Swamp? A mirage? It feels eerie.
There ... what is that? What—or—who?

Shouting! But nobody's hearing.
Failing to balance, he falls—
Lake-water shakes—pale-appearing
Mirror Venetian—it calls.

142. Old Country Estates

They haven't changed, the old two-story
Homes, yet askew, the cattle yard
And threshing barn—the geese in glory
Parading, prattling, keeping guard.

Nasturtium-garden, or of roses—
A pond: bright-colored crucians glide ...
Old riddling Russian land discloses
Antique estates on every side.

Nikolay Gumilev

At times, at noon, along the border
Of woods, you'll hear a cry—of fright?
The voice will not reveal the order
Of creature. Human being? Sprite?

Or, you might view a church procession
With singing, ringing, booming bells:
An icon has arrived to freshen
The village mood as water swells.

Old Russia raves of God—red flaming
Of angels hinted in the haze—
Has faith in sign and strange proclaiming,
Living and loving olden ways.

Here comes our neighbor for a visit:
His coat—his pride—long-waisted, tight.
His daughter, bowing, is exquisite,
Just turned eighteen. The age is right.

"Though my Natasha has no riches,
She'll wed no beggar—I insist!"
Her clear gaze clouds. Her body twitches—
She'll do no more than clench her fist.

"Father says no ... it seems a wedding
Is something that will have to wait."
Those mermaids' life—not bad, I'm betting,
Down in the pond by our estate.

QUIVER

In days of vernal languor, yearning,
Of many a white and dancing cloud,
In giddiness the heads are turning
Of elder men and daughters proud.

Let men enjoy the monastery:
'Tis gold-domed, holy, wide and white ...
But, though for maidens necessary,
Their sequestration is a blight.

Old Russia, wizard-witch relentless,
You take what you have named your own.
Flee? Loving novelty ... yet—friendless?
To live apart from all you've known?

Our amulets are with us always.
Our luck will alter—one more throw!
There, on the shelves in olden hallways,
Are pistols, Brambeus, and Rousseau.

143. Fra Beato Angelico

A land where happy hippogriffs invite
Wing'd lion cubs in azure land to play,
Where wreath-crowned fury, crystal dryad bright,
Fall from the sleeve of night, in snow or May,

A land where, though each master-grave be mute,
The will yet lives, the prior strength felt clearly,
We find great painters, famed and resolute—
But one of these alone do I love dearly.

Celestial Raphael is great, I grant—
Ágnolo, favored of the spirit-being
Who lived in cliffs—da Vinci, hierophant;
Cellini, gleam of flesh in bronze foreseeing.

Raphael dazzles, though, and never warms—
While Buonarroti fright'ning splendor granted—
And Leonardo's ardor quite alarms
The soul who thought the blest felt calm unscanted.

In Fiesole, among the poplars thin,
Where poppies burn amid the em'rald grasses,
And in the depth of Gothic churches dim
Where many a martyr-shrine the pilgrim passes—

On all the master made, you find the seal
Is love of earth, simplicity, submission.
His draftsmanship was not the Grand Ideal,
But what he knew, he drew with hand-precision.

Past cliff, and grove, a knight upon a horse—
Where is he headed? Churchward? To his dear?
On city wall, a dawn—the flocks, of course,
Along half-rural streets are trotting near.

The Virgin Mary holds her little son,
A curlyhead, with noble pink complexion—
On Christmas Eve, yes, even such a one
A barren wife may get, hope's resurrection.

The executioner in dark blue smock
Will not perturb the saints who're bound for
    brightness.
With golden haloes, they delight to walk
In worlds illumed by intimated lightness.

But color, color!—radiant-brave and pure:
With him the hues were born, with him
    extinguished.
The oils, that blessing gained of prelature,
Were holy, with a grace yet unrelinquished.

Tradition also told: a seraph came
Down here to rival him, loud laughing, shining—
Took brushes, got to work—yet, feeling shame,
For all his art, disheartened, went back pining.

There is a God, there is a world, they live
Eternal, though our life is grim with grief.
But we receive the deeps that it can give
If we but love the world and hymn belief.

144. Conversation
for Georgi Ivanov

When ray of green at last, after the sun goes down,
Glimmering hides away and goes we know not where,
The spirit, rising, like a madman, roams around
A garden gone to seed, an empty public square.

The soul now owns the world, and never envying
A bird or angel, walks the quiet avenues.
The body drags behind—resentful, hidden sting
Lamenting, pain of fate—and tells the world the
    news.

"Superb to lounge and sit around the fine café
Where gas may crackle in the lamps above the
    throng—
To have a swig of beer, to hear the keyboard play
'La p'tite Tonkinoise' or some such other song.

And then the cards start fluttering above the table
To seek the bored and lost, to make them want to
    live:
You know I love to touch, hot-handed, when I'm able,
Whatever gold I've gained—less taking than I give.

You know how hard it is to deal with all this raving,
To listen to imagined voices in the air,
To stare at trifling stars that leave an unknown
    craving:
How simple, poor, the God-lent decorations there!"

The earth, from time to time, in sympathy is
    sighing—
Aromas of the the sap and dust and shrubbery—
It ponders, always profitlessly rueful, trying
To pacify the soul's unwearied mutiny:

QUIVER

"Return to me—be dirty clay again, my child,
In deep of marshes cold and dark and slippery,
And choose whichever you prefer, Nevá or Nile,
To be a fitting home for your tranquillity.

We know each ear, each eye will close a dying door;
Surrendered to the foe—your brain will rot away—
But you'll become a plant or animal once more,
And that's the best you can expect, I have to say."

The spirit wanders, lauding yet its lofty lot
But yearning for fictitious, long-enduring fields.
The body runs behind it, halting, tired, and hot.
A fragrance of decay the earth, alluring, yields.

145. Rome

She-wolf with muzzle of crimson,
On pillar of purest white,
You merit glory-hymns on
The ground of your royal right.

I see two infants, brothers,
Struggle to get to your breast—
Mere boys, and each the other's
Wolfish image at best.

Didn't you love them harder,
The boys, long ago, when they,
Snarling with battle ardor,
Burnt cities in a day?

When, to the realm of nightfall,
They, sigh-like, sped off soon,
With moanings long and frightful
You dug a triple tomb.

She-wolf, the rapid river
Rolls while your city stands.
Though loggias last forever
And columns may dominate lands,

Though faces of fine Madonnas
Appear in St. Peter's Square,
There yet looks down upon us
Your darkly yawning lair.

The brambly reeds and grasses
Grow from the fragile stone—
And a bloody moon-sphere passes
In a night of steel and bone

The caesar city wondrous
Of papal decretal laws,
Made strong by your rumbling thund'rous,
By your shaggy, beast-like paws.

146. Iambic Pentameters
for M. L. Lozinsky

The night, a naiad black—on sea-waves dashing,
A boat below the shining Southern Cross:

QUIVER

I traveled southward—mighty breakers, crashing,
The powerful propeller-vans would toss.
The vessels that we met, amid the splashing,
Would enter darkness, and we'd sense our loss.

I pitied them—it felt uncanny, thinking
That they were going back, could not retain
Their boats within the welcome bay, unsinking—
Don Juan to hooded woman no more winking—
Nor diamond hill would Sindbad now attain—
Still worse what fates the Wand'ring Jew constrain.

But months had passed … Again I was returning—
With many a tusk of finest ivory
And leopard skin that gleamed appealingly—
And Abyssinian art for the discerning,
And—something I did *not* expect—a burning
Scorn for the world. My dreams had wearied me.

Though I was hungry, young, to fear resistant,
The spirit of the earth—still, haughty, distant,
Had made my blinding dreamings die away,
As birds will die, and flowers will decay.
My voice became well-measured, uninsistent.
My life had failed me. You—what can I say …

In the Levánt, for you, I wandered, buying
Rich, royal purple robes, their age belying—
But you I lost as, into frenzy flying,
Had Damayanti lost his Nal—loved well …

Nikolay Gumilev

The dice were tossed, and down like steel they fell:
Their pattern showed my fate—O heavy spell!

For it was then that, pensively and strictly,
You said, "I loved, believed in you too quickly.
I'm leaving, no more crediting your love.
And on my path bestrewn with perils thickly,
Before the face of Providence above,
You I deny. Alone I'm doomed to rove."

To kiss your hair I was too broken-hearted;
And ev'n your hands—how slender and how cold!—
I felt too loathsome, spiderlike, to hold—
Each tone alarmed me, who had been so bold.
You, darkly, simply dressed, had then departed ...
With crucifying hurt my spirit smarted.

With heat and stuffiness unheard of, too,
My summer filled with storms, wild, unretreating,
The world seemed darkened to a dreary view:
At times my heart would suddenly stop beating.
In fields the sheaves their seed about them threw;
The sun stood red—a heavy hammer heating.

And then, amid the roaring of the crowd,
Where rumbling ordnance I would soon be meeting,
'Mid sound unceasing of the trumpet proud,
A sudden hymn—my fate!—I heard aloud
And ran to where the populace were fleeting—
"Amen, amen, amen" I, meek, repeating.

Quiver

"Move on, go forward! If we die, we die!"—
The chant of soldiers—though their words unclearly
Came through, they reached my heart, which loved
    them dearly:
"Above our beds the grass will wave—the sky
Will watch, green leaves will curtain us—on high
Archangels benediction lend, heard clearly."

The sweet, outpouring song had such allure
I signed right up, my feeling, mood so pure—
A horse and rifle were my armature.
The fields were filled with sanguinary foes—
Loud-rumbling sounded bombs, and bullets rose—
Red-flashing light the heaven would disclose.

My Soul, enkindled by a happiness
Remaining—widened by a new largesse
And clarity and wisdom—glad would talk
About the Lord while stars arrived—to bless;
It listened to the Lord—in war's deep shock,
It called divine the ways it had to walk.

Most honored of the honored cherubim,
Most gloried of the gloried seraphim,
Of earthly hope the heaven-consummation,
It lends each moment grandeur, jubilation—
And simple words, it feels, are heard by Him
Who listens with benevolent elation.

There is, along the desolating tide,
A monastery, golden-domed and white,
Illumined with a glory, day and night.
There would I go, to leave this world of spite,
To look at spreading currents, heaven wide—
O gold-white refuge by the waterside!

147. Pisa

Sunburnt walls arise of henna:
Roofs, bazaar, piazzas are a
Pride—and the marble of Siena
Amber! And milky-white—Carrara!

All is quiet below sky's burning:
Having completed their psalm, the last,
Red-clad children you'll see returning
Home right after the evening mass.

Where are now the somber thunders
Deep in ravines, gold Tuscan valleys?
Bazzi's Sodom-passion that sunders?
Ugolino's devouring sallies?

Soon for torment, pleasure, whether
Noble or base, fate judgment lays on
Ghibelline, Guelf—they're laid together,
Each in his grave with brandished blazon.

Everything, like a shadow, passes—
Time, with its pow'r of retribution,

QUIVER

Burdens dark of the past amasses—
Present—and never a diminution.

Satan, with fire-gleam hard to bear,
Himself will from the fresco tear,
Down-bending with unending fear
Over the tower leaning here.

148. Judith

What wisest of wise pythias will inform us
What truly happened in that olden story
Of brave Judaean Judith's deed enormous
Of bringing Holofernes down in glory?

Judaeans many days had known misfortune,
Inflamed with Babylonian desert breezes,
Before the dawn-red glare of tents; impórtuned,
They'll neither fight nor do what tyrant pleases.

The satrap was a mighty man and splendid,
Strong body, roaring voice, the tone of battle:
And yet the maiden did what she intended—
No frenzied fear could steely nerve-calm rattle.

Yet in that blest-curst hour of searing weather,
When whirling winds tranquillity would sunder,
Love's angel, Syrian wingéd bull—together
In Judith rose, a union rare, a wonder.

Could it have been amid the incense glowing—
The shouting, strutting, to a tambour clangor—
A Salomé was adumbrated, showing
The head of John the Baptist, cold with anger?

149. Stanzas

With such high terror is the island smitten—
   Mist grand and wide!
The Book of Revelation here was written,
   Great Pan here died.

Near islands differ—there, with happy humming
   The reapers dwell:
Near palm and palace can they stroll—and summon
   With shepherd bell.

I took a fiddle, curved, superbly fashioned—
   Held breath—to play:
The strings I heard exhale with faintest passion
   Her soul away.

Yes! It is purely magic that I'm feeling—
   Alone, subdued:
That star-rain seems to fall by night—down reeling—
   A moan, a mood.

For I am free, believing in my labor—
   The world my home—
Can kiss a lovely girl, can win her favor,
   Make her my own.

Quiver

A moment, from my land to Yours to turn me—
    Bridge, opened—shines:
Star, cross, and chalice of the stars can burn me
    Like fiery wines.

150. Return
for Anna Akhmatova

They slept as I parted, a stealthy rover.
My traveler-friend by the hedges hid.
Perhaps in the morning they'd look all over;
Too late—we had gone where the fields might bid.

My yellow-skinned, slant-eyed friend was slender.
How madly I loved him—and him alone!
His cloak-concealed pigtail, his look not tender—
He stared with his adderlike eyes and moaned.

He moaned for the old, for the strange, the painless—
He moaned that he longed for eternity.
I heard a faint bell-ringing, pure and stainless:
I fainted, was seized by a syncopë.

Hill, forest, and mountain we passed, unending—
We slept in rough huts in remote ravines.
To years, it appeared, was our time extending—
Then suddenly shrunk to a day of dreams.

But when we'd arrived at the Chinese border,
My traveler-friend said, "Farewell, I go.

Two journeys: while yours of a sacred order
Must be, I have rice-seed and tea to sow."

Upon a white knoll over tea-field, seated,
The Buddha we saw in pagoda frail—
To him in rapt silence I bowed, I greeted
The sage—never sweeter a pilgrim's tale.

How softly, how softly, above the stainless
Wide valley, with adderlike eye, he sang.
He sang of things ancient, eternal, painless,
And strange. Brightened air! And the chanting rang.

151. Leonardo

Three years of plague and famine
Ravaged the widespread land.
The people begged Leonardo:
"Save us, you're wise and good."

Scrolls that were hidden, treasured,
Were things Leonardo knew.
And he, in one brief summer,
Had saved the country 'round.

Conflict and feuds erupted:
The king had passed away.
The people told Leonardo,
"Now you will be our king."

QUIVER

Leonardo was acquainted
With war, the royal art.
Poets were quick in writing
Appropriate victory odes.

Soon the land was tranquil,
The plowman back at the plow.
The people told Leonardo,
"You're young—you need a wife."

Peaceful, clear, and somber,
Leonardo did not reply.
By night he was gone from the castle.
No one knew where he went.

But a shepherd-boy, aslumber
That night in the gloomy hills,
Claimed he had heard, distinctly,
Harmonious vocal tones:

It seemed a hovering eagle,
A ram, a lion, a man
Cried, and sang, and summoned—
All at once in the dark.

152. Bird

I can no longer recite a prayer …
The words to the litanies I've forgot.
A bird moves menacing through the air;
Bright fires make her eyes white-hot.

Nikolay Gumilev

I hear how she restrains her screaming,
A cymbal tone now buried deep—
Rumble of far-off waters gleaming
Beating against a boulder-heap.

Now I can see: claws' steely glimmer
Inclining close above my head,
As river currents at night will shimmer,
Moonlit, when all is quieted.

I'm scared. What *can* the bird be wanting?
I am no youthful Ganymede.
On *me* no sky of Hellas, haunting
In loveliness, can shine—indeed!

And if this dove be truly godly,
Having flown down to declare, "It's time,"
Why does it differ so very oddly
From local doves of our garden-clime?

153–154. Canzonas

I

Fine, strong winds from a lucky region,
Lovers' plainings abroad are sent:
Like ripe sheaves in a wheatfield, legion,
Bow the heads of the never-bent.

Sings the Arab in wildernesses,
"Out of my body the soul is torn."

Quiver

Over the ocean the Greek confesses,
"Seagull! you came to my call forlorn."

Well may you marvel how love has hearkened!
Nightly, a lamp lights the Greek girl's eyes.
Seeds aromatic in chamber darkened
Burn where the Arab's beloved lies.

One great call—every land had blessed it—
Spreading yet further, more wondrous, pure.
Haven't you heard it, dear, and guessed it,
Though my chant be so awkward, poor?

Darling mine, with the summer smiling,
Slender-armed, and so weak, indeed—
Black hair, fragrant, the mind beguiling,
Like a myriad-year-old mead!

II

Above Adonis, lunar-graceful, proud,
Narcissal youth and Hyacinth the slender,
And over Danaë, that golden cloud,
The Attic heights breathe gentle morning, tender:

Iambic ocean moanings piteous—
The flock of crying cranes, a-trailing, swaying;
The palm, whose legend had Odysseus
Recounted when with Nausicäa staying.

That old sad world will not be charmed for good
By fragrant curls, or by alluring glances,
By heart-warmed petal-lips, by heated blood
To beat triumphantly in love's advances.

Death tells the truth; and life—but stammered lies.
And you, for whose fair sake each day is dear—
Your body, music—you will go, with sighs,
Will leave me—and, unsparing, disappear.

I, to my grief, don't know the lasting word—
An earthquake it would be, cascade, or thunder—
To keep you living, let your name be heard,
Like youth and maid of Hellas, long gone under.

155. Perseus
sculpture by Canova

The muses loved him from of old.
He's young and blazing and heroic.
Medusa-head he raised up, bold—
Swift, steely-handed he, a stoic.

Of course, he cannot ever see
(In whose bright soul were storm and lightning)
How fine, filled with humanity,
The eye once mad in wrath, and fright'ning.

The features of that pain-wrought face
Are traits, now, of a thing of beauty—

But boyish willfulness abates
No boundary, no bond of duty.

Waits nude Andromeda, enwound
With dragon sinuosity—
And Victory, while distant found,
Will come, as light, as wing'd, as he.

156. Spirit Sun

How could we have gone along, unrattled,
Never given happiness or harm,
Never dreaming of a fire embattled,
Triumph-trumpet, after war-alarm?

Though the end's not yet—we're nowhere near it—
Yet a spirit sun inclines to us.
Menacing, benign, that light of spirit
Pours through heav'n a radiance bounteous.

Now the soul's abloom, like May-time roses—
Like a flame, it threads the darkness through,
While the body, to whom fate discloses
Naught, must bow. For spirit will subdue.

Wild the charm of major field-expanses—
Gentle, muffled secret of the wood—
Nothing hard holds back the soul's advances:
Torment has it ever well withstood.

Now I feel the autumn's adumbration
Culminate our sunlit, bright pursuit.
From the spirit tree the woken nation
Soon will pluck the ripened golden fruit.

157. The Middle Ages

Patrollers pass, their swords rap-rapping.
The evil monk steals to his dear one.
Over the gabled homes a-napping,
Reposes the Unknown, quite near one.

But we are peaceful, we'll be fighting
With guards of the Almighty's anger:
St. Genevieve, your cloak, inviting
To rest, breathed starry, sea-like languor.

Do you remember how, before us,
Above the altars in the gloaming
Arose a temple dark, where, aurous,
Burnt many a fiery sign and omen?

Triumphant, stone-wing'd, overawing
Our town kept safe in grave complacence!
Within it hammer sang, with sawing
Tones of the industry of masons.

With speech they're casual but sparing;
Their looks are stubborn, strict, and pure—
They know the ancient secrets, caring
To build a church that will endure.

Quiver

We kissed the threshold crafted finely,
And kneeled, transgressions then confessing:
We asked for what is giv'n divinely—
For you, for me—a heaven-blessing.

The Master, with a spirit-level,
Stood firm amid the roar unruly
And whispered, "Go in peace: the Devil
Beëlzebub we'll vanquish, truly."

So long as in the world they're living
They set the rules for holy sowing.
So, Genevieve, our love we're giving,
Kept safe in coming and in going.

158. Cathedral of Padua

Amazing—holy church, yet sad with yearning.
Temptation, yes, and joy—a storm of fire.
In windows of confessionals are burning
Torménted eyes new-widened by desire.

A swell—subsiding—organ's mighty musing—
Then growing fuller and more awesome yet,
A rebel bloodstream, drunkenly refusing
In darkened temple-vein to quell its jet.

From purple, from a martyred saint expiring,
Whose half-bared body pale is laid to rest,
How good to flee (dark-swallowed vault, immiring)
With soul yet unabducted, unpossessed!—

In quiet tavern of an ancient quarter,
On terrace lounging, drink a little wine:
The wall's become quite green where streaming water
Washed past it from the channel maritime.

Out, quickly! Real departure needs the leaven
Of effort!—in the yard, you'll feel quite weak.
The Gothic towers fling their wings to heaven—
Catholicism-Powers at their peak.

159. To One Departing

I'm trying not to feel deep envy
(What injury the fates have sent me!)
Because you're leaving—soon you'll be
On Mare Nostrum, heaving sea.

You'll love both Rome and Sicily
(These Vergil loved—devoted, he).
In lemon-scented, overgrown
Corner you'll pen a lover's moan.

Myself, I've felt this many a time
While breathing of the sea-air brine—
Like Dante on the Arno, I
To Beatrice would testify.

The envy that's invading *me*
Spoils nature and antiquity.
The Muse of Distant Travel *you*
Will meet along some avenue:

QUIVER

For you, in that enchantress' land,
Filled crystal nectar glass will stand—
Fine lively conversation waiting—
Delirious lightning, high-elating.

But I, as if by ogre giants,
Am locked away, despite defiance—
Old folio-tome, I silent sing
And never hear or see a thing ...

160. Again the Sea

I was happy again, believing
That a hefty anchor'd been raised—
While the ocean, delighted, receiving
A five-decker steamboat, gazed:
I felt that the sun was breathing,
That the earth was chanting, amazed.

Can even a rat, exploring
In a kitchen—a worm in a hole—
Or a toothless old man deploring,
In dementia, how dull days roll,
Not have heard how the singing, soaring
Of Ulysses had summoned the soul?

He has called me to play with the trident
Of old Neptune—with Nereids' hair,
While the bow-waves are breaking, strident,
As if strings, to the trembling of air,

Of the foam, of the breasts of the silent,
Of the sweet Aphrodite fair.

I am leaving my home—I'm slated
To encounter my destiny.
For a universe, known—strange—fated,
Is prepared to come close to me:
Shores bending—with peril baited—
And the water—the wind—the sea.

And the sun of the soul is unsetting,
And the earth—it will lose the war.
I will never return, I'm betting.
Weary flesh I'll encourage more
If the summer is mild, unfretting—
If the Lord loves what I'm for.

161. African Night

Midnight comes down, with a dark unbroken—
Only the river the moon has lit.
Kindling their watchfire, to vigil woken,
Tribesmen hidden-hushed tones emit.

Morning will come, and we'll all be clearer
Who is the master. To ward off loss
They have a flintstone. To us, much dearer
A soldier's personal golden cross.

Mapping, I'm crossing the ditches: ammo
Here, supplies—and the mules right there.

Wretched, the hell of the land Sidammo:
Never a tree in the stifling air.

Comforting thought: if we win the battle
(Many's the struggle we've won, out here),
Reaching the winding highroad that'll
Lead past the hillocks, we're "in the clear."

But if the fevered Uebbi river,
Roaring, will greet my expiring sigh,
Dead, I will marvel as, fierce forever,
Fire-god and night-god contend for sky.

162. On the Offensive

Land attractive—and so extensive—
Might be Eden—but now is fire:
Four days famished—a long offensive;
Four days' starving and tiredness' ire.

Earthly food's not a prime objective
In this brightening, frightful time:
God's own word, our divine directive,
Feeds me better than bread or wine.

Blood-wet weeks have gone by, they bound us,
Blind us—yet, they are somehow light.
Shrapnel tears through the air around us—
Blades much faster than fledglings' flight.

Now I shout, and my tone is tameless,
Bronze, a bell that is rung on high.
I, the bearer of bold thoughts blameless,
Cannot die—no, I *can not die*!

Like the blows of the hammer-thunder,
Wrathful sea-waves that never rest,
Russia's heart must the foemen sunder,
Steady, beat in emboldened breast.

Like a maiden who, grateful, graces
Friends in triumph is vict'ry sweet:
Let us follow the hazy traces
Left by enemies' quick retreat.

163. Death

Varied lives have their varied riches—
One death only may claim great worth.
Under bullets in quiet ditches,
You have faith in God's banner, Earth.

For this reason you know quite clearly:
In that singular, stringent hour
When, red cloud that will leave austerely,
Day is yielding a rosy flow'r,

Heaven's vault will be cleft by forces
For the soul, and the soul will rise,
Borne, for glory, by snow-white horses
Climbing heights that will blind the eyes.

There the Master, in armored raiment,
Most dread helmet of stellar rays,
To the warriors' entertainment
Calls: a fire-wingéd trumpet-blaze.

But below, here on earth, quite equal
Is our death to the rites above:
One true friend will, in grieving-sequel,
Kiss the dead on his lips in love.

Here the priest, in a tattered cassock,
Softly, low, will intone a psalm—
Over valley and hill and hassock
Martial songs being borne along.

164. Vision

Exhausted, the martyr had lain on the sickbed
(What burden more bitter to bear than the sickbed?),
When suddenly, light is awakening, flaming,
He sees and he hears in a rapture, a *gloria*,
That, leaving the darkness, the night beyond
    naming,
Come Saint Panteleimon and George the wise
    warrior.

He hears the grave words of great Saint Panteleimon
(Sweet-breathing, the speaking of Saint Panteleimon):
"How sleepless and red are your eyelids—what
    loathing

Bespoken—hot, smothering pillow-sedation.
But once you are touched with the hem of my
    clothing,
Bright health will enliven your warmed circulation."

Right after his friend, arrives George the wise warrior
(High triumph's own trumpet-voice, George the wise
    warrior):
"Renouncing all wars, you had sought for salvation;
But tears from the mighty the Lord is not prizing:
God hadn't accepted your sad supplication.
You'll rise in the morning, and glory in rising."

They vanished, a pair of bright stars disappearing
(In darkness of night, two bright stars disappearing);
The rushing of oncoming day is beginning:
By glimmer of dawnlight, the tired one's arising,
High-spirited, smiling, his gaiety winning,
Heart open to bottomless life he'll be prizing.

165. Courteous ...

Courteous to contemporary
Life, I observe a certain limit.
It mocks what I find valid—very!—
And laughs at what has merit in it.

Victory, glory, valor—pallid
Words that today have lost their meaning—
Sound in the soul—a storm-stroke mallet:
The voice of God, Who scorned mere seeming.

Quiver

Always unneeded, unrequested,
Rest will come at a wretched hour.
I swore to be an arrow, tested
By Nimrod's or Achilles' power.

But—no, I'm not heroic, tragic—
I'm dry, sarcastic—feeling cloys.
As with metallic idol-magic,
I rage among frail china toys.

The idol thinks of heads bent, curly-
haired, of the boys below his altar—
Of priestly pray'r, in forest early—
'Mid stormwind where the tall trees falter.

He'll sadly laugh at scenes beguiling,
As at a swing where, tranquil, mute,
A buxom maid is list'ning, smiling
At shepherd-tootling on the flute.

166. What a peculiar ...

What a peculiar pall:
The gray before the dawn—
The spring snow thawing; all
That passed, and wisely, on.

To read on a gold-eyed night,
Dante was what we chose.
Winter's curls were white
When we dreamed a Levántine rose.

In the morning I wake up sad,
Wary of woe and bliss.
Can a kiss yet make me glad
From a sweet and silly miss?

Flowers I plucked as a child
In the deep green dragon marsh,
Where *are* you—thin-stemmed, mild,
Spreading—in times so harsh?

There's a shining life to be had,
Less pining—free, at ease—
Where laughs an Athenian lad
Reading Euripides.

167. I've not so much ...

I've not so much lived as languished
The half of my life away.
You, Lord, appeared—but I'm anguished
By that dream—what it seemed to say.

I beheld a light at Mount Tabor—
And a madness seized me, seeing
I to land, to sea lent favor—
Mere sleep—crazed dream of being—

For none of my youthful power
Has bent to do Your will—
And your daughters' beauty, each hour,
With pain my heart would fill.

Quiver

Yet can love be a blossom, learning
To breathe but a minute and die?
Is love but a flamelet burning,
Then quenched with a waning sigh?

How sad, that quiet thought,
As I'm dragging this life along.
You deal with the next; I can *not*—
One's álready turned out wrong.

168. Happiness

I

The sick believe in Maytime roses—
Tender, the tale of beggary.
Sleep by a wall in jail discloses
An Eden-gift to you, to me.
How could a mind be more dejected
Than when engaged in silken strife?
Pea-princess, pampered, not neglected—
And yet would I surrender life.

2

"Hunchback, what are you after?
Want to swap lives with me?—
Learn play, delight, and laughter,
Uncaged, like a bird on the sea?"
But his eye showed mere despite

As he measured me, head to toe:
"I pray you, get out of my sight.
There's nothing I need. Just go!"

3

Torment has many lute-strings playing—
There's only one will do for bliss.
You'll feel more homeless, heaven-straying,
Than if you'd entered the abyss.
The banisher of leprosy
Who said unto the virgin, "Rise!"
Found Lazarus more dear to see
Than preachers all with kindly eyes.

4

I've not been a sinner, O Lord;
I'm not an apostate or thief.
So hide not Your presence adored
From me, a true man of belief!
I'm not of the saints, the elect—
I'm young, I am happy, I sing ...
I know You will surely reject
My soul, my poor soul, O my King!

5

That was my brightest day, so fair,
The day of Christ's own resurrection:
Redeemed I felt my soul's election

QUIVER

Which I'd been seeking everywhere.
I, sudden, thought I'd come to lie
Deaf, naked, wounded, in a wood …
For every earthly life to cry
In tear-filled bliss ill-understood.

169. Eight-Liner

The whisper of the midnight distance,
The hymn that Mother sang to me—
Each finer thing our dull resistance
Will undervalue willfully.
But, symbol of our greater station,
For kindly-minded testament
The high, opaque articulation
Of poets' making must be meant.

170. Rain

Through the rain-splashed windowpane the world
    Seems a pockmarked, speckled place.
Look again: in tranquil air that swirled—
    Scene revealed—unfaded face.

Though the leafage-gleam bespoke an omen,
    Wet with trickling vitriol,
Yet the bush, blood-roses in the gloaming—
    Sharply outlined, shines for all.

Drops in meadows drip more quietly,
   Muttering their measured psalm.
Nuns at vespers, with rapidity,
   Chant like this amid the calm.

Glory be to heav'n for sable cloud!—
   Making spring's new river, where
Not the fish, but hilltop trees that crowd
   Sway in turbid rain-filled air.

In a stagnant pool of millwheel magic
   Steeds can neigh in frenzied glee.
Now the soul, immured in prison tragic,
   Feels at ease, at liberty.

171. Evening

The evening hangs—how heavy—lacking wings!
A sunset—melon cracked. And nothing sings.

One wants to shove things forward just a bit,
To budge the waning, fading clouds, ill-lit.

On wearied evenings, dilatory, dull,
Will steeds in harness gallop to the full—

Through rivers fishermen row rapidly;
And woodsmen? Angry, hacking down each tree,

They fell the curly-headed oaks that tow'r—
And those who harbor knowledge of the pow'r

QUIVER

That moves the fate of things, unknown and known,
Who feel their rhythm, fathoming their tone,

A lyric will be making, freed by wings,
Unchaining hymns of elemental things.

172. Genoa

The doges' grand palazzo seen
In Genoa brags of art antique:
A canvas shows a brigantine,
Swanlike and floating, gliding, sleek.

Alongside ships that crowd together
The fishermen and fittings-men
Still carry on, in any weather,
Their age-old gossip. Grinning, then,

Their eyes agleam, they chat with ease
About the living, dead … The bay
Attracts the damp—you see the breeze
Entangling strands of beards gone gray?

We soon find something quite surprising:
An eager man appears to see us:
"Where are you from, Signor?" (tone rising)—
"Maybe Livorno, or Pireus?

If, in the coming summertime,
My Brábant brother you'll be meeting,

Give him this keg—Chanti wine!
Tell him I send a friendly greeting."

173. Chinese Maiden

On the river—midstream—
Is a bower, light blue—
Cage of wicker, 'twould seem,
Where the moths are on view.

From this bower I see,
When I look at the dawn,
Every twig of each tree
Sway and swing. Further on

Past the waving of trees
Boats will bend around bowers—
Gliding gently, with ease,
They can idle for hours.

There are porcelain blooms
In this dungeon of mine;
Metal birds—yellow plumes
In the tails of them shine.

From enticements I turn.
Silken ribbon—I write
Songs of love and concern—
Taut-lined *tanka,* just right.

QUIVER

My betrothed loves with zeal.
Though he's bald—needing rest—
He has passed (wise ideal!)
Every government test.

174. Paradise

Apostle Peter, kindly get your keys:
A heaven seeker knocked. Reply then, please.

Ecclesiastic synods made it clear
That I've been upright, held each dogma dear.

St. George will testify commendably
That in the war I fought the enemy.

St. Anthony, it's true, will have to say
My flesh I couldn't humble *every* day,

Cecilia, though ... her lips will whisper, soft:
My spirit, pure, directed thought aloft.

And Eden gardens blooming may appear
To me, red-fruited branches bending near—

The charming angels' light, their voice, where all
The marvels of the height united call.

You know so well: a paradisal dream
Must ring the bell of rising Eden gleam.

Apostle Peter, don't reject me: you
Can't send me down to hell—what would I do?!

My warming love will melt infernal ice,
My tears make hell-fire liquid, in a trice.

Dark seraph soon before you, Lord, will be
A mediator who can plead for me.

Don't wait though, Peter, let me see your keys:
You clearly heard me rapping—answer, please.

175. Islam
for O. N. Vysotskaya

We had Chianti wine in a café
When in came, asking for a *sherri-brendi,*
A tall and grizzled elderly effendi,
Levántine foe of Christians, in his day.

Then I approached him bravely, saying, "Stay!
My friend, it's bad to play disdainful dandy
Right now when legendary Damayanti
Is here beneath the green of twilit ray."

But, tapping with his toe, he made a moan:
"Do you not know the holy Kaaba stone
The faithful venerate this very week?"

He sighed then, with a deeply thoughtful air,
And whispered, "Mice are getting what they seek:
Three strands they've eaten of the Prophet's hair."

176. Bologna

Pure Romagna water is the sweetest;
In Bologna, ladies are most fair.
Billets doux on hazy nights are fleetest,
Amorous aromas in the air.

By a roaming noble's lantern, flaring,
We can just detect, amid the gloom,
Skimpy lace the pink of skin half-baring,
See a mústached troublemaker loom.

Now the lantern's gone, but love yet glances:
Fragrance hinted in the maiden's hair—
Look: her lover, confident, advances,
Kissing her—behold her trembling there.

Want wine strong? You'd better get the sweetest
Though the comely ladies be more coy.
Comes an old professor, not the neatest:
Fame that he had dreamt of as a boy

Yet evades him, but he likes to wander
Through the city till the break of dawn.
Planning lectures, he's intent to ponder
Roman codes of law he's working on.

All hunched over, scarlet gown a-wagging,
Seeking order in the disarray,
Even *he'll* keep pace, if slightly dragging,
In Bologna's decked-out streets today.

Nikolay Gumilev

177. Tale
for Teffi

On a crag, where Elizabeth River
Bares her boulders, like teeth, there was never
A more awful old castle to look at.

Each embrasure and cold crenellation
Hosted hordes of the avian nation,
Gaunt and cawing, and boding misfortune.

On a lower declivity lying
Was a lair, where a dragon was spying.
It was six-legged, wool-covered, reddish.

Pitchy-black was the lord of the palace—
Having claws that went well with his malice,
And a flexible tail, always hidden.

He lived modestly, never austerely,
And his neighbors would tell you sincerely,
"He's the Devil, quite simply the Devil."

Of these neighbors I'll note, in addition,
That their hides had attracted suspicion:
A hyena, a werewolf, a raven.

Once they met by Elizabeth River
When the moonlight was merely a sliver,
To play dominoes—dominoes, really.

Quiver

And the time went so pleasantly, quickly,
That a single small thistle-grain thickly—
No, a nettle it was—grew and flourished.

Before Adam, occurred this adventure,
Before God ... Only Brahma would venture
To be boss, and he looked through his fingers.

Let them live as they wish—never worry!
But one night slept together the furry
Scary werewolf and hairy hyena.

And their offspring—bird?—cat?—duly born in
Greatest haste on the following morning,
Was a welcome new family member.

So they gathered quite early, quite proudly,
Having howled by the river quite loudly,
And expecting their common amusement.

Well, they played, and they played, so intently,
Such a game was too much, evidéntly:
They were stupefied, breathless, exhausted.

And the child, for a prize, got some money,
And a bottomless barrel of honey,
And the fields, and the lands, and the castle.

And he cried as he puffed out his chest,
"Go away, I'm the boss, I'm the best:
You get nothing! I'm keeping my winnings.

One thing more: with a will that's unflagging,
To the lair where I first met the dragon
I will take, and will dump, my old mother."

Second night, by Elizabeth River,
Such a carriage of black you will never
Have envisioned—within it, the Devil.

And behind it the others were lagging—
Sick and worried, their feet they were dragging,
Coughing softly, lamenting and whining.

One was bragging, one angry, one grieving.
Then came Adam, you'd best be believing.—
God save Adam and Eve from such mischief!

178. Naples

Waves, enameled, gleam like fire—
Wingéd crimson sunset-flare
Over each cathedral spire—
Harpies darting through the air.
But the ancient city dirt
Will delight the tourist less:
Hardly can the walker, hurt,
Love the golden ugliness.

Lemon-, fish-aroma rise—
Pérfume of a Parisienne
(Parasol to shade her eyes)

Quiver

With a shrimp jar—two rough men,
Near a dung-heap, cut their bread.
Salvatore Rosa caught
This vignette, one might have said,
Drew it on the very spot.

Here it isn't warm: from sea
Tow-haired hazes brought a shade.
Midnight—people don't feel free
Yet to enter in the glade
Which the gray and menacing
Cliffs embrace, a wreath of rocks,
Where malaria is king—
Frenzied, yellow-faced, it mocks.

Like a bird with pipe in beak,
Lifting up its hackles, crest,
Heav'nward splatter will bespeak
Old Vesuvius, moved in rest.
Climbing to the zenith, cloud
Steeds will stamp. But he'll ignore
All—a homeless beggar, bowed,
He will sulk and smoke and snore.

179. Spinster

Life is sad, its anguish great—
Wide indifference appalls:
Every ornamental plate,
Parlor vase, the frames on walls—

Dead. These pages—dusty, gray,
That I'm riffling listlessly;
Knights in novels, every day,
Fall in love, but not with me.

Yet my mirror seems to show
Someone different, as I pass:
I, a moonlit naiad, go
Gliding on the liquid glass.

In a medieval gloom
I'm a princess who, astir,
Learns about her beauty's bloom
From a page who flatters her.

At a banquet, in Versailles,
While the world is slumbering,
Handsome men despondent lie.
I'm the idol of the king!

My romances next entwine
The Parisian demi-monde—
Poets, long-haired, leonine,
Write me strophes noble-toned!

I'm a Lady! I will be
A devoted, spiteful wife—
And my dream, decidedly,
I'll not alter in my life:

QUIVER

When that life will start to tire—
Galloping upon a horse
Death will come, with rose of fire
On his armored breast, of course.

180. Postal Clerk

She's gone ... Blue lilacs, ag'd,
Have withered from the tree.
And ev'n the siskin, caged,
Is weeping over me.

The worries that would hárass
Our lives, fool siskin, are
In vain. She's now in Paris,
Berlin, or somewhere far.

More frightening than bogeys
This honor to the fair—
'Tis not for us, old fogeys,
The runaway to snare.

In church, the grizzled reader
With stovepipe hat askew,
Big, bony, thin, and meager,
Will come: it's tea for two.

His wife her life had left,
The world had worn her out.
We'll chat, as friends, bereft,
Do always, I've no doubt.

Our cup of woe is full—
There's nothing more to mull;
Life is unlivable—
The mind is clouded, dull.

Let, spirit-lifting, swell
A melody at hand:
"Farewell!—ah yes, farewell
Predicts a different land."

181. The Sick Woman

Delirium tormént s me with a sense
Of lines extending on, unendingly,
While, summoning an emptiness immense,
The church bell's ringing, unrelentingly …

It seems to me that, after death, like this,
With teasing, testing hope of resurrection,
The eyes will open to a circling mist
And search for objects known from recollection.

But in the ocean of the primal tangles,
Appear no voice, no grass, no flower-blooms,
But only cubes, and rhombuses, and angles—
With evil and unintermittent *booms*.

If only sleep would bear me far away!
I'd hope to go, as to a feast of healing,
To yellow sands where sea waves, grayish, play—
To count the big brown boulders, hard, unfeeling.

QUIVER

182. Ode to D'Annunzio
on his appearance in Genoa

Again the she-wolf on the pillar
Will roar in fires of crimson light:
The future Italy's fulfiller
Must ever be her poet bright.

Augustus' age was lofty, and
Knew golden lines of poetry:
More tranquil than the rivers grand
Old Vergil spoke with Italy.

Sad times arrived, and it was then
That foes would knock on every door.
One left his civil work—of men
Most homeless: Dante—exiled, poor.

At length brought low, the country 'round
Was soon to know a celebration—
Torquato's body duly crowned
With laurel, fit though late laudation.

In these—how wondrous!—days of war,
To which I bow in deep devotion,
And which would Alexander or
An Agamemnon cross the ocean

If but to envy, now when all
The best in us comes out of hiding,
And power rises, there will fall
Our fetters, many years abiding.

The words, "Arise, great Rome, and take
Your rifles, children of great sadness,"
May be our thunder: they can make
A crowd a sea of swelling gladness.

Cerulean swaddling-cloth or shroud,
The sea lay 'round us, might and glory
Of Italy, shield sacred, proud,
Of free men famed in ancient story.

Cold mountains in the upper sky—
Unknown, such force, and enigmatic—
The forest-lightnings ripen—high,
Keen thunders hide, kept vital, vatic.

Great steed that, rising, prancing, rears,
The folk believe in truth and light,
Entrust their fate, throughout the years,
To poets, with a proud delight.

The song that one abroad can sense
Proclaims the fact that free men áre
Embodying the elements—
The flame, the water—wind from far.

Nikolay Gumilev

183. Trees

I know that to the trees, and not to us,
The grandeur of a rounded life is granted:
To earth, star-gentle sister generous,
We are the strangers—they at home are planted.

In depth of autumn, in an empty field,
Bright lessons they can learn, of coloration:
Dawn-amber, bronze-red dusk, instruction yield
To this green, pleasant, peaceful population.

You'll many a stately Mary find, a palm—
Or Moses in the oak ... A soul may surely
Transmit a message to another—calm
Their call, by streaming water sent, securely.

Corroding diamonds deep below the ground
Break up the granite—springs are babbling quickly—
They'll chant and shout if any elm is downed,
Or sycamore with leafage covered thickly.

I feel, if I could find a quiet land
Where never would I need to cry or sing—
I'd—wordless—want with lofty height to stand
Multimillennially sheltering.

Pyre

184. Andrei Rublyov

I've gained a sweet-strong knowledge and
Am grounded in monastic art:
The face of woman's like the land
The Lord had promised to the heart.

Her nose compare to sapling stem;
Her fine, twin eyebrows, curved and tender—
They're bending—you may liken them
To gentle palm fronds, rounded, slender.

Owl-wise, prophetic sirens are
The eyes—their depth unseen can sing
Enchanted narratives afar,
And secrets of the spirit ring.

Her open brow—the arch of sky;
The curls that, cloudlike, stray beneath—
A seraph coming, soft and shy,
May touch them, like a holy wreath.

Above the tree's white pedestal,
Her lips—a paradisal flow'r
Where Eve, bold mother of us all,
A law broke—in a primal bow'r.

Rublyov, whose brush attained all praise,
Had taught me—gone the cry and strife!
He led me onto lighter ways
And godly blessing lent my life.

Nikolay Gumilev

185. Autumn

The heavens are flaring red-orange …
Rumbustious and brusque, wind a-swaying
The berries, the bloody-red rowan.
I urge on the horse's careering:
The orangery—we'll go past it,
The glasswall, the lattice, the railing
Of park and of pond, swans a-gliding
Alongside—while, ruddy and shaggy,
Is running my dog, my companion,
Who's dearer to me than my brother,
And whom I will always remember
Long after the day of his passing.
The sound of each hoofbeat is hastened—
    The dust rising higher.
How hard to keep up with a horse of
The purest Arabian blood!
We'll have to sit down, exhausted,
To rest on a rock, wide and flat—
    To wonder, dully,
        At red-orange heavens,
    To wind dully listen—
    Piercingly shrieking.

186. Childhood

As a child I loved to be facing
Big fields, air-honeyed, full—
Dry grasses, interlacing,
And, among them, the horns of a bull.

PYRE

By the roadway, bushes dusty
Would cry, "I'm teasing you:
Be careful with me, or my trusty
Branches may pierce you through!"

But the autumn west-wind, savage,
Would bluster and halt the play.
What a happy feeling of ravage!
I thought I'd die right away—

Not alone, but with friends arising—
Fool-stepmother not left out—
And beyond the last horizon,
I would grasp what life's about.

The rougher and riskier playing—
Warlike!—I'll never refuse!
Blood's not more sacred, I'm saying,
Than the grasses' emerald juice.

187. Small Town

Over a calm, wide river
Well cinched by a bridge, for ages
A small town stood. It was never
Mentioned in chronicle-pages.

I know that in this town
Human life is real,
Like a boat that is guided down
To its goal—that's what I feel.

Nikolay Gumilev

The stripy columns stand
By the guardhouse, where soldiers march
To the blaring trumpet-command
Like lunatics—life is harsh.

At bazaars you'll find all sorts:
Madmen, gypsies, transients;
They buy and sell, of course—
And the preachers go off on tangents.

In Samarkand-kerchiefs bright,
In their homes, where such order I see,
Wait modest wives, pale white,
But their eyes are dark as can be.

Each gas-lamp—comes the night—
In the governor's palace blazes.
What a stallion—the guiding light
Of the nobles: he amazes.

In springtime, hidden—since
'Tis a churchyard—the young find bliss.
A winsome whisper: "My prince!"
And above a tomb—a kiss.

A cross on the church looks down,
Embleming Fatherly eyes—
A mellow chime will sound
In language human, wise.

188. Ice Drift

Already are the islands dressed
In March-transparent greenery;
Nevá, more fickle than we guessed,
May frown again, though, frowardly.

Stand on the bridge—and look straight down:
The ice floes leap and play and push—
Green-copper, poison, they won't drown:
Like rustling horrid snakes they rush.

Geographers, in troubled dreams,
View frightful things no man can love:
They trace the outlined shadow-schemes
Of unknown continents that move.

There is a smell of mushrooms, raw—
And other odors, not yet strong,
As if we a cadaver saw,
With beetles scampering along.

The river's ill—it, frothing, raves.
Yet confident, within the lairs,
To sense a coming thaw that saves,
How pleasant for the polar bears!

They've come to know it isn't real—
Their weighty, dull imprisonment:
The Arctic Ocean, filled with zeal,
Flows, for their liberation sent.

189. Nature

Well that's the way that nature is—
Although the soul may think it harsh:
The honeyed meadow-fragrances
With odors mingle from the marsh.

The wild cries of the wind, come early,
Are like the moan of wolves in crowds—
What leaps above the pine-tops curly?
Alone the patchy, piebald clouds.

In shadows, bad extrinsecations,
When gripped with anger, I can view
The meager, scant variegations
Of seed-germs the Creator threw.

Say, earth! why joke and play with me?
Become the being that you are:
Throw off the rags of beggary
And rise, fire-penetrated star!

190. You and Me

Yes, I know, we are not well suited,
I don't favor the tame guitar—
Far away my desires are rooted,
I sing songs to the wild zurnah.

Pyre

Not for me the salon, dark dresses,
High-class ballroom and high-toned crowds—
I write poems in wildernesses,
Chant to waterfall, dragon, clouds.

I'm an Arab when heat is raging!
Falling prostrate on shore, he drinks—
Not a knight who, his love assuaging,
Waiting, looks at the stars and thinks.

I won't die on a bed, surrounded
By dull doctors and notaries—
Some ravine, in a land unbounded,
Ivy-cushioned, provides fine ease.

I won't head for a heaven neatened,
Proper—Protestant—welcoming.
No, my afterlife's glory-sweetened—
Brigand, publican, whore will sing!

191. Dragon

In the days when the sky and the earth
Were enchanters, the magic was stronger—
Marvels marvelous coming to birth,
Wonders wondrous—we'll see them no longer.

When the rumbling ravines of Cathay
And the great Golden Horde were forgot,
Wingéd dragon!—in garden he lay,
And would hide, on May nights, in a grot.

When the maidens, to look at the moon,
Would approach with tread gentle and measured,
He would seize one, shoot upward, and soon
Disappear—then return, at his pleasure.

How he glittered and blinded and burned—
Armored snake—in the moon's greedy light!
Over woods of Old Russia, he yearned
And would cry—silver toned—in his flight:

"These delectable maidens, so fair,
With complexion more pale than a swan,
Do not breathe our sublunary air
Overseas, in the East, or beyond—

But not one of them ever could be
In Lahore, in my manor-home splendid:
When we're crossing the Caspian Sea,
They'll get ill—and their days will be ended!

They are crazy indeed!—to prefer
To repose with the sea-beasts that crouch,
Not to rest with their mighty seigneur
On his regal, luxuriant couch.

So I envy the shepherd's fine fate
When with shepherdess-maiden he'll toy
On a meadow where, early and late,
He'll make jokes that a girl may enjoy."

Pyre

Having heard the lament, Prince Volgah
Found a cord. To his bison-horns, bent,
He attached it—and then, aiming far,
From that bowstring an arrow he sent.

192. Peasant

Thicket and marshes before us,
River the color of tin,
Mossy, dark huts in the forest—
Odd, every peasant within.

Here's such a man in a region
Roadless, with feather-grass wild:
Cries of Stribogue!—winds are legion—
Tale he was told as a child.

Here, long ago, the impulsive
Pécheneg paused, and then passed:
River-smells raw the emulsive
Rot in the shallows amassed.

Now, with his backpack, he's singing,
Walking the not-trodden ways—
Tunes, long and languidly ringing,
Filled with the mischief he'll raise.

Varied his path—bright, then darker—
Fields hear him whistling, it seems;
Quarrel, then bloody brawl, starker—
Tavern more fierce than your dreams.

Nikolay Gumilev

Into our capital vaunted,
Entering—Help! Lord Who saves!—
He has ensorceled and haunted
Russia's mad empress who raves.

Childlike and smiling and charming—
Mild yet conniving, his chat—
Now he will show—foes alarming—
Gold royal cross—quick as *that*!

How can they still remain standing
Straight, not destroyed by their loss?—
Isaac Cathedral, commanding,
Topped by a woebegone cross!

Over the capital, shaken,
Gunshot! and cry of alarm:
Here may a lioness waken,
Shielding her babies from harm.

"Christian! Believer! No matter
Whether my body you burn—
After my ashes you scatter,
Where will the orphan child turn?"

Wretched the region surrounding …
Many such peasants abound.
Roads are already resounding:
Trembles—with treading!—the ground.

PYRE

193. Worker

There he stands, before a searing furnace:
Old he is, and of a middling height,
Seeming tranquil, though he's made to turn his
Blinking reddish eyes to blinding light.

Friend and comrade—all of them are sleeping.
He alone, alert, a man of worth,
Molds a bullet that will soon be sweeping
Me away from life upon the earth.

Now, his eye asparkle, he is finished.
He can leave. The moon shines overhead.
Tired, but with a bliss yet undiminished,
Warm, his wife awaits him in their bed.

Over the Dvinah, gray-foaming river,
Whistling by, the bullet he had cast
Fated aim will seek—foreknown forever—
Reach my breast, and enter it at last.

I'll be falling—destined—as when dreaming,
Feel my lifetime in a moment pass—
Blood upsprung outgush—then see it streaming
Over dusty, trampled, faded grass.

God, in fullest measure, will reward me
For my brief and bitter years. At night
I can see the bullet coming toward me,
Molded by a man of middling height.

Nikolay Gumilev

194. Sweden

Land of a chill that, rousing, calls—
Of sounding wood and mountain, where
Disheveled, tousled waterfalls
Alarming roar in upper air—

Land to which we are ever grateful,
Do you remember yet the day
When stern Varangians their fateful
Trip underwent, that led our way?

What meant the bronzen targe's fate—
To witness hateful injury—
And then at golden King's-Town gate
Forgot by brave Olyég to be?

Why, in a wild, a torment-raving
Again appeared, as yesterday,
Your strong and gloried sister, saving
With aid to conquer fear, dismay?

And did your winds, fresh, unresisted,
In vain reveal a sweeter truth?
In vain can Ryúrik have assisted
Slav, Pécheneg, of Rus's youth?

PYRE

195. Norwegian Mountains

I cannot ever comprehend you, mountains—
Is it a hymn you chant, or blasphemy?
While staring down to view cold lakes and fountains,
Are you absorbed in prayer? sorcery?

Here, with the cry of savage desecrations—
How like a Satan on a steed of fire!—
On an enchanted deer his levitations
Peer Gynt accomplished, climbing ever higher.

The unacknowledged heir of worldly glory,
The man whom only principle might claim,
Was it not Brand who, preacher minatory,
Moved avalanches with the Maker's Name?

Eternal snow, more blue than any chalice
Of sapphire-stone! You are a land like ours—
A treasure-home of ice, a winter palace—
But nothing bring to birth in frozen bowers.

Yet marvels are the faces made of dreaming:
Their curls are snow, hell-ent'ring holes their eyes,
And down the cheeks that storms erode, a streaming
Wide waterfall, and beard of mountain wise.

Nikolay Gumilev

196. On the North Sea

Oh yes, we're of the race
Of olden conquerors!—
Who raised on the Northern Sea
Broad, decorated sails
And leapt out from the longboats
On level Norman shore—
Invading ancient princedoms
While bearing flame and death.

More than a hundred years
We've ranged around the world,
We roam, and blow our trumpets,
We wander, beat our drums:
"And don't we need strong arms,
And don't we need firm hearts?
Is not red blood demanded
By monarch, or republic?"

> Hey, boy, go get us
> Good wine, and quickly!
> Málaga, port-wine,
> And, best of all, whiskey!
> Say, whát's over there?
> A boat under water,
> A floating weapon?
> For that—you need sailors!

Oh yes, we're of the race
Of olden conquerors—
We roam about forever,
Storming from towers high,

PYRE

Drowning in gray-waved oceans,
And with our wilding blood
Quenching a drunkard-thirst—
Iron, steel, and lead.

Although in different dialects
Poets may shape their songs
In western land and eastern—
And though the monks are praying
In Athens and Madrid

As candles go down before God—
Yet still the women dream
Of us, and us alone.

197. Stockholm

Disordered, disturbed was the dream; for no reason
It rose from the depth of an era long gone,
An odd dream of Stockholm—though sad, nearly
      pleasing—
Upsetting and and baffling—and then it moved on ...

It seemed like a feast day—the memory's fading ...
I heard a big bell—a big bell—the tones poured!
The city, an organ—sound louder, upbraiding—
And shaking. It prayed, and it rumbled—and roared.

As if I had wished to be louder and clearer
To preach a bold word, on a hilltop I stood:

Calm, quietened water I saw—'twas a mirror—
The groves all around—and the fields, and the wood.

"O Lord!" I cried out in distress, "Tell me whý here
I find myself—surely the land of my birth?
For did I not love here, and did I not die here,
Upon this green, sunny, blest part of the earth?"

I knew I had strayed and for ages had wandered
In passages, blinded, of space and of time.
Though someplace were flowing dear rivers, I
> pondered
The path, now cut off, that I never would find.

198. Creativity

Born of my word, the giants
Guzzled their wine all night.
The word was crimson—defiance
Made it a threat, a fright.

If *my* blood they had drunk,
I'd surely have been less wan.
To sleep I had finally sunk,
Stroked by the fingers of dawn.

I woke on the darkening leas.
High swamp-fog—it was late.
A warm and worried breeze
Breathed from the southern gate.

PYRE

Suddenly, with a sigh,
I rued the empty day
I'd lost—it had passed me by
On its self-determined way ...

To run, catch up with the light!
But I lack the strength to tear
My notebook of the night—
Whatever the visions there ...

199. Solace

Hearing wonder-sound,
Sensing lilies white,
Lying underground,
That is your delight;

Lying underground,
Viewing endless light:
Seraph wings abound,
Snow-hues charm the sight.

You are dying, yes—
Cold your arms and hands;
You the spring can't guess
Of unearthly lands.

By my pow'r of prayer
Heaven waits for you;
Soon will you be there—
What I swear is true.

200. Prememory

And that is life! A whirling, singing—
The sea, the city, wilderness;
All things reflected flittings flinging—
Forever lost to emptiness.

A flame is flaring, trumpets blaring,
And restless, reddish horses fly.
Arousing lips their joy unsparing
Aver, affirm: delight is nigh.

And now my woe, as earlier—
And old allurements—come again:
The gray-maned sea with whirl and whirr,
The cities, and the desert plain.

Revived, I'll be myself, the "I"
Arising from a lifelong dream—
A Hindu that would, dozing, lie
On holy night beside a stream?

201. First Canzona

Many the seas of the world have I swum:
    Frolicking, foaming, and old
Oceans; how often would caravans come:
    Many-day travels untold.

How we would laugh in those seasons gone by!
    Muse, to the height we would mount.
Free as a flock, rhyme and rhythm would fly:
    Memory cannot recount.

PYRE

Love never left me: her heavenly strings—
    Harp of an angel—would call,
Piercing the spirit with needle-thin stings—
    Eden-blue light over all.

Now you alone are my lot—wide awake,
    Watching the sun of the night,
Days in the world I remain for your sake—
    You are my life and my light.

You're the Jerusalem pilgrims would view:
    Calm to the worried you teach.
I must acquire, using words about you,
    Six-wingéd seraphim-speech.

202. Second Canzona

Lord, your temple is in the skies,
Yet you dwell in the world as well.
Hear, in woods, on the linden rise
From the birdsong a heaven-swell!

As our carillon comes the spring,
Sweeping over the happy meads—
Sleeping, souls hear the voices ring,
Angel-tone that the spirit needs.

If, O Lord, You confirm it so,
If my song can the truth instill,
Grant a sign that will let me know
That I aptly have grasped your will.

Please appear to the one who grieves,
You whose form is the Unviewed Light:
Hear her pleas, ere the vision leaves—
Grant an answer beyond our sight.

Sweeter far than the birds aloft,
Than an angel-apocalypse,
Are her eyelashes, trembling, soft,
And the smile of her well-loved lips.

203. Third Canzona

How nature's uproar lightens!
Nothing but hearing and sight.
Our final freedom frightens,
But our spirit seeks it aright.

The earth will forget the ruin
That fighter and merchant made;
The Druids will be pursuing
Their truth in the verdant shade.

The Druids will be meeting
To guide all hearts to the heights,
Like angel, comet, leading
To a goal beyond their lights.

I then will cry, "But where
Are *you*, my fiery being?
I sing the selfsame air—
Unchanged, my way of seeing.

I am your beauty's servant,
Partaking of your pow'r:
You are my ardor fervent;
Light of the final hour."

204. Victory of Samothrace

When thoughts in fevered nighttime race,
You bold appear before the eyes:
O Victory of Samothrace,
With arms outspread to claim the prize.

The nightly quiet shies away:
My thoughts, a gyroscope, awhirl—
Blind, wingéd flight that none can stay,
Illimitable skiey swirl.

Within your gazing, mad and bright,
A something laughs, while filled with flame:
Our shadows, fleeing, seek the night—
To follow us they're yet too tame.

205. Rose

The rush of pleasing flowers and of song
Is now forbidden (antiquated dreaming!)
To poets. Only pure and virgin-seeming
Words are allowed, that cannot lead to wrong.

This rose, brought here to the hotel not long
Ago and then "forgotten" by intention,
Left on a book of lyrical invention,
Rudel's canzonas, medieval song,

Called for a sonnet, honor not amiss:
The book had shown again the strength of love,
Both in the thirteenth century and this.

On petal-velvet if my lips may rove
(More sad than death, more heightening than wine)
Perhaps I do not quite commit a crime?

206. Telephone

Unexpected, confident,
It's a woman on the phone—
Sweetest harmonies unpent
In her voice—no form, all tone.

Now I needn't feel so grim
When you leave and I'm alone:
Like the lute of seraphim
Is your telephonic tone.

207. South

Because I once again have felt
Calm, since my liberty has died,
Of all most bright, and smooth, and svelte,
I'm hearing nature, mild, confide.

Pyre

Plunged into sultry summer light,
I'm wildly glad to see the sun—
Of all most clear, and svelte, and white,
Uninterrupted crickets hum.

On glimpsing foam-drift thrown aloft
By silver swell of ocean surf,
Of all most white, and live, and soft,
Memory's musing in her mirth.

Night, sail outspread and dark yet clear,
Is gliding—through the sky she streams:
Of all most calm, and soft, and dear,
Whisper the colored wings of dreams.

208. Star Scatterer

Alien, proud—not always are you so
And ... not always telling me to go.

Softly, dreamily, and quietly,
You may even come, at times, to me.

Tresses lie quite thickly on your brow:
I am not allowed to kiss them now.

Burning are your eyes—how large and bright!—
Each a magical and lunar light.

Tender friend, relentless enemy,
Blest is every step you take, to me.

Nikolay Gumilev

On my heart you step, in nightly hours,
When you scatter stars and colored flowers.

I where you acquired them cannot know ...
Why do you with such a brightness glow

That whoever wants to be with you
Finds the time for love on earth is through?

209. About You

About *you*, about *you*, about *you*—
But not me: here I've nothing to do.
In humanity's fate-darkened night
You're the bright-wingéd cry to the height.

Like an ancient and prized coat-of-arms—
Thus your heart, proud and noble. Our days
You made sacred. No fatal alarms
Can affright us poor mortals. All praise!

Should the stars, in their brightness and pride,
Turn away from the Earth that they serve,
Yet her loftier objects abide—
She will keep your brave gaze in reserve.

If the seraph's own trumpet of gold
Should announce that our time's at an end,
Your white kerchief, our guard, we will hold
Out before him, our lives to defend.

PYRE

When the trumpet-tones tremble and die
And the seraph in ruin must lie ...
About *you*, about *you*, about *you*—
But not me—here I've nothing to do.

210. Dream

I groaned in a dream malignant,
For it seemed—by the pow'rs above!—
You'd been hurt (I felt indignant!)
By another man—whom you love!

I awoke and jumped out of bed,
Like a killer escaped from the block.
The lamplight was dully shed
As from animal eyes that mock.

There was never more hopeless blight
Than my homelessness would shed
On the darkened street that night
Like a dried-up riverbed.

I am waiting in front of your door:
I've nowhere else to go.
But I never will dare to implore
Admittance, that much I know.

He hurt you—I understand—
In a *dream*, but, all the same ...
I am dying, while I stand
By your tight-shut windowpane.

NIKOLAY GUMILEV

211. Ezbekeeyeh

How strange—ten years, already, passing by
Since I had visited at Ezbekeeyeh—
A Cairo garden, large, by full-grown moon
Triumphantly illumined on that evening.

I had been feeling tortured by a woman.
Neither the salty vigor-wind from sea
Nor murmur from exotic trade-bazaars,
Nothing had any strength to comfort me.
I had begun to pray to God for death
And was prepared, myself, to bring it near.

This garden, though, in every way was like
The holy groves the early world had known:
Thin palm-trees raised their branches to the heights,
Like virgins, whom the Lord might favor soon—
On hillocks, the prophetic Druids stood—
In crowded majesty—the plantain trees.

A waterfall was whitening the gloom,
As if a rhino on two legs might stand;
Nocturnal butterflies would flit about
Among the flowers growing straight and tall,
Or, 'mid the stars—the stellar height seemed low—
Barberries, ripened, might the glows have been.

I shouted—I remember—"Worse than woe,
More deep than death is life! Accept, O Lord,

Pyre

The oath I freely give: whatever happens,
Whatever grievances, humiliations
May come my way, I never will consider
Again the thought of light and easy death
Until the moonlit night when I return
To see the plantain, palm of Ezbekeeyeh."

How odd—ten years, precisely, now have gone,
And yet I can't stop thinking of the palm-trees,
Or of the plantains, or the waterfall,
That standing rhino in the whitened mist …
Then, suddenly, I'll glance about me, hearing
In windy rushing, or in distant talking,
And in the horrifying nighttime quiet,
A single word of wonder: Ezbekeeyeh.

Yes, only ten years gone—but, somber stranger,
I must depart again, must lay my gaze on
The sea, the clouds, and all the foreign faces—
All things that can no longer flatter me—
Then to that garden go, repeat the promise,
Or say that I quite faithfully have kept it
And now am free …

PORCELAIN PAVILION

Nikolay Gumilev

CHINA

212. Porcelain Pavilion

Arose in artificial lake
A porcelain pavilion white
With convex bridge, like tiger spine
That leads to it, of jasper made.

To this pavilion, friends have come,
In festive clothing brightly dressed—
From cups, with dragon patterns fine,
They drink a wine that's freshly mulled.

They happily will talk awhile,
And write their verses after that,
Each wearing yellow well-cocked hat
And rolled-up sleeves, in working style.

We see, upon the clear-waved lake,
A bridge, concave, a jasper moon,
Where friends, with cups their helpful boon,
A topsy-turvy picture make.

213. Moon on the Sea

The moon from height of clifftops willed to float
And with translucent yellow filled the sea—
The friends are drinking, on the sharp-prowed boat,
Their well-warmed wine, but not too hurriedly.

Porcelain Pavilion

Observing how the clouds are passing, light,
The lunar column, mirrored in the sea,
One dreamy comrade feels the objects might
A train of Bogdykhanian women be.

But others think: to groves of heaven go
The shades of pious men, from earth set free—
A third opinion's heard: the upward flow
Of swans—a flying caravan—they see.

214. Heart so joyful ...

Heart so joyful, my soul is a-flying:
Light the boat that the lake-water laves,
Floating over the swell of the waves—
Move from dawn to the sundown replying,
Mirrored hill-view the spirit awakes,
Opened onto the purest of lakes.

Thousand days of a grieving insistence
Heartbeat speeded, as animal-chased,
Soul had yearned for a never-known distance,
Wanted more ... By a heaven-beam graced,
Mirrored hill-view the spirit awakes,
Opened onto the purest of lakes.

215. Nature

The little lake, in tranquil rest—
A cup well filled with water calm.

Bamboo appears a group of huts,
The trees are like a sea of reeds.

Sharp-bordered crags pagodas are:
They're looking down on flower-blooms.

It cheers me up to think how much
Eternal Nature learnt from us.

216. Road

Before me I beheld a road.
In shade, the straggling oaks among.
Ah, such a lovely little road
Along the fence, 'mid flowers flung.

I glanced and felt an anguished load.
While on the path a mist appeared ...
To stones I gratitutde had owed—
They each felt near me, and endeared.

Should I bestride the road—why dare?
I know it nevermore can lead
To where I cannot breathe, and where
My dearest one is trapped, indeed.

The day that she was born, in chains
Of iron they her legs had placed:
All roads to her made foreign—pains
In shade of outspread bough she faced.

The day that she was born, her heart
In iron fetter they'd confine.
The one I love—how harsh that art!—
I know can never now be mine.

217. The Mandarin's Three Wives

Legal Wife

In the goblet deep, some wine remains,
There are swallow-nests upon the plate ...
To his legal wife the mandarin
From the meal's beginning showed respect.

Concubine

In the goblet deep, some wine remains,
On the platter, goose that's big and fat.
Should the mandarin no children have,
These the concubine will glad supply.

Servant Girl

In the goblet deep, some wine remains,
On the platter, plenty of preserves.
For the mandarin, you do your best,
Yet he wants another girl each day.

Nikolay Gumilev

Mandarin

Wine in goblet deep no more remains,
On the plate but one red feather lies.
Quiet, stupid chatterboxes all,
Stop your laughing at a poor old man.

218. Happiness

My boat is brand-new, of the reddest of wood,
    And look at my flute—all of jasper.

The water is cleaning the silk from a spot,
    And wine cleansed the fear from my heart.

If you but possess a nice, light-floating craft,
    Made better with wine and a woman,

What more could you want? You're in every respect
    The same as a genie in heaven.

219. Unifying

The moon's arising in the nightly heaven:
It's bright and, deep in love, relaxing, tranquil.

Across the lake at evening wind-breeze wanders,
The water kissing, filling it with gladness.

How blessed is the holy, kind uniting
Of friends who were created for each other.

But people who were fashioned for each other
United are, we know, alas! too rarely.

220. Stranger

Stranger, far away from your homeland,
Money gone, and bereft of friends,
Never you, in your search for music,
Hear the tongue of maternal joy.

Yet there's nature, so dazzling, blinding—
I consider you lucky still.
Tuneful birds, in the branches nesting—
Speech like this, can it alien be?

Merely hearing the flute of autumn,
Overpouring cicada chirr,
Merely viewing a cloud in heaven,
Spreading, stretching, and dragon-long—

Comprehending the grief unending
Gathered up in your heart till now,
You in thought will be homeward rushing,
Aiding eyes by enframing hands.

Nikolay Gumilev

221. The Poet

I heard: from the garden a woman was singing,
  But I—I was watching the moon.

So, now, of the singer I couldn't be thinking—
  The cloud-favored moon was my love.

No stranger I've been to the deity splendid,
  Responsive am I to her glance.

No branch of a tree, neither bat flown above me
  Could ever conceal me from her.

At eyes of the poets oblivious of women
  The moon is delighted to gaze,

As onto the radiant scales of the dragons,
  Each holy, a bard of the sea.

222. Home

The home where I played in my childhood
A merciless fire has burnt down.

I got on a boat that was golden,
My woe for awhile to forget.

A flute, with its wondrous adornment,
I played, to the moon at her height.

But quickly with cloud she was covered—
The moon—I had made her too sad.

Then back I returned to my grieving,
Yet couldn't recall any song.

It seemed all the joy of my childhood
Had gone up in smoke with my home.

I, too, was desirous of dying—
I lightly inclined toward the sea.

But into the boat slid a woman
By moonlight that newly appeared.

And if she is eager and willing,
And, too, if the moon will allow,

I'll get back my home, build a new one
Within her unknowable heart.

INDOCHINA

223. Annám

The moon is encompassed by heav'n
Spread out in a wonder-huge way,
'Mid thicket-bamboo is the wind
And, fragrance conveying, the air,
Surrounding the family blest.

The elders take tea in the grove,
And drink, while they lyrics declaim ...
A ruckus they hear from the house
Where children are active at play—
A newborn is crying, and loud.

The one who can lead such a life
Knows blessing perfected, entire.
To him, what are money and fame?
A faith he maintains: to survive
He must, for the children's dear sake.

224. Girls

The girls are fond of rupees,
With birds on them engraven:
They'll leave their parents gladly—
Go off to follow Frenchmen.

225. Song of a Child

Why do beetles have so red a mouth—
Hasn't this one chewed a lot of betel?
Let the one come quickly who is wanting
To become my father's wife and helper!
Dad will make her welcome with a greeting,
Serve her rice, and certainly won't hit her—
Mother, though, will surely rip her eyes out,
Grab her guts and tear them from her belly.

Porcelain Pavilion

226. Laos

Girl, your cheeks are tender, gentle, blest,
Then—soft restful hill for me, your breast.

Love me, girl, and we will go away—
Then forever we'll together stay.

Pick a swift and light pirogue—you can!
Meanwhile I will map a travel plan.

You can ride an elephant, and I'll
Be your true karnák; you'll ride in style.

If you say you'd like to be the moon
I'll be cloud, and playful mood attune.

If you'd rather turn liana-vine,
I'll be bird or ape you may entwine.

If you'd like to look from mountaintop
Down the pit, and estimate the drop,

Folks might tie my feet in iron bond—
Still I'd climb to reach you, and beyond!

Yet—it's all in vain, my wistful thinking—
Into bitter torture I'll be sinking,

Knowing you don't love me, I will die
Like a youthful bull deprived of grass—

Not a single kiss for such as I,
Of your fresh pink tender cheek, alas.

NIKOLAY GUMILEV

227. Kkha

Where are you gone, pretty girls—
You, who can never reply—
Leaving me always behind,
Stuck with a weakening voice,
Rousing an echo too loud?

Or, have the tigers devoured you?
Or have your lovers entrapped you?
Pretty girls, answer me, answer!
Filled with my love, to the forest
I have gone searching for you.

Reaching a hilltop, I saw you...
Naked you played by the lakeside—
Down I came racing—forgetting
You are the daughters of moonlight,
I am the raven's black son.

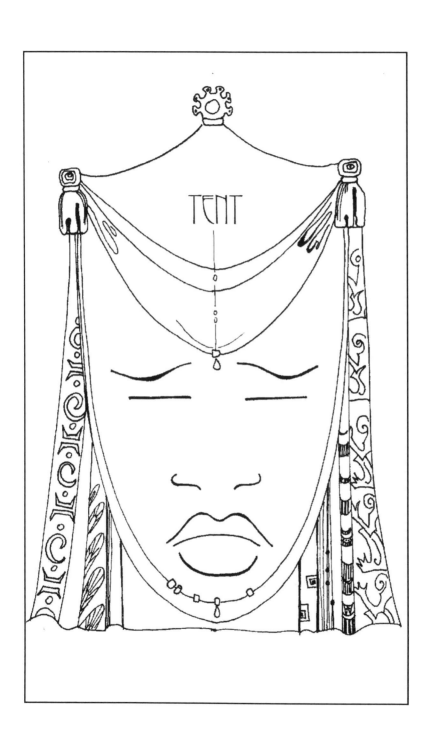

Nikolay Gumilev

228. Introduction

Ever deafened by trampling and roaring,
And enshrouded with flame and with haze,
There are whispers, O Africa, soaring
In the sky where the seraphim blaze.

When they read your evangel, invested
With such wonder and awe and affright,
They recall the young angel, untested,
You were lent, to bring order and light.

I will tell of your deeds—a fantasia
I'll portray—and of creature-sprites there
On the ancient, great tree of Eurasia
Where you hang, ripe gargantuan pear.

I'm predestined to speak to you, chaunting
Of your leaders in leopard-skin, who
In a forest, their victory vaunting,
Lead the hordes of the warriors through.

Immemorial idols are smiling,
With a laughter that bodes little good,
While the lions, their victims beguiling,
Later tail-whip their ribs in the wood.

May my journey be smooth and unruffled.
Where no roads are, I pray that a river,
In the jungles where language is muffled,
May be named in my honor, forever.

Tent

And—a great, signal mercy for me
Looking forward to heaven, the blest—
Let me die by the sycamore tree
Where the Virgin and Christ had known rest.

229. Red Sea

I salute you, Red Sea, giant fish-broth of sharks,
Broadest bath-pool of black men, hot kettle of sand!
On your high-rising banks are no damp, mossy
      parks:
Limestone crags—giant petrified cactuses—stand.

On your islands embraced by a blistering sand,
Quite forgot by the tide when it swells in the night
Are the beasts of the sea—tritons, desperate, grand—
Where the swordfish make octopods die in a fight.

When pirogues from the African shoreline set out,
In their hundreds—for pearls are the prize of the
      bay—
The Arabian shore sends feluccas to rout
The competitors—equally numberless they.

If a black man is caught, he'll be taken away
To Hodeida, the slave market, burdened with
      chains—
The unfortunate Arab, though, once in the bay,
Tepid refuge of muddy-red water sustains.

Like a teacher the schoolboy rebuking, at times
Will a vast ocean-steamboat pass through in a trice:
From propeller-stirred water cold gurgle-tone
    climbs—
On the deck, there are blooming red roses, with ice.

You are powerless here: let the hurricane fret,
Let the wave roar and rise in a crystalline hill—
With a sigh of relief, with a new cigarette,
Says the captain: "Thank God!—can't stand *heat!*—
    had my fill!"

On the sea—as in dragonfly-swarms, aureoles—
Flying fish may be seen in a glimmer ahead:
At the landspits, in sickle-shaped curve, sandy
    shoals
Are like flowers in blossom, in green and in red.

In the glittering air, with its hyaline fire,
Sun is glaring, a magical bird, from his height:
"O my sea! You are queen in diurnal attire,
But at nighttime you're even more blindingly bright!

Puff of cloud, exhalation of vapor drift by,
And the shades of the mermaids may darken the
    waves:
Constellations unknown—axe and cross—rise on high—
They're enkindled undwindling in heavenly naves.

Bengal lights in the night will begin to bewitch
You, Red Sea, with their firework, their streams of
    bright blue,
As if, envying Sky, you had fantasies which
Would make possible stars molded only by you.

TENT

Rising wind-breeze will waft tree-aromas around
When the moon to the zenith ascending will sing
And from Súez to Bab-el-Mandéb can resound
A melodious wind-harp—your surface will ring!

Your abrupt, jagged bank will the elephants mark
When they hear the invasion—the spray of the sea:
They approach, though they're deeply afraid of a
    shark,
Lunar light to admire, bowing reverently.

You recall, long ago, how, unique among seas,
Your high breakers and bow-waves were parted, put
    down:
You fulfilled ineluctable godly decrees
So that Moses might cross and the Pharaoh might
    drown."

230. Egypt

Like a cherished old booklet's dear scenery
Deep-instilled in my evenings of calm,
Are these fertile ravines, with their greenery,
And their many-branched fannings of palm.

The canals, the canals, the canals—
Flowing on along walls made of clay:
On Damietta, and nearby locales,
Pink-white sprinkles of foam they would lay.

And the camels are so entertaining,
Each with fish-body, serpentine head—
Giant monsters, enchantment sustaining
From an sea's ancient colorful bed.

Thus will Egypt appear even now
At the thrice blessed hour when the sun
Has drunk up mankind's day, to allow
The bewitchment of sea-haze to come.

Toward the plantain-trees, blooming afar,
You approach, as a magian once came
Who would talk to a bird or a star
As to comrades—and call them by name.

Is it water so restively groaning
Between burdensome wheels of a mill?
Or the snowy bull Apis a-moaning,
Rose-bedizened, adorned for the kill?

Is it Isis' benevolent glancing—
Or the gleam of the new-risen moon?
High pyrámidal powers, entrancing,
You will view, black and frightening, soon.

To the pyramid-slopes' graying mosses
Fly the eagles who stay through the night.
Hardened covering safely embosses
Bound-up mummies protected from light.

Tent

Keeping watch at a fane that is holy,
Lies a sphinx—a vague smile I can see ...
From the desert come guests, moving slowly,
Unfamiliar to you and to me.

But, as leader, old Egypt has seen a
Stronger lord—regal surge of the Nile,
Overflowing in Elephantina,
Memphis, Thebes, then withdrawing awhile.

Overlooking the desolate river,
You will cry, "It is really a dream!
To the present not fettered forever,
I can time-travel, triumph supreme!

When the monarchs, commanding and mantic,
Forced the slaves the vast boulders to draw
To be wrought into columns gigantic,
I was watching that labor—I saw!

I for centuries watched, in attendance:
Lauding crocodiles, priest-ladies danced
While they chanted. At Ibis' transcendence
They fell prostrate, enamored, entranced.

With her hope for Mark Antony mounting
While she raised her bright, wandering eyes
To the Nile, Cleopatra was counting
Preening sails that her lover so prized."

But enough! Too much time to be spending
On remembering pleasure long past:
Come alive, your attentiveness lending
To delight of the night, of the grass.

Let no underfoot crypt-fragment ringing
Be a marker, a sign, of your bliss—
The true spirit of Egypt is singing
For a feast more enheartened than this.

Like a Fata Morgana, immured,
Is the city, held captive by night,
And the moon appears minaret-skewered
By the mosque of Hassán in its might.

On the terraces, open, delighting,
Women sing, combing golden-bold hair;
Female friends with dark eyes they're inviting,
Snacks of rose-jam and ginger to share.

They are frowning and strict in their praying—
All the sheikhs—with their gorgeous Qur'an
Where, like butterflies, fable-made, straying,
Persian miniatures lead us on.

Every poet's revising a strophe,
And on soft-covered sofa he'll sprawl
Before hookahs and flaming-hot coffee
In cafés while the night starts to fall.

Tent

Not for nothing this country created
Words of wisdom, your favor to earn:
"Who his thirst has with Nile-water sated
To sweet Cairo will long to return."

For although it's the English who govern,
Playing soccer, imbibing their wine;
Though the weakened Khedive is not sovran,
With divan that's no longer divine,

Yet the ruler is never the white man
Nor the Arab—to *him* the land yields
Who, with plow made of wood, or with bright ram,
Leads black buffaloes onto the fields.

For although he's a poor hovel-dweller
And in forest he, beastlike, will die,
As the Nile's own beloved, the fellah
Remains ageless—to her his deep tie.

'Tis for him that, each year, inundations
Of the Nile's ruddy water suffice:
In the wheat-field the rich irrigations
Offer generous harvesting—thrice!

With his threshold defended, protected
With a sharp ridge of boulders heaped high,
He can sleep, free from threat unexpected
Of the Nubian daggers nearby.

But the hawk will keep watch, like a warder—
For the river will cover the land,
Which is edged with a foliage border,
And another one, golden, of sand.

If a stork should fly, pensively, nearer,
To repose on your field in the spring,
Write a message in English (it's clearer)—
Put it carefully under his wing.

If the stork, toward a eucalypt striving,
Should return here betimes and beguiled,
A short message may soon be arriving
From a plowman's delighted young child.

231. Sahara

Through the ages, of deserts alike we would tell,
    But the Gobi, Arabia, Syria—
These are quieter waves of Sahara's grand swell
    Which arose in satanic deliria.

When the rising Red Sea and the Persian Gulf rush,
    When Palmyra's deep snows melt, unseen,
Yet the sandiest floods of their ocean will push
    To Siberian borders of green.

Not the sea in her flood nor the calm, drowsy wood
    To the desert will ever compare:
Where the absence of men is the ultimate good
    You'll love only the sun and the air.

Tent

There the sun bent his head from the brightest blue
    height,
    And his pure, youthful countenance blooms,
While like currents, decanted, of liquefied light
    Are the yellowy sands of the dunes.

There are porphyry palaces, turreted, fair,
    Bounding fountains, palms leafy and lush—
A mirage on a surface of mirroring air
    Sun will paint with a radiant brush.

And the heavenly painter of landscape at eve,
    At the feet of the cliffs and the plants,
Will on sand—the most golden of icon-planks—leave
    Shades of lilac, attracting the glance.

When the singer of heaven, new sound to inspire,
    Gives the signal, in time, that he must,
You hear crackles of limestone quite bursting with
    fire—
    Darkly scattered, and carmine, the dust.

Though the cliffs are yet glittering, farther below
    Rocky riverbeds blacken at last;
When the sable of sea will in thunderstorm grow—
    So the desert—her day overpast.

Look again: the perpetual glory of sand—
    The reflection of heat from the hill
Is like heaven, with clouds over-drowsing the land,
    And with rainbow—our spirit to thrill.

Nikolay Gumilev

The wild wind, in this land, is the next in command;
   How it hurries, in bursts, like a beast—
Among sizable hills, wide ravines, over sand,
   He's a pedigreed steed from the east.

How the sand sings, arisen! Her master is there,
   Whom, familiar, she loves all the more.
Like a soft, solar iris will glimmer the air;
   Pomegranates possess such a core.

Immemorial stems have the palms, monster-tall—
   Sweeping whirlwinds of dust puff them out
While they bend as they sway, through the dust-
      heavy pall,
   All their enemies ready to rout.

Winds will wander and roam to the end of all time,
   And their menace will ever increase—
Each a deadly gray serpent, unrivaled, sublime,
   With a head lost in heavenly fleece.

In a moment, though, trembling, the wind becomes
      tired,
   And a vast heap of sand settles down.
What's the meaning of that? It has stumbled, been
      mired
   By a frightened, tired camel it found.

When, within the now clarified, smoothened ravine
   All the dust heaps lie down, forming hills,
Toward the Mediterranean Sea the khamseen
   Will ascend to foment further ills.

TENT

When a caravan halts, the poor leader, perplexed,
    Whirls a rod in the air, in dismay.
He knows well there's a waterspring near, but—
    behexed—
    He'd forgotten the place, and the way.

Horses neigh in oases—in comforting grots—
    And the palms waft aromas of nard—
But these isles in the flame-sea are rare as the spots
    On a cheetah—to find them is hard.

And you often will hear a quite deafening shout:
    Lances glimmer, and burnooses wave—
For the western Tuáregs, who live farther out,
    Scant affection the Tibbusites have.

While they struggle and fight for a palm-grove, a hill,
    Or a camel, or slave-maiden graced,
Their loved Teebesti, Murzuk, and Gáddamës will
    Be swept over by sand from the waste.

Next the wilderness-winds, which are proud as
    can be—
    Never recognize limit—won't halt—
Crushing walls, gardens littering, wanton and free,
    Poison ponds with their whitening salt.

And perhaps we have not many centuries more
    Till our olden green world will be struck
By the down-rushing winds, wanting plunder, and
    more,
    From Sahara, still young in its luck.

They will cover the Mediterranean Sea—
   Moscow, Paris, and Athens they'll tame—
And like camel-borne Bedouins, truly then we
   Will believe in the heavenly flame.

When the Martians, at last, in their spacecraft arrive
   On our sterile terrestrial sphere,
Golden ocean they'll see, but with nothing alive,
   And they'll call it "Sahara" in fear.

232. Suez Canal

Flocks of nights, and of days,
Overswaying the mind—
Yet in Súez bright rays
Never brighter I find

Than when boats move on land,
Not by sea or by brook—
Long-time brought, caravanned,
With a sea-camel's look.

On the stony inclines,
Birds in numbers arrive
As from fairy-tale times—
Waders goitrous, they thrive.

Then the lizards are seen:
Like the surf-wave they dash,
Being golden and green—
A solidified splash.

TENT

To each blackamoor boy
We toss fruit as we go;
By the waves, they enjoy
Being "pirates," we know.

Shouting, catching their loot,
Voices vibrant, they run.
But—the mad maraboot
Hissed a curse—and we're gone!

Comes the hungry-hawk night—
On the sand settles down.
Fading flamelets' dim light
Back, ahead, all around,

Coral-red, blue, or green—
Water-carnival mild—
An improbable scene
In the African wild.

From the hills, distant, higher,
By a current pursued,
From each Bedouin fire
Winds are smoke-mist-imbued.

From the walls fallen down
And canal-turns, are heard
The hyena—shrill sound—
And the jackal's wild word.

While the steamboat replies,
Pining stars may grow wan.
Sleepy Africa sighs ...
The piano plays on.

233. Sudan

There's a frightening sound in the morning
When the drums are untiringly beaten
On a crocodile drumhead stretched tightly,
The enchantresses calling so loudly
On the cliffs of the Nubian Nile-land—
Shrunken heart!—and the forehead is fevered,
With the eyes getting darker and darker,
And we dream of the harbor we hope for
'Mid the tawny-skinned mariner-voices
While the sea leaps in foam-shred and tatter—
Beyond seas, Darfour-dream of deep canyons,
And of Cordofan's gallery-forests,
And the shallower brooks of Bornu.

Then in cities, illumined by sunlight,
Each a storehouse in overgrown verdure,
There are threatening hands raised to heaven—
Each a minaret bravely ascending.
On the ivory thrones, sitting stately,
New delirious dream of the ancients,
Are the sovereign Sudanese monarchs;
Next to each of them, fettered with chain links,
Eyes screwed up, there's a lion, head lifted,

Tent

Licking bright human blood from its whiskers.
Next to each, with an axe or a hatchet,
Standing, thick-lipped, the skin black and shining,
We've the soul, as it were, of the ruler—
Executioner, tunic bright red.

Then the slave-traders came, showing proudly
All their wares to the hoped-for consumer—
Heavy stocks have produced a great groaning,
Victim-eyewhites agleam in the sunlight,
While the leaders arrive from the wildland,
With their close-woven, pearl-threaded turbans,
And with feathers of ostriches waving
On the backs of the heads of their horses:
Supercilious, then come the Frenchmen,
Smoothly shaven, in whitest of garments—
From a pocket, sealed papers are peeking,
Which the Sudanese rulers, in envy,
Rise, from thrones, all the better to see.

On the veldt-land surrounding the village,
Where giraffes are concealed by the grasses,
God's own gardener once felt empowered—
Dressed in moon-colored mantle of bird wings—
To create a true paradise-mirror:
With capricious mimosa, acacia,
Spreading coppice-dark over the country,
He made baobabs grow on the hillocks,
Forest gallery show—cool yet sundrenched
As an elegant Dorian temple—

Many-currented rivers, directed,
In a burst of serene exultation,
To debouch into quiet Lake Chad.

This completed, he, youthfully smiling
As if proud of a charming amusement,
Had collected some creatures undreamt of,
Unbelievable animals, birds, and
Taking color from jungle at sunset,
He bedaubed the fine feathers of parrots,
Gave the elephant tusks that were whiter
Than a cloud of the African heaven,
Clad the lion in aureate garments,
Dressed the leopard in spot-scattered clothing,
Gave the rhino deep horns made of amber,
The gazelle gave soft, maidenly eyes.

Then to faraway stars he departed,
To adorn them, perhaps, in addition.
Beasts are roaming—so God had appointed—
To assemble at watering-places,
Unaware that their beauty's a wonder,
That their nonpareil lives are unrivaled,
And the hunter knows nothing about it
While he hides in the full-flaming noonday
By a bush, with his venom-tipped arrow;
Crying Triumph—the beast well-subjected—
While he revels in venery, dancing—
Carries off, to a Sudanese ruler,
All the glorious plunder he gains.

Tent

But the plain-dwellers often occasion
Conflagrations on grassy, dry meadows.
On the day when the sunlight is darkened
By the ashes invading on wind-breath
And—an animal nameless and crimson—
Flame on veldt-land will shimmer and tremble—
On that day, there is great celebration
Which the affable Devil arranges
For Dame Death and her brother, bright Horror!
On that day you won't recognize humans
In the crowds of inflamed ones, all roaring;
Tusk and horn striking wildly about them,
They are conscious of nothing but Fire!

It is evening. The eye can't distinguish
Threads of red on the white of a waistband—
Sign of twilight, a time for the Muslim
To complete his ablutions for Allah,
Taking water in woods by a river—
Taking sand in the water-gone wasteland.
From the sand-scattered cliffs looking over
The unruly Red Sea's perturbation
To the bow-waves, the broad-foaming breakers,
Of the fathomless, far-off Atlantic,
People pray. The Sudan becomes quiet.
And above—like a child who's a giant—
I believe, I believe, God leans down.

234. Abyssinia

Right between the broad shore of the stormy Red Sea
And the mystery dark of the sylvan Sudan,
Four plateaus that converge we in overview see—
Like a lioness lies Abyssinian land.

To the north is a bottomless marsh without end,
Whose approaches are guarded by serpents of black
And where yellow-faced flocks of the fever, their
 friend,
Have found refuge. The walker does well to turn
 back.

And above it, morose, have the hills knit their brows,
For in Tigre old conflicts live on, people fight,
Where the pits bare their teeth, and the forests are
 tous-
-led and mountain peaks climb to a snow-silvered
 height.

In the fruitful Amharra, they reap and they sow;
Zebras gladly join cows where they wander in calm.
In the evening, the cool-bringing winds will bear low
Tones of guttural songs and of thrum-comfort balm.

Abyssinians chant as they strum the baganna,
Resurrecting the past, bringing charms from afar—
Tell of times when, before the great lake known as
 Tanna,
Rose the capital city, the royal Gondár.

Tent

As he captured the crowd with a resonant line,
Under plantains, the sage would explain holy writ:
Flanked by peaceable lion and Sheba's queen fine,
In a portrait, King Solomon, stately, would sit.

But, allured by the Shoanite's flattering things,
From his fatherland, lovely, of poet and rose,
Abyssinia's elephant wise, King of Kings,
Took his throne down to Shoa, the stone-land of foes.

Shoa's fighters are sly—they are cruel and grave—
They smoke pipes and sip tedzh, a euphorial aid:
They love trumpet and drum in the music they crave—
And to grease up a gun, and to sharpen a blade.

Danakilian, Harrarite, Gallan, Somali,
Pygmy, cannibal—these the grim Shoan derides
To King Ménelik. Meanwhile the big palace hall he
Is adorning with king-symbols, leonine hides.

While beholding the streams at the feet of the
    mountains,
And the triumph of trees that the noon-light will
    give,
Europeans will marvel how rose from the fountains
Both the traits of the men and the land where they
    live.

Land of spells! In the depth of the hollow, you gasp
When the fire is poured forth in full strength from
    the height—

Nikolay Gumilev

Though the hawk's cry be heard overhead, one can't
  grasp
What is happening, such the broad sultriness' might.

Palm and cactus and herbs of the height of a man—
And too much of the searing-hot grass, heavy sleep ...
But be careful! The boa constrictor might plan—
As may panther and ruddy-maned lion—to leap.

From ravine and from steep by a burdensome way
You ascend, then quite startlingly, suddenly see
All the roses and sycamores, villages gay,
And the folk scattered wide over mead, over lea.

There the wizard will work his habitual spell—
To a melody, meekly, snakes writhe in their place:
In the open-air court, a man's ready to tell
Why he sold a sick camel—the judge hears the case.

But go higher! How cool it's become! As if late
In the autumn, the fields look so empty and old ...
Streams are frozen by dawn, and the flock dread
  their fate,
Huddling cautiously under the roof of the fold.

Amid bushes of milkweed, the peacocks cry out,
Getting messy in sticky and whitening smear—
Aiming lances, the horsemen dash by as they shout,
And their rifles ring out in their headlong career.

TENT

Higher now remain only the precipices,
Where the winds are asway, gladdened eagles will
 come—
Not a man has yet reached them, each
 mountainpeak is
White with snow while it stands in the tropical sun.

Men in caravans ride, when more bright the air's
 grown,
Whom the ever-expanding immensity thrills,
Having left for a country they never had known,
Seeking ivory, striving for gold in the hills.

How I love roaming free over pathways like these—
Longhorned goats won't be caught as they're leaping
 aloft!—
Seeing stars that are heavy and rounded, like peas,
Then, at night, lying down on the moss, gray and
 soft.

Ethnographic museums you'll find in my town
Where the currents of Nile-like Nevá love to flow;
During times when poetical life gets me down,
The museum's my haven. It's there that I go—

It is there that I go to stroke savage-made things
That, myself, I had, many years back, carried home;
Their strange odor, portentous yet cherished!—it
 sings
Both of beast-wool and laudanum—roses in loam.

Of the tropical sun can the flare never set,
And the leopard is crouching and crawls toward a
    foe;
And my servant awaits me, equipment all set,
In the smoke of the hut—it's a-hunting we'll go!

235. Galla

I'd been leading the caravan out from Harrár
    For eight days: the gray monkeys I'd shoot
When we passed the Checherian mountains afar
    Might collapse on a sycamore root.

On the ninth day we rode, from a hill I could see—
    What a strange, unforgettable sight!—
On a faraway plain, fires were shining for me
    Like unnumbered red stars in the night.

And they followed each other, in lively array,
    As if clouds in the radiant blue.
Every night was thrice holy, distinct every day
    On the broad plain of Galla we'd view.

It appeared that whatever I looked at, out here,
    Was so large I kept feeling amazed—
As I watched, it appeared giant women came near
    And, by ponds, their huge camels they grazed.

Then in leopard-skin clad, or in bright lion-hide,
    The enormous Gallanians came.

Tent

Running ostriches each, on a charger astride,
   Would hack down, never pausing, aflame.

Dying snakes would be fed with fresh milk every day
   By old men ... But since whites were yet strange
To the bulls, they would bellow while running away
   When I happened to come within range.

Near a cave, on occasion, I'd listen to loud
   Singing, chanting, the beat of a drum.
I was feeling like Gulliver, formerly proud,
   When to Brobdingnag country he'd come.

Next, the tropical Rome, town mysterious to men:
   Sheikh-Hussein would come towering high—
First I bowed to the mosque and the palm-trees—and then
   To the place of the prophet came nigh.

The fat black man was seated on Persian rugs fine,
   In a hall that was bare and half-dark,
Like an idol, with bracelets and earrings' bright shine:
   In each eye was a marvel, a spark.

First I bowed, then he smiled in reply, and his whim
   Was a slap on my back, lucky sign.
Novel pistol from Belgium I offered to him
   And my sovereign's portrait, quite fine.

Back in Russia, he wondered, in foreigners' hearts
   Was he valued appropriately
For beneficent deeds, for medicinal arts,
   That were famed all the way to the sea?

If you've lost your best mule in the depth of the wood
   Or your slave had escaped and you're sad,
You'd receive what you needed, if only you could
   Bring some gift—Sheikh Hussein would be glad.

236. Somalian Peninsula

There's a night I remember, a dune-covered land,
   With the moon lying low, near the sand.

I looked steadily up, not averting my eye
   From the moon's yellow pathway on high.

It is bright there, birds probably singing, beyond—
   There are blossoming plants by a pond.

You won't hear any wandering lions—wild scenes!—
   For their roaring resounds in ravines.

Dead of night: dreaded thorn of mimosa won't scratch
   Nor the unaware traveler catch.

On that night, as the bush-shadows crept—couldn't see—
   The Somalis came closer to me,

Tent

And their shaggy-haired leader, commander-cap red,
   Now declared that I soon would be dead.

He was trying—with eyelids half-lowered—to see
   Just how many my helpers would be.

In the morning a merciless battle began,
   With the howling of many a man—

Beneath camel-feet, bodies entwined on the ground—
   Venomed lances and arrows rained 'round:

On the moon, I thought strangely, would never a foe
   Launch attack with a terminal blow ...

I precisely at midnight my caravan stirred:
   Past the hill, roaring ocean we heard ...

Men had perished at sea: one expected, on land,
   Sudden death at the enemy's hand—

But we ran, and the damp, odoriferent grass
   Smelled of lion-hide sweat as we'd pass.

Among rock-relics holy shone blindingly white
   Piled-up skulls and dead bones in the night.

The Somalis are Africa's deadliest—and
   Her most comfortless country, their land.

For, by wells in the sand, lances thrown in the night
   Have meant death for so many a white

That their exploits the hungry hyenas again
   And again sound throughout Ogadén.

When the moon bent at morn, it was altered—instead
   Of the white we had viewed, it was red.

And I knew that for heroes in glorious fight
   It was gleaming, the shield of a knight.

Granting camels a rest by a watering hole,
   To my gun I commended my soul.

237. Madagascar

Pounding heart—it was woeful, wholly—
Daylong roaming, and aimlessly,
Then I dreamed I was floating, slowly,
Some big river supporting me.

Every moment it's wider, wider
(Strange the world of the dream has grown)—
Now the river is brighter, brighter:
Light I lie in my boat alone.

Red the idol on pure white pillar—
It has offered the riddle-key.
This red idol on pure white pillar
"Madagascar!" proclaims to me.

TENT

Golden-rich palankeens enclosed them;
Carven watercraft bore them on ...
Broad-backed oxen to wind exposed them:
Riding loud-neighing steeds they'd gone—

Gone where, flutter-wing'd, singing, humming,
Lightly myriad swans would fly,
Dark-faced crowds every hour were coming,
Looking forward to plays nearby.

They'd compose entertaining dramas,
Then perform them immediately:
That old man made the maiden promise—
When, he asked, will the wedding be?

Finely uniformed, free of shyness,
Face benign, the hussar looks down—
Styled "Her Bright Madagascan Highness'
Faithful General"—serves the Crown.

Heavy bulls—they are Tomatavan—
Looking much like a boulder-pile,
Graze away in their grassy haven:
Fresh aromas the fields beguile.

Then I sighed: what's the point of gliding?
Why not stop—just remain at rest?
Could I not, in the calm residing,
Write good poems—my very best?

Yet my words drifted off, unhearkened—
In the quiet my voice was drowned.
On the wings of a bat, now, darkened
Skies came warmly and softly down.

Wood and sky into darkness wandered—
Swans had sounded their final note.
Lying, still, in my bed, I pondered,
Grieved the loss of my dreamed-of boat.

238. Zambezi

As if bronze onto iron were welling,
Flaming needles cut deep into night.
The Zambezi's broad breakers are swelling,
And they roar when they're borne out of sight.

Through the fury and frenzy of lightning,
Something's visible over the height—
A black body is bending; a bright'ning
Mighty battleaxe, glintingly white.

Soon a guttural song will resound.
When the muses that circle our sphere
Issue orders, there's no getting 'round
What they'll say, so the Zulu must hear:

"I have dreamt, in the kraal, with a start,
That a lion had roared on the range:
Happy sadness contracted my heart—
It was quick—made my head whirl—that strange!

TENT

Then a sword, sweeping into my hand!
Wind unseen a door open would fling!
Roaring lion had died on the sand—
Then a mist-hidden spirit would sing:

'May your anger be gloried forever!
Like a lion, you kill and destroy:
You're a scion of Díngan—you never
May deny the bold life you enjoy.'

Since that moment, I always keep ready,
And at night I'm reluctant to rest—
With my blood-thirst unquenchable, steady:
I'm prepared for the ultimate test.

Beyond mountains, more wide than the clouds are,
By the river-mouths, over the marsh,
Where the ware-trading Arabs' great crowds are,
I'd rip guts with my assagai harsh.

I'd go down to the storm on the plain,
I would show, where the forest arose,
My adornments—eight wounds, worth the pain,
And—eleven—the heads of my foes.

Thirty years I have roamed: long ago
I have stopped fearing people and flame
And the gods ... But I know—yes, I know—
There is one whom I never can tame.

He is living in thickets unknown.
He's an elephant: strangers he'll pierce
With his long, broken tusk—he's alone
And he's great, just like me, and he's fierce.

And I dream of him, night after night,
And I know he'll be crossing the plain,
For the spirits of mist, in their might,
Have proclaimed my long-prophesied pain.

He will kill me, this last of my foes—
'Tis a fate that my heart cannot doubt.
The abyss of the heav'n will disclose
Dingan-Father, and then he'll cry out:

'Yes, you never were craven or tamed,
But a lion—made enemies blench!—
So between me and Chaka, well-famed,
Sit down here on your foeman-skull bench.'"

239. Damara
Hottentot Cosmogony

Human pride is a sin, 'tis flighty:
Human power, a little thing—
Once, on earth, ruled a bird, most mighty,
Stronger far than a human king.

Seeing sunrise, the bird would follow;
Crag and cliff it would swiftly swallow.

TENT

Then it flew to the ocean shore,
Swallowed islands, and looked for more.

Later on, in the holy gloaming,
See? The bird that is soaring, roaming
Heads aloft—hear the music ring?—
Sings to gods of a godly thing.

Drawing signs with its feet, it soon
Lit the underworld's murky gloom:
All the future and all the past
Lay revealed on the sand at last.

Sweet to hear, and superb to see—
Sign and song in a harmony—
Soon it pondered, the foolish bird,
If to gods it should be preferred.

God, who reckoned the world below,
Guessed its impudent thought, and so,
Proper penalty well in view,
Knife-divided the bird in two.

First, the part where the music rings,
Singing, godlike, of godly things:
Hottentots, from the upper part,
Sing all day with a carefree heart.

From the part where the signs had soon
Lit the underworld's murky gloom,

Bushmen entered the earthly light,
Decorating their hut-walls bright.

Feathers, feathertips blown away
Where the breakers of ocean lay,
Drifted—seemingly people, white:
When enough of them come to light,

Then the bird, with its halves combining,
Happiness to the people chiming,
Feather-spreading, will settle down,
White-wing'd, nesting upon the ground.

240. Equatorial Forest

Abyssinian mountains were stretching far
    westward—
On a rocky-hard slope I erected a tent,
And I watched, free of care, while the sunset was
    flaring
On the roofs of green trees in the broadened
    expanse.

There were birds heading toward us, in light
    unfamiliar,
With their emerald tailfeathers trailing, quite long—
And exuberant zebras ran up in the nighttime—
You could hear their loud snorting, the thud of their
    hooves.

TENT

When the sunset, one evening, was redder than
    normal,
And a pungent aroma swept in from the trees,
To my tent came, in pain, a distraught European,
Who was haggard, unshaven, requesting some food.

He kept eating till nightfall, voracious and awkward,
Put sardines on a thick hefty slice of hard meat;
You would think they were pills, the cubed bouillon
    he swallowed,
And he drank undiluted, unwatered absinthe.

When I asked what had made him so morbidly
    pallid—
Why the wild agitations were shaking his hands
Like the leaves in the fall—"Forest fever," he
    answered,
And with fear in his eyes he looked down at his feet.

When I asked him concerning the big open blood-
    wound
Turning black under rags on his sunken-in chest,
"It's the forest gorilla that did it," he said and
Was reluctant to look at me, loth to say more.

It appeared that a pygmy was with him, black, naked,
And as high as my waist, but unable to speak—
Like a dog he was sitting, obeying the master,
With his great bulldog face—glancing down at his
    knees.

As it happened, my servant once playfully poked him,
And he suddenly clenched his horrific white teeth:
For the rest of the day he kept snorting, excited—
With a javelin, angry, he'd beat on the ground.

So I made up a bed for my guest, now exhausted,
And myself lay on panther fur—sleep, though, had
    fled.
From his feverish raving I soon pieced together
All the terrible tale of this man from the woods.

He was sighing: "So dark ... there's no end to the
    forest ...
I am sure we will never again view the sun ...
Where's the diary—under your shirt? Pierre, find
    it! ...
I'm convinced that our lives matter less than that
    book!

Woe is me! All the blacks have abandoned us, left
    us ...
Why is that? And they went with our compasses, too.
What to do? There's no animal visible, nothing ...
Only whistling and rustling, above and below!

Have you noticed the pyres? There are certainly
    people ...
Say, Pierre, do you think there's a chance we'll be
    saved?
Those are pygmies ... so many, so many together ...
Shoot, Pierre! At the pyre, I can see a man's leg!

Tent

We'll have hand-to-hand combat! Their arrows are
    venomed ...
Hit the one on the stump ... that's their leader, he
    shouts ...
Woe is me! Smithereens—all that's left of my rifle!
Now I'm done for ... they've got me, I think.—it's the
    end—

No, I'm living—but, wait! I can't move. Villain,
    villain!—
Let me go! Oh my God ... I can't bear it, won't look! ...
They are burning Pierre ... Now my memory takes
    me
To Marseilles, where like children we played by the
    sea ...

What is happening, dog? On your knees you are
    walking?!
You are bestial, disgusting, I'm spitting on you!
Now you're licking my hands? And undoing my
    fetters?
Ah, it's clear to me now—you must think I'm a god ...

Well, let's run for it, run! Let the human meat *stay*
    there:
That's a thing the all-powerful gods don't consume ...
Woods ... O forest eternal ... O Akka, I'm starving ...
If it's practical, capture a snake for some food!"

He was wheezing and groaning, he grabbed at his
     chest, and
In the morning it seemed he had simply dozed off—
When I quietly tried to awake him, however,
I caught sight of the flies, how they crawled on his
     face.

At the foot of a palm-tree I buried him quickly
And erected a cross on a heap of big stones,
And I wrote on a wood-plank an epitaph, simple:
"Here a Christian has died; say a prayer for him."

And I read, a year later, in France, in the paper—
And in sadness I nodded while scanning the lines:
"From the trade expedition to far Upper Congo
Not a single survivor has ever returned."

241. Dahomey

To his captain-commander the king's proclamation
Said, "Dahómean elephants you in your height
Have outrivaled, yet higher in glorification
Is the tall heap of heads you've piled up in your
     might.

Like your valor, well tested and tried and all-
     knowing,
Is my favor to you—grace benign, without end:
See the sun on the water? It's there you'll be going:
You will serve my Gold Father, my old, worthy
     friend!"

TENT

They are beating the drums; tambourines are
          resounding—
As they bow, all the people unite in their moan:
There's a long-drawn-out amazon song, and a
          sounding
Of a trumpet-call piercing the ocean's dull groan.

When the captain had bowed, mutely, meekly
          inclining,
From the cliff, toward tempestuous waves, he jumped
          down;
And he drowned in the sea, and it seemed, in the
          shining
Of the gold of the watery sunset he drowned.

He was deafened by drums and by shouting that
          simmered—
He was blinded—by splattering wave-salt
          unmanned—
And he vanished. The face of his overlord glimmered
Like the shining black sun of the underworld-land.

242. Niger

Under longitude, latitude, netlike, extended
On a map of our boredom, I've noticed a line
That appears like a blackening branch oddly ended
In a wide-reaching, curving, and wandering vine.

Nikolay Gumilev

Like a cluster of grapes are the cities around it:
They are Bussa, and Gomba, and King Timbuktu.
The mere sound of each name makes me glad I had
    found it—
Like the sunlight, or drums, bringing dreams into
    view ...

But the map is so dull, is it possible? Never!
Yet I've checked in the book, and it really does say
It's the Niger ... O royal, magnificent river,
How the insolent mapmakers dimmed your array!

Through Sudan you flow sealike, triumphant your
    motion—
And you fight with the predator-flock of the sand—
And, approaching the welcoming, bountiful ocean,
You have spread out so far, we no longer view land.

Your behemoths' pink snouts architectural piles
To uphold an invisible bridgework might be:
The propellers of steamboats your wild crocodiles
With a blow of their tails can demolish with glee.

O my Niger, for you I'm preparing, emboldened,
An unheard of new map, best that ever was seen.
A brocaded, long ribbon—the sheen will be golden—
I will place on a wide satin sheet, tender green.

Then below, on the left, bloody rubies will be
A procession of strange rocky gods in Benín.

TENT

Who, 'mid ivory, skulls, the first idol could see
In some gloomy, obscure, and forgotten ravine?

On the right, where Sokotto's thick grove may be
    found,
On the satin an emerald, splendid, I'll place:
Here the hamlets are rich, perfect hunting around,
And the people are free—singing birds—loving space.

Further on, a pale opal is gleaming discreetly
Hiding whimsical fires with a gleam red and blue,
Of the plain of Songayya reminding me sweetly
And recalling the sultan's clay domicile, too.

By the sign of a pearl marked in radiant wonder
Timbuktu, with luxuriant roofings, will loom
While the hawk's puzzled cawing shows thought rent
    asunder
When it's viewing the desert mimosa in bloom,

Every maiden as lithe as the vine and more charming—
For their breaths than the balsam are headier far—
And the fountains in gardens, the roses of carmine
That enwreath each poetical school's guiding star!

Filled with ardor's the African heart, and with song—
And I know, if at times we've a dream that allures
But whose name can't be known, though we search
    for it long,
Then the wind that has brought it is—Africa—yours!

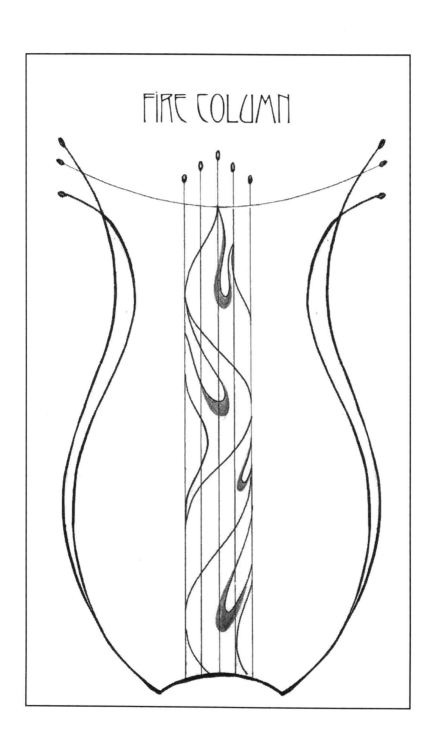

NIKOLAY GUMILEV

FOR ANNA NIKOLAYEVNA GUMILEVA

243. Memory

Though a snake may throw a skin away,
Getting older, and the soul will grow,
We diverge from these, I'm sad to say—
Changing soul, not body. Be it so.

Memory, with giant hand sublime,
Guide our lives—like horses—by the rein!
Tell me who, in now-forgotten time,
Used my body long before I came.

"Well, the first, unhandsome and quite slim,
Loved a gloomy grove in twilight-frame—
Fallen leaves ... He loved a child whose whim
Was, with magic word, to stop the rain.

Tree, or rufous dog—such were the kind
He would choose for friends, unfailingly."
Memory, you'll never find a sign—
Won't convince the world—that I was he!

"And the second ... loved the southern wind—
Heard in faintest reed a lyre-tone sweet—
Used to call his life his 'ladyfriend'—
All the world a carpet for his feet.

He's the one I cannot like at all—
Wanted to be god, and king, and more—
Even hung a placard, 'Poet's Hall,'
On my taciturn and tranquil door.

Fire Column

Freedom's chosen one I love the most—
Archer, and a swimmer of the seas:
Him, when waters chanted on the coast,
Every cloud would envy, every breeze.

High his tent, the mules impatient, strong:
He would love to drink, like bracing wine,
Sweet, fresh air—in draught so deep, so long—
Of a land that whites could never find."

Memory, each year you're weaker, right?
This man, or one after, or before,
Traded off his freedom's long delight
For a sacred, long-awaited war.

Hunger, thirst, he knew, and knew full well—
Troubled sleep, and travel void of rest:
Yet St. George, with twice-effective spell,
Warding off the bullets, touched his breast.

I'm a stubborn builder—never tamed—
Of a temple risen in the mist.
Both in sky and earth, God's glory—fame—
These I envy, these will I resist.

Ardent, filled with fire my heart must be
Up until the day when, bright, arise
New Jerusalem's high walls for me
In my homeland, reaching to the skies.

Then a wind—great stranger—worlds to thrill,
Heaven-light will perilously pour—
That's the Milky Way, where gardens will
Bloom with dazzle-planets evermore.

Then before me will appear, unknown,
Hidden-faced, a traveler ... Yet I—
I'll know all, and see the lion lone
Follow him—the eagle in the sky ...

I will shout!—but how can anyone
Help my spirit keep from dying then?
Skin a snake may shed in warming sun:
Soul we change, not body—we are men.

244. Woods

Whitish trunks, emerging unexpectedly
Out of mist, appeared for everyone to see.

Root then followed root, climbed quickly, making
    room:
Grasping hands arise of dwellers in the tomb.

Under foliage as bright as any fire
Lived the giants, and the dwarfs, and lions dire.

Traces fishermen could view upon the sand—
Imprints of a big six-fingered human hand.

Fire Column

Nowhere was a path to lead a peer of France—
Or a knight of Arthur's Table Round, perchance ...

In the brush no brigand hideaway had sunk—
Nor were cave-cells excavated by a monk.

Only once, from here, one evening storm-bestirred
Came a lady strange—cat-headed, I have heard—

And a crown she had, of molded silver pure—
Moaned till morn, as if some woe she must endure ...

Quietly at dawn she died—the vicar gave
Her the eucharist, then laid her in the grave.

All this happened, all this happened, in a place,
In a time, of which you'll never find a trace.

All this happened, all this happened, in a land
Even dreams will never help you understand.

I invented it, just looking at your hair—
Fiery tresses—burning serpent nesting there—

At your greenish eyes I looked, as at an ill
Persian turquoise, making pain my spirit fill.

Now I think: that forest may have been your soul.
Or, it may have been my love, entire and whole.

Or, it's possible, perhaps, that when we die,
To that woods we'll head together, you and I.

Nikolay Gumilev

245. Word

When, above the world at first created,
God inclined His face, began the time
Words would make the sun halt, subjugated—
Make a city drop into the slime.

Eagles didn't dare to wave a wing,
Stars with horror at the moon would stare
When—some rosy flame a hearth might fling—
Floated by a single word in air.

There were numbers for the lower world
As for yoked, domesticated cattle—
All the hidden hints would be unfurled
By a number—numbers won the battle.

Good and evil taming, knowledge-bound,
Rose a patriarch, gray wizard—and,
Lacking courage to employ a sound,
With a reed drew numbers on the sand.

We forgot that words alone would grant
Deep relief, unique, amid our woes …
In the gospel, John, the hierophant,
Told us that the Word as God arose.

Limited, our words are not alive—
Nature's soul a miser, limited:
Like the bees that die in empty hive,
Rots the odor of our words long dead.

FIRE COLUMN

246–248. Soul and Body

1

Above the city hovers (hushed) the night.
No swish or whisper—all is muffled, muted.
And you, my soul, remaining silent, quite—
My God, a quiet more to marble suited!

But now may come the answer—faint and slight,
As if an airy lyre-tone growing bold:
"Why did I open eyes to being's light
In such a scorned and scoffed-at human mold?

Insane, I think, I left my home behind,
To see if heaven-splendor might be bettered.
The earthly sphere's a heavy ball, I find,
To which a convict will be tethered, fettered.

And love I certainly have come to hate!
It is an illness, you its victim, surely:
It early fogs the world, beclouds it late—
A world that's odd—but might be viewed more purely.

A single thing may keep me yet akin
To wisdom past that glints in planet-chorus:
That thing is woe, my shield of hope within.
Though cold in scorn—woe forms a focus fór us."

2

The sunset, golden, then went copper-red.
The clouds were covered with a greenish rye.
"To everything the spirit lately said"—
I called upon the body now—"Reply."

And then my body duly answered me,
My simple body, but with blood that burns:
"My life has left me in perplexity,
Although I know of love, in human terms.

I love to splash about in salty waves
While hearkening to hawk-shriek, raucous, coarse—
To cross, on never-ridden steed that raves,
Fields—carroway—endearing to that horse.

I love a woman … When her lowered eyes
I, modestly approaching, dare to kiss,
I'm drunk, as if a storm-wind should arise,
Or holy spring had lent me heaven-bliss.

For all the things I have or want today—
For all the grief, the frenzy, the elation—
The lot of men is such—I yet must pay
With ineluctable annihilation."

3

However, when the word of God on high
Gleamed forth in brilliant Bear's great constellation

Fire Column

To pose the question, "Who are you that sigh?"
Both soul and body rose to lofty station.

'Twas then I raised my eyes to mitigate
Their boldness, gentling it as best I might:
"Does one expect a dog to cogitate
When howling at the limpid lunar light?

Interrogating *me*? How can you dare?
My life is brief, a moment in duration,
From starting-day on earth, first breath of air,
To final flaming world-representation.

Within this mortal mind, for good and ill,
The seventy and seven worlds find rest,
As in the mighty ash-tree Yggdrasil:
All fields are dust—of mortals, of the blest!

I am the one whose challenge, though supreme
Beyond expression, will descend. I sleep.
You each are the reflection of a dream—
Awareness brief, and streaming to the deep."

249. First Canzona

In the yard was a feathered
And a thunder-voiced fire—
Blue-black sleep it untethered
When the shrieking rose higher.

Though they'd flown, gently dipping,
From the moon, seeming meek,
Winds were painfully whipping
At tranquillity's cheek.

Over cliffs while it clambered,
Youthful dawn quickly fed,
With the barley-hue ambered,
Cloudlets ravenous, red.

I was born in that hour,
In that hour I will die.
If no path gave me power
To do good, that is why.

And my lips, ever heedless,
Love to kiss, with delight,
One with whom it is needless
To ascend to the height.

250. Second Canzona

Now, we've left the world—we're somewhere new—
Nowhere, really … shadows in a maze …
Summer, sleepily, is leafing through
Pure blue pages of serener days.

Diligent, the pendulum, insistent—
Bridegroom, never recognized, of time—
Bluebeard chops the heads off, unresistant,
Of the plotting seconds, in their prime.

Fire Column

Every highway here is merely dusty,
Every bush desiring to be dry,
No white seraph, dreamed of, coming, trusty—
No white unicorn will be led by.

But, within your hidden sadness, dear,
There is yet a fiery frenzy, and—
Curst in boondock-gloom—it yet is clear,
Freshened breeze-breath from a legend-land

Where are movement, shining, song, affection …
Dream of *that*, the favored isle afar.
Captive here is held our twin reflection
In a rotting, stagnant reservoir.

251. Imitation of the Persian

Right behind your words like nightingales,
Right behind your words, each pendant pearl,
My words crouch, with beastly, bristling tails—
Tusk'd and woolly—and with horns that curl.

I think I'm going mad, my lovely one.

For your cheeks, twin Shiraz-blooming rose,
Both my cheeks are faded, fallen in.
For your hair that, softly golden, flows,
All my gold I gave, your love to win.

Naked, bare am I, my lovely one.

To obtain a single, treasured glance
At your turquoise—no, your beryl eyes,
Seven nights of vigil, in a trance
At your door I sat, and didn't rise.

Blood-red weary eyes, my lovely one.

Just because you never leave your home
Never from the tavern do I roam.
Just because your honor gives you pride,
Toward a knife my hand's inclined to slide.

I'm a public nuisance, lovely one.

If there's sun—and timeless God—up there
You will cross my threshold: that I swear.

252. Persian Miniature

When I complete this hide-and-seek
With frowning death, my God, I'm sure,
Will make of me a quite unique
Perfected Persian miniature.

You'll see a turquoise heaven rise—
A prince with glances beckoning
To glimpse her almond-shapen eyes—
A youthful maiden on a swing.

Fire Column

A shah, with bloodied lance, rides far—
His road rough-rising to a height
Vermilion, maybe cinnabar—
Behind a chamois in its flight.

Not on awaking nor in dream
Was ever known such tuberose,
And vines in evening sweet would seem
To bend to meet the lawn-repose.

And over on the other side—
Tibetan cloud, so light to see—
My valued sign will be espied,
My emblem high of artistry.

A pleasant, older man, perfumed,
A merchant, or a man of state,
Will feel by loving glimpse illumed
With love that's hard and won't abate.

His days, unchanging, light that lend,
A beacon star, I'll regulate:
First wine, then sweethearts, then each friend,
Will I replace, for there's my fate.

And that is when I'll sate at last—
Not drunk, and not in suffering—
My olden dream of years long past:
To be adored by everything.

Nikolay Gumilev

253. Sixth Sense

Delightful is a wine in love with us,
A well-made bread-loaf, in the oven waiting,
A woman who, delayings torturous
Endured, at last our passion may be sating.

What shall we do, though, with the rosy dawn
Below the heavens growing slowly colder—
With all the wide, unearthly, quiet calm—
Immortal verse, more strange as we get older?

All these we cannot kiss, or drink, or eat—
The moment flees and cannot be constrained.
We wring our hands, condemned to feel defeat:
We miss, and miss again, our senses lamed.

Ev'n as a boy, oblivious of a game
And gazing at a bathing girl instead,
Knows naught of love, for which he has no name,
Yet feels tormented by a want unsaid—

And just as, in a thicket overgrown,
A gliding reptile, roaring, getting bolder,
Was tortured by a weakness yet unknown,
And felt a wing-to-be upon each shoulder,

So, through the ages—Lord, O Lord, how long?—
A scalpel nature wields, an art intense:
The soul cries out, nor is the body strong—
Sixth organ birthing of a stranger sense.

Fire Column

254. Young Elephant

My love for you's an elephant, just that.
A young one, born in Paris, or Berlin:
He'll gallivant, with padded feet and flat,
In zoo attendant-rooms and raise a din.

Don't give him rolls or any French cuisine:
A cabbage-head to him is not a treat—
He'll gladly try a slice of tangerine,
Or sugar cubes, or candy, something sweet.

Don't weep, my darling, that in narrow cage
He's mocked and troubled by the chuckling crowd—
Cigar smoke up his trunk—as if his rage
Might charm the milliners, who laugh out loud.

Don't think, my dear, that soon will come the day
When, truly angry, he will break his chain
And run and, like a bus that broke away,
Ram down the people, make them wail in pain.

Envision him instead in early dawn,
Brocaded, ostrich-feathered, far from home,
Like that Resplendent One who, stately, calm,
Bore Hannibal to face a trembling Rome.

Nikolay Gumilev

255. Strayed Streetcar

I strolled on an unfamiliar road
And suddenly heard a raven cry,
A lute plucked, far-off thunder explode:
A streetcar, near me, was flying by.

I leapt to the footboard—I managed to find it,
But how? It's a puzzle—I couldn't say.
The vehicle left a trail behind it,
Fiery, right in the light of day.

It speeded away, dark, wingéd, stormy,
Within the abyss of ages it strayed ...
I called to the tram conductor before me:
"Stop the streetcar! It's been waylaid!"

Too late. We leapfrogged a wall meanwhile.
We flew ahead through a grove of palms,
Across the Seine, the Nevá, the Nile:
Three bridges we roared along—no qualms ...

Flashing by, in a window frame,
A beggar threw us a glance of woe:
An oldster—naturally, the same
That died in Beirut a year ago.

Where *am* I? Anxious, exhausted, wry,
My heart was answering—I could hear it:
"You see the station where one can buy
A trip to the India of the spirit?"

Fire Column

A sign ... in letters of blood poured out:
"Greens." But I knew that—never fail—
Instead of cabbage and sauerkraut,
Heads of cadavers would be for sale.

Red-shirted executioner—
Face udderlike—my hacked-off head
Would lie with the rest like a thistle-burr
In a slippery box at the bottom, dead.

A wood-board fence on a narrow lane—
A house, three windows, and a lawn ...
Conductor, stop this crazy train!
Stop it! I'm sorry I ever got on!

Masha, you lived here, sang, rejoiced!
For me, your bridegroom, a rug you wove.
Where is your body, your ringing voice?
Might you have died, my dearest love?

Loud you moaned—in your chamber—while
I, peruke well powdered, went
(Never to see you again!) in style,
Myself to the empress soon to present.

Freedom—now I could understand!—
Is only a light beating down from beyond:
People and shades at the entry stand
Of the zoo of planets, in space unconned.

At once a wind, familiar, calm ...
Flew to me from the bridge, of course,
Harsh, the iron-gloved horseman's palm
And the two huge hooves of the rearing horse.

Orthodox stronghold, certain, true,
St. Isaac's, outlined for all to see ...
Mashenka, I'll say prayers for you!—
Then—a requiem mass—for me.

My heart is heavy when I sigh:
It's a pain to live, and it's hard to breathe!
Masha, I never had dreamed that I
Could love so much and so deeply grieve.

256. Olga

"Helga! Helga!"—the tone would pierce
Where foe smote the spine of the foe,
Their eyes light blue and fierce—
Veined arms, that stalwart show.

"Olga! Olga!" the ancients wailed,
Their hair as yellow as brass;
In the baths they scratched and flailed,
Bloody-nailed, pushing, en masse.

Beyond seas from which they came
It would jangle and clang and peal:
Again that ringingly challenging name,
Byzantine bronze on Varangian steel.

Fire Column

Forgetting all I could ever quote,
I forgot every Christian name—
Only yours, Olga, yet in my throat
Is sweeter far than wines' high claim.

Bloody eras have set the tune strictly,
Year by year, as they measure the time.
Ancient burden intoxicates quickly—
Scandinavian skeleton, mine!

Ancient regiments' backward warrior,
I hide my dislike for this life—
Mad Valhalla I want, battles gorier;
I want banquets—and glory—and strife!

I see mead-filled skulls—I am weary—
Rock-ridges, a taurine spine:
Above me, a high Valkyrie,
You whirl, Olga, Olga mine.

257. With the Gypsies

Stout, he was swaying, as if in a trance.
Gleam-teeth—predator-mustached face.
Red hussar jacket. Catch a glance
At the braided knots of golden lace.

A string ... and a guttural wail ... Right away
My blood felt sweetly unsolaced fate.
I believed in the story that used to say:
Strange lands, dearer to me, would wait.

Nikolay Gumilev

Vatic tones are the bulls' own veins—
But the bulls have fed on a bitter grass.
A guttural voice—and a girl complains:
A hand is squeezing the mouth of the lass.

Pyre-flame! pyre-flame! and columns high,
Red pillars—hey!—unbearably loud:
A loved guest tramples rust-leaves nearby—
A Bengal tiger whirls in the crowd.

Blood-drops, from prickly whiskers hanging—
He's tired, he's drunk—but at least replete:
Too many tambourines crash-banging—
Bodies too many, strong-odored, sweet.

How spot him, in cigar-smoke ripe,
Where corks are popping, and people yell?—
On a table, wet, does an amber pipe
Tap the beat of a heart from hell?

I remember him on a diamond-boat, fleet,
On a river he fled to Creator-Land,
In an angel storm, seduction sweet,
With a bloody lily in a slender hand.

Girl, who are *you*? Here's a wealthy guest—
Stand before him—a comet at night:
A wingéd heart in a hairy chest—
Rip out the heart—rip it out!—that's *right*!!

Fire Column

Circling, circling, wider and wider,
More and more, wave your hand till it tires—
The evening smoke is a meadow-glider
When past the wood there are fires and fires ...

Bull-strings left and right—their horns
Are death, their bellowings make you bristle—
They've pastured on bitter grasses, thorns,
Wormwood, goose-foot, prickle-thistle.

Wants to get up, can't ... Jagged—see?—
A jagged flint—like a guttural cry—
In a velvet paw, raised threateningly,
Pierced his wingéd heart. With a sigh

He falls face down, tangling aiguillettes:
Can't drink, can't see ... gone to his rest ...
Attendants are busy—with what regrets?—
Carrying off the drunken guest.

Gentlemen, half past five—what say?
Asmódeus, reckon up the bill!
Laughing, slim-tongued, a girl, in play,
Licks a drop from the flint-blood spill.

258. Drunken Dervish

In the cypresses are nightingales—the moon begins
    to shine.
Little black stone, little white stone, I have drunk a
    lot of wine.

Than my heartbeat louder far, my bottle melody has made:
"All the world is friendly smiling eyes ashine, the rest but shade."

I've not come to love the cupboy just today or yesterday.
Not today or yesterday have I been, drunken, laid away.
But the triumph of my knowledge is a thing I'll never trade:
"All the world is friendly smiling eyes ashine, the rest but shade."

I'm a wanderer, a loiterer, a wayward man as well.
Everything I've ever learned I have forgot, it so befell,
For a single rosy smile and one refrain, I am afraid:
"All the world is friendly smiling eyes ashine, the rest but shade."

Now I'm going to the graveyard where my friends are lying low.
Need I be ashamed to ask the dead what *they* of love may know?
Hear a skull proclaim a secret from the pit where he was laid:
"All the world is friendly smiling eyes ashine, the rest but shade."

In the moonlight rise the welling streams from out
 their misty lake.
In the cypresses no melody the nightingales will
 make
Save a single one who never sang before in darkened
 glade:
"All the world is friendly smiling eyes ashine, the rest
 but shade."

259. Leopard

If you fail to singe without delay
the whiskers of a killed leopard,
the spirit will persecute the hunter.
—Abyssinian belief

Working spells and wizardries,
There's the leopard which I killed
In my chamber, if you please,
In the night when all is stilled.

People come and people go.
Last of all departs the one
In whose veins will ever flow
Darkness of a golden sun.

Late. You hear a squeaking mouse
And a purring, never stilled.
To the wheezing of the house-
Goblin, purrs the leopard, killed.

"In a Dobrobrán ravine
Floats a fog that's dove-grey, wan.
Red as any blood-wound seen
Is the sun of Dobrobrán.

Smells of copper and verbena
Winds are driving eastward, and
Howls and howls the wild hyena,
Nose well-buried in the sand.

Brother—foe—you see the haze,
Smell the odors, hear the howl?
Strange that you should spend your days
Breathing air that's harsh and foul.

Murderer, you'll die forlorn,
In my country, as I plan,
So that I may be reborn
Fitted to the leopard clan."

Till the dawn begin to rise
Must I hear this crafty spell?
Should have listened to advice—
Should have singed the whiskers well.

Much too late! The enemy's
Led me to a sorry pass.
He is trying, now, to squeeze
Down my head!—that hand!—like brass!

Fire Column

Palms ... A fearful, skiey flame
Burns the sandy reservoir ...
Danakeel would seem the same
As such fiery lances are.

He won't ask and cannot know
Why my spirit was so proud.
That same spirit he will throw
Anywhere—for all's allowed.

I am rising while he laughs.
I'm incapable of strife ...
By the well of the giraffes
I'll await the end of life.

260. Prayer of the Masters

There is a prayer I recall the masters said:
Preserve us, Lord, from all disciples who are led

To tell us that our genius, meager though it be,
Should blasphemously ask for new discovery.

We'd honestly prefer a straight and open foe,
But these men follow us wherever we may go.

These men will gladly see us struggle till the day
When Peter will deny and Judas will betray.

The limit of our strength the Lord alone will know:
Posterity can weigh how far each man could go.

What we in future make is in the Father's power:
But what we have attained is with us every hour.

To injurers a humble kindness we will show.
To those who put on airs we firmly answer, No!

A flattering reproach, the praises of the crowd,
In the creative sanctuary aren't allowed.

No master will be crazed by henbane, like the corps
Of elephants from Carthage prior to the war.

261. Ring

A maiden dropped a ring
In a well—in a well at night—
That drew from a cooling spring:
She stretched her fingers light.

"Return, dear well, my ring
With its ruby from Ceylon:
Undines don't need such a thing,
Nor triton damp at dawn."

In the deep, the water darkened.
"We like your ring," she heard,
"With its body-warmth." She hearkened
To the uproar of that word.

"My bridegroom's tormented, defeated.
Into your water clear
He will dip his arms, noon-heated.
He will shed a burning tear."

Now she could see the faces
Of tritons and dewy undines:
"This ruby we like replaces
Real human blood, it seems."

"My bridegroom always repays her
Who'll flatter a lover's pains.
If I ask, with a steely razor
He will gladly open his veins."

"It must have a healing magic—
That ring ... You beg? What zeal!
You'd buy it with all the tragic
Pure love a man can feel?"

"A body's less precious than gold.
A ruby is redder than blood.
What's love? Yes—I've been told—
But I've never understood."

262. Bird-Maiden

A shepherd hailed
The sun that dawned.
And drove his cows to the shady vale
Of Brocéliande.

Letting them feed,
He played a joyous tune
On a flute of reed.
Suddenly, soon,

He clearly heard
From a tree a voice, not birdlike at all.
He saw a flamelike bird,
With a maidenlike head, and tall.

As at night a baby cries,
Broken-toned her song—
Soft black eastern eyes
As of one imprisoned long.

His heart is stirred.
Attentive is he:
"Such a pretty bird
And moans so bitterly."

Her answer he
Hears with a troubled mien:
"There are none like me
In this land of green.

If a bird-lad,
Filled with passion fond,
Were born, I would be glad
In Brocéliande.

But a vile
Fate has made us forlorn.
Consider, shepherd, I'll
Die before he is born.

Fire Column

I don't love the sun.
The moon I don't seek.
My lips are not needed by anyone—
Nor my pale cheek.

Here's what is sad—
What I most rue—
I want the bird-lad
To be unhappy too.

He'll flutter about, he'll bend
Toward an elm—he'll sit, forlorn,
And call to his ladyfriend
Who hasn't yet been born.

Shepherd, you are rough,
But this I'll forbear to check—
My lips you'll kiss well enough,
And my delicate neck.

You'll wish to get married—you're young—
Have children, too.
The bird-maid's memory will be sung
Centuries through."

The shepherd inhaled the scent
Of her sun-warmed skin.
Ringing gold bracelets on bird-claws bent—
He takes it in.

He's fevered, yearning,
Perplexed altogether.
His knees are burning
From a bright red feather.

A moan made she,
A single moan.
Her heart stopped suddenly,
Still as a stone.

She will not rise again,
On her eyes, a filmy glaze.
And tunes of pain
Upon his flute the shepherd plays.

If wind will rouse,
Gray fog may rise beyond.
He drives home the cows
From Brocéliande.

263. My Readers

An old roamer in Addis-Abába,
Who had conquered many tribes,
A black spear-carrier sent me
With a greeting, made of my verses.
A lieutenant, who led cannonades
Under enemy battery fire
All night by a southern sea,
Recited my lines by heart.

Fire Column

A man who, 'mid crowds of people,
Had shot an imperial envoy
Came up to shake my hand,
Thanking me for my verses.

There are many—strong, angry, and glad—
Who have elephants killed and men,
Who have died of thirst in the desert,
Frozen by edge of perpetual ice,
The faithful ones of our planet,
Which is glad, strong, and angry;
They take my books in a saddlebag,
Read them in a palm grove,
Forget them in a sinking ship.

I don't offend them with neurasthenia,
Don't lower their spirit with tepidness,
Don't wear them out with wearying hints
At something not worth a plugged nickel:
But when bullets are whistling around
And waves are shattering ship-decks,
I teach them how not to fear—
Not fear—and to do what's needed.
And when a woman, with a lovely face,
Uniquely treasured in the universe,
Says, "No, I do not love you,"
I teach them how to smile,
And go, and not return.
And when their final hour approaches,
And an even, red haze comes over their eyes,

I will teach them to remember
All of their cruel, kindly days,
All of their dear, strange homeland
And, appearing before the face of God
With wise and simple word,
Calmly to await His judgment.

264. Starry Horror

Happened on a night of golden shining—
Golden shining, though the night was moonless:
Over plains he ran, and kept on running,
On his knees he fell, but rose, continued—
Like a harried, wounded hare he scurried.
From his eyes, hot streaming tears were flowing
On his cheeks, long hollowed out by wrinkles,
Down his aged beard, thin, stringy, goatlike.
After him were running all his children,
After him his grandkids, too, were dashing—
In the tent of unbleached cloth, one grandchild
Who had felt ignored had started squealing.

"Please come back," his children called. Imploring,
Folding palms together, children's children
Shouted, "Nothing bad has really happened:
Sheep have not devoured the struggling spurge-
    plants—
Nor have sacred flames been quenched by rainfall—
Nor did lion, or the Zend most cruel
Come toward our tranquil tent to scare us."

Fire Column

In the black, a steep, a slope looked blacker.
Old, his vision weak, he couldn't see it.
To the ground he crashed, his bones were cracking—
Nearly lost his life, so great the shock was.
Then he tried to crawl a little farther,
But his children—they'd already grabbed him.
Here is what he said to them in anguish:

"Dreadful, dreadful! Snares, a pit, a terror—
That's the lot of every living creature—
For the black one, with a hundred eyebeams,
Looks at every one of us from heaven,
Seeking out the closely hidden secrets.
Being fast asleep last night, as always,
Wrapped within a fur, face pointed earthward,
I had thought I saw a cow, a good one,
With a hanging udder, puffy, swollen.
Crawling underneath her, I had wanted
Fine, fresh milk—but, suddenly, a terror:
While I tried to sleep, she might have crushed me.
Turning 'round, I happened to awaken—
Now without a cover, facing heaven.
Lucky thing for me, a skunk some putrid
Viscid juice had squirted, burned one eyeball—
Or, with two eyes frighteningly wakeful,
I'd be staring, but—no longer living!
Dreadful, dreadful! Snares, a pit, a terror—
That's the lot of every living creature."

Children in embarrassment looked downward.
Grandkids hid their faces with their elbows.

All were standing, motionless, awaiting
What the eldest son would say, the graybeard.
Here is what he said to them, confounded:

"Quite a while I've lived, but nothing evil
Ever happened to disturb my quiet.
Now my heart is pounding with impatience,
Wanting reassurance of the future.
I would like to see, eyes open, clearly,
Who it is that wanders in the heavens."

Having finished the asseverations,
Down he lay at last, not prone but supine.
All remained immobile, barely breathing.
Still they listened, and they kept on waiting.
Then an old man said, aquake with terror,
"Tell me what you see." But—stubborn?
      thoughtful?—
Still the graybeard son declined to answer.
Yet when all his brothers, bending over,
Looked at him, they saw he wasn't breathing.
Darker-hued than copper now, the visage,
Twisted by the heaven's fatal fingers.

How the women then vociferated,
How the children wept and wailed and mourned him!
Wheezily the old man uttered curses
While he tugged his beard, enraged, insistent.
Jumping to their feet, his eight big brothers
Powerfully pulled their tightened bowstrings:

Fire Column

"Let avenging arrows reach the heaven—
Shoot him down—the one up there who wanders ...
That, for us, can be no dreadful danger!"
But the newly widowed wife protested:
"Vengeance can't be yours—be mine the vengeance!
I'm the one who wants to view him clearly—
With my teeth to rip his throat asunder,
With my fingernails to scratch the eyes out."

So she cried and heavily fell earthward.
Yet her eyes were narrowed—long the time she
To herself yet muttered quiet curses,
Scratched her breast, and gnawed upon her fingers.
Finally, she looked about her, smiling.
Like a doll's, her head was nodding, nodding:

"Lin! The lake is dangerous! The liver
Of the antelope, how's that progressing,
Eh, Linoia? Children, look, the pitcher—
Lost its spout: I'll *get* you! Father, quickly,
Look, get up! The Zends are bringing branches—
Mistletoe—a basket made of rushes.
Trade is what they want—they crave no fighting.
Look how many fires are here—and people!
All the tribe has come! Tremendous feast-day!"

Now the oldster, fingering his kneecaps,
Reattained his former calm demeanor.
Children twang the bow—the children's children
Now emboldened, dare to smile: they're charming.

But the widow won't keep quiet, jumping
To her feet, she terrifies the young ones.
They are turning green—from fear they're sweating.
Black, with big white eyes, she's tossing wildly—
Frenziedly she wails, her cry ascending:
"Dreadful, dreadful! Snares, a pit, a terror!
What is this? Where *am* I? Red—a swan is
Chasing me ... A huge, three-headed dragon—
Look, it's crawling ... Go, the beasts are coming!
Crayfish, don't you touch me! Goats! I'm done for!"

While, insanely, she continued wailing,
Wailing like a maddened dog made rabid,
Leaping to her ruin from the cliff-top,
Not a one ran after her to save her.

To the tents returned the people, troubled,
Sat about on rocks and felt their terror.
Time marched on to midnight. The hyenas
Howled and then, as suddenly, were quiet.
Now the people said, "The one in heaven,
God or beast, will surely want a victim.
Let us sacrifice to him, and quickly.
It must be unflawed, an adolescent,
One on whom no man has looked with longing.
Har has died, Harayya is demented—
And their daughter's only known eight springtimes.
She, perhaps, may win the heavens' favor."

Women ran as fast as they were able,
Bringing back at length the little Harra.

Fire Column

Lifting up his flinty axe, the elder
Thought it would be best, her crown to shatter
Just before her final look at heaven—
She—his grandchild, and he—sympathetic.
Yet they wouldn't hand her over, saying,
"Shattered crown? A sacrifice unworthy."

So they put the girl upon the altar,
Just a big black rock on which, befóre this,
Dedicated flames had burned, unstopping,
But in times of turmoil were extinguished.
There they put her and they bent their faces,
Waiting: soon she'd likely die. Right after,
They would hurry home and sleep till sunrise.

Nonetheless, the maiden didn't perish.
First she glanced above, and then looked rightward
Where her brothers stood—again looked higher,
Finally attempted jumping downward
To escape the altar. But the elder
Wouldn't let her—asked, "What are you seeing?"
Earnest, her reply was quick in coming:
"Not a thing I see, but just the heaven
Bent and curved, as ever, black and empty,
Little fires that everywhere are scattered,
Like the flowers on the swamp in springtime."

Then the elder, thoughtfully, made answer:
"Look again!" Again did little Harra
Stare into the sky, looked long and slowly.
"No," she said, "they can't be little flowers,

They are simply little golden fingers,
Calmly toward the flatland downward pointing,
To the sea, and to the Zendish mountains.
They are indicating what has happened—
What is happening—what yet will happen."

All the people hearkened well and marveled:
No adult had—not to speak of children—
Ever uttered words of such a wonder.
Harra's cheeks were flaming, they were scarlet:
Sparkling were her eyes, her lips were ardent.
Raising heavenward her arms, it seemed she
Wanted to fly off at once for heaven.
Suddenly—her song reverberated,
Like a wind within a reedy thicket,
Wafting from Iran to the Euphrates.

Mella had as yet lived eighteen springtimes,
Never had she known a man. And now she
Prostrate fell upon the ground with Harra,
Looked at her and then began a chanting.
After Mella, Akha—after Akha,
Urr, her bridegroom—now the tribe's entirely
Lying on the ground: they're singing, chanting,
As the larks may croon in blaze of noonday,
Or the frogs upon a turbid evening.

Only to the side now stands the elder—
Hands on ears, he hates the happy music.
Shedding, single-eyed, tear after tear, he
Wails the pain, the fall from rocky slope, and

FIRE COLUMN

Mourns the burning sores on knobby kneecaps,
Harra, and his widow, and the time when
People looked upon the plain serenely,
Pasturing their cattle, looked at water,
Sails aglide, at grass with children playing,
At the heavens black where, bright and alien,
Unattainable, the stars were shining.

BOOKS OF ORIGINAL AND TRANSLATED VERSE
BY MARTIN BIDNEY

Series: East-West Bridge Builders

Volume I: *East-West Poetry:*
A Western Poet Responds to Islamic Tradition in Sonnets,
Hymns, and Songs
State University of New York Press

Volume II: J. W. von Goethe, *East-West Divan:*
The Poems, with "Notes and Essays":
Goethe's Intercultural Dialogues
(translation from the German with
original verse commentaries)
State University of New York Press

Volume III: *Poems of Wine and Tavern Romance:*
A Dialogue with the Persian Poet Hafiz
(translated from von Hammer's German versions,
with original verse commentaries)
State University of New York Press

Volume IV: *A Unifying Light:*
Lyrical Responses to the Qur'an
Dialogic Poetry Press

Volume V: *The Boundless and the Beating Heart*
Friedrich Rückert's The Wisdom of the Brahman
Books 1–4
Dialogic Poetry Press

Volume VI: *God the All-Imaginer:*
Wisdom of Sufi Master Ibn Arabi in 99 Modern Sonnets
(with new translations of his Three Mystic Odes,
27 full-page calligraphies by Shahid Alam)
Dialogic Poetry Press

Volume VII: *Russia's World Traveler Poet:*
Eight Collections by Nikolay Gumilev:
Romantic Flowers, Pearls, Alien Sky, Quiver, Pyre,
Porcelain Pavilion, Tent, Fire Column
Translated with Foreword by Martin Bidney
Introduction and Illustrations by Marina Zalesski
Dialogic Poetry Press

Other Books by Martin Bidney

*Shakespair: Sonnet Replies to the 154 Sonnets
of William Shakespeare*
Dialogic Poetry Press

Alexander Pushkin, *Like a Fine Rug of Erivan:
West-East Poems*
(trilingual with audio, co-translated from Russian and
co-edited with Bidney's Introduction)
Mommsen Foundation / Global Scholarly Publications

Saul Tchernikhovsky, *Lyrical Tales and
Poems of Jewish Life*
(translated from the Russian versions
of Vladislav Khodasevich)
Keshet Press

*A Poetic Dialogue with Adam Mickiewicz:
The "Crimean Sonnets"*
(translated from the Polish, with Sonnet Preface,
Sonnet Replies, and Notes)
Bernstein-Verlag Bonn

Enrico Corsi and Francesca Gambino,
Divine Adventure: The Fantastic Travels of Dante
(English verse rendition of the prose translation
by Maria Vera Properzi-Altschuler)
Idea Publications

[For e-books of verse and works of criticism see martinbidney.com]

This is the fourteenth poetry book by Martin Bidney, Professor Emeritus of English and Comparative Literature at Binghamton University. He has also published *Blake and Goethe* and *Patterns of Epiphany*.

Marina Zalesski, Lecturer in Russian at Binghamton University, is artist and translator for Global Scholarly Publications in Manhattan. She is co-editor (with Bidney and Katharina Mommsen) and co-annotator of *Like a Fine Rug of Erivan*, a trilingual collection of Pushkin's verse, and has translated Mairam Akayeva's *Hope Has No Light*.

Made in the USA
Middletown, DE
10 January 2017